Learning to Teach Using ICT in the Secondary School

A companion to school experience

Second edition

Marilyn Leask and Norbert Pachler

Routledge
Taylor & Francis Group

LONDON AND NEW YORK

First edition published 1999
This edition published 2005
by Routledge
2 Park Square, Milton Park, Abingdon, Oxon OX14 4RN

Simultaneously published in the USA and Canada
by Routledge
270 Madison Ave, New York, NY 10016

Routledge is an imprint of the Taylor & Francis Group

Typeset in Bembo by
HWA Text and Data Management, Tunbridge Wells
Printed and bound in Great Britain by
TJ International Ltd, Padstow, Cornwall

British Library Cataloguing in Publication Data
A catalogue record for this book is available from the British Library

Library of Congress Cataloging in Publication Data
A catalog record for this book has been requested

ISBN 0–415–35104–9

Contents

Illustrations

FIGURES

TASKS

TABLES

Contributors

Andrew Burn is a senior lecturer in media education at the London Institute of Education. He has worked in comprehensive schools for over twenty years, as a teacher, head of department, assistant head and AST. His most recent post in schools was as Director of Media Arts in the first specialist media arts college in the UK. He teaches a Masters' course in digital video in collaboration with the British Film Institute.

John Cuthell is Director of Research and Implementation for MirandaNet. For the past three years he has co-ordinated MirandaNet action research projects with teachers funded by Promethean, evaluating the impact of interactive whiteboards on teaching and learning. He has taught and worked in education for more than thirty-five years. During the past fifteen years he has researched and evaluated the impact of new communications technologies on teaching and learning. He also runs Virtual Learning, a consultancy specialising in research, evaluation and change management aspects of e-learning. With a background in Language, Communication Studies and Cognitive Psychology, he has just completed a long-term research project on the impact of ICT on thinking, learning and working, published as 'Virtual Learning' (2001, Ashgate, Aldershot). Dr Cuthell is Visiting Research Fellow at the School of Education and Professional Development, University of Huddersfield and works with the Centre for Educational Innovation & Technology, Bath Spa University College, as a Field Consultant for School Improvement projects.

Yota Dimitriadi is a senior lecturer on ICT in Education at Reading University and the associate researcher of SENJIT at the Institute of Education, University of London. She also chairs the Inclusion and ICT Experts Panel of the British Computer Society. Yota has worked at the British Dyslexia Association and currently supports international dyslexia organisations on teacher training courses on multilingualism and ICT.

Allison Freeman has taught English in secondary schools in England for twelve years. She is currently a Research Assistant in the Department of Educational Studies at the University of York. Her research interests include systematic reviewing and issues involving the use of ICT in the teaching of English.

Colin Harrison is Professor of Literacy Studies in Education at the University of Nottingham School of Education, and is also a member of the Learning Sciences Research Institute. He directed the Multimedia Portables and ImpaCT2 evaluations for DfES/Becta. More recently, he has become interested in researching teachers' use of digital video for staff development using the Interactive Classroom Explorer (ICE) program, and in evaluating Internet research performance using artificial intelligence approaches with the Intelligent Online Reading Assessment (IORA) project.

Marilyn Leask is Head of Effective Practices and Research Dissemination at the Teacher Training Agency in London. She has responsibility for developing the use of the internet to support the training of teachers and she has commissioned web-based materials to support new teacher trainers. These cover a wide range of subject specialist areas as well as cross-curricular themes. Her work is focused on making the evidence base underpinning practice in education more accessible to teachers and teacher trainers. Previously she was a teacher trainer and a senior manager. She has worked on a number of national and international educational projects focused on the use of ICT in education. As well as an advisory role in an LEA, she has been a full-time researcher both at the University of Cambridge and at the National Foundation for Educational Research. She has recently held a senior management post in an inner London secondary school and as TVEI co-ordinator she had email in her classroom in 1985. She was involved in the start of the European SchoolNet in 1996 (http://www.eun.org); TeacherNet in the UK (http://www.teachernet.gov.uk) and initiated the teacher training resource bank supported by the Teacher Training Agency. She is co-author of the best-selling text: *Learning to Teach in the Secondary School* and co-edits the Routledge Learning to Teach in the Secondary School series and the accompanying practical texts.

David Litchfield is Headteacher at Castle View School, which serves a challenging area of Sunderland. Previously he was a head of English and deputy headteacher as well as an advisory teacher for Secondary English. David is a MirandaNet fellow and has wide experience of new technologies in schools. He has been using computers in classrooms since 1981 and has been involved in various research projects including studies of mobile technology for management and of ICT, language and learning. Castle View School has taken a lead in the development of learning policies and in the use of interactive technologies; several staff have been involved in national projects and published studies of their work on improvement through the use of technology. David's previous publications include *Promoting Language Development Through IT* (MESU 1989) for which he was a contributor and design consultant.

Tom Moore is an assistant headteacher at King Edward VII School, Melton Mowbray, Leicestershire. Originally a science and ICT specialist, he now holds the role of Director of Learning and Achievement. Tom has recently led an initiative to re-engineer learning at KS3. This involved creating 'state-of-the-art' e-learning bases for students. Tom also specialises in making student performance data impact directly upon teaching and learning in the classroom.

Norbert Pachler is Associate Dean: Initial and Continuing Professional Development and Co-director of the Centre for Excellence in work-based learning for education professionals at the Institute of Education, University of London. He is currently

Course Leader for the Institute's Master of Teaching. Previously he was Subject Leader for the Secondary PGCE in MFL and Course Leader for the MA in Modern Languages in Education. Apart from the application of new technologies in teaching and learning his research interests include computer-mediated professional teacher learning, all aspects of MFL and comparative (teacher) education. He has published widely in these fields. He holds a Dr Phil degree, has taught in secondary and further education and has worked for an LEA inspectorate and advisory service on curriculum development and in-service training. His PhD/EdD supervision is in teacher development, language education and ICT (particularly computer-mediated communication). Norbert is currently co-editor of the *Language Learning Journal* and *German as a Foreign Language*.

Nick Peacey is co-ordinator of the Special Educational Needs Joint Initiative for Training (SENJIT), Institute of Education, University of London. SENJIT is a consortium between the Institute and thirty-six LEAs working on disability and SEN issues. Nick is frequently involved as a consultant in development and research work for government agencies, most recently leading on curriculum issues for the DfES national Accessibility Planning Project which supports the implementation of the Disability Discrimination Act across schools and LEAs. He has been a member of many national steering and working groups on inclusion.

Christina Preston, the Founder and Chair of the MirandaNet Fellowship, advocates the application of new media as a catalyst for change in teaching and learning. Recent research and development reports focus on innovative models for ICT Continuing Professional Development and practice; the building of international web-based communities of practice; supporting teachers as peer ementors; new ways of supporting supply teachers and international exchanges in citizenship and ICT leadership. Practice-based research is the preferred methodology for teacher education (www.mirandanet.ac.uk).

Ana Redondo is lecturer in education in the School of Culture, Language and Communication at the Institute of Education, University of London. She has mentored PGCE students from various ITE providers, is an experienced in-service trainer and has published in the field of MFL teaching. Currently she is a part-time tutor on the secondary PGCE in Modern Foreign Languages and is also a part-time Head of Modern Languages and senior teacher in a London secondary school.

Michelle Selinger is an executive adviser for education at Cisco Systems. She draws on her academic experience from the UK Open University and the University of Warwick to research and disseminate effective solutions for e-learning in all aspects of education and training.

Carole Torgerson has a background in English teaching and research, having taught English in secondary schools in England and Scotland for ten years. She is currently Research Fellow in the Department of Educational Studies at the University of York, where she is involved in undertaking systematic reviews and randomised controlled trials in a variety of educational fields. She has a methodological interest in systematic reviews and in the design, conduct and reporting of randomised controlled trials in educational research.

Ros Walker was the Project Manager for the REVIEW Project (Research and Evaluation of Interactive, Electronic Whiteboards), a two-year project, funded by NESTA and Promethean Ltd, based at the University of Hull. The Project aimed to find and disseminate good practice in the use of interactive whiteboards and over the course of the Project more than 200 classroom lessons were observed and recorded. Ros now works full time for Promethean Ltd, advising on the use of interactive technologies in the classroom.

Mary E. Webb is a Lecturer in Information Technology in Education at King's College London and Director of the secondary PGCE ICT course. Previously she has taught ICT, Computer Studies and Science in secondary schools as well as all subjects in primary schools. She provided advice and professional development on ICT for schools in Hertfordshire as a member of their advisory team. While based at the Advisory Unit for Microtechnology in Education, Mary co-ordinated the Modus Project, developing software and curriculum materials and conducting research into computer-based modelling. Her main research interests include professional development of teachers in the use of ICT, use of computer-mediated communication for Initial Teacher Education, formative assessment, computer-based assessment, computer-based modelling, and ICT and pedagogy.

Lawrence Williams is Head of ICT at Holy Cross Convent School, Surrey. He has been guest lecturer at Baylor University (Texas, 1996) and at Osaka Kyoiku University (Japan, 1997, 1998). Lawrence has given presentations at conferences in the UK (Media '98), the Czech Republic (Poskole, 1997, 1998) and Japan (Schools and the Internet, Tokyo, 1998). His work in cross-curricular ICT methodology is published as part of the National Education Centre's guidelines for Head Teachers throughout Japan in Mizukoshi, T. (1998) *Unique Educational Methodologies in Foreign Countries*, Tokyo: National Education Centre; and his pupils have been on television programmes made by the BBC (Blue Peter) and by NHK Japan (Media and Education).

Sarah Younie is a principal lecturer in Education at De Montfort University. Sarah has been involved in a number of international research projects in ICT and education, including EU-funded projects researching effective practice with ICT: notably the 'European Schoolnet Multimedia Project', 'Schoolscape of the Future' and 'Web@ classroom' projects. The latter was awarded the ESchola 'ICT Best Practice in European Education' by the European Schoolnet in 2001. Sarah has delivered research papers at international conferences and published articles on ICT and education.

Introduction

The teaching methods in twenty-first-century classrooms where ICT is integrated across the curriculum are considerably different to those used in the nineteenth century. In other schools, the difference is barely noticeable. Practice in teaching and learning in UK schools is changing radically in those schools which have leaders and leading teachers who have embraced the opportunities offered to learners and teachers by ICT. But the gap between these innovative schools and schools which see ICT as just an add-on to the curriculum and the province of an expert few is unacceptably wide. All children are entitled to leave school fully equipped to use ICT in their work and in their leisure and to achieve this, schools need to ensure pupils develop appropriate problem-solving capabilities and are familiar with the wide variety of ICT tools and how they can be used.

In this text, we are not talking about moving to teacherless classrooms but about schools where it is natural for pupils to choose from a wide range of technologies in order to engage in work of high quality, satisfying a range of learning outcomes.

The contributors to this book come from a variety of backgrounds – schools, universities, LEAs, industry and government agencies. Each addresses the issues from their perspective based on their experience and the research relevant to their field. All have a long history of being involved in developing and testing out innovative practice in the use of ICT in education and for teachers' professional development. All are involved in international exchanges of ideas either through international collaborations between their pupils and others, through collaborative research and development projects and through international conferences. It is this experience which leads us to feel confident in sharing the ideas expressed in the book.

We believe that there is enough evidence that the appropriate integration of ICT into the curriculum enhances pupil learning and the contributions to this text acknowledge the evidence for practice where it exists. However, teachers need to work and learn together to establish new and high-quality professional practice in their own schools. This has to include assessment methods as well as teaching methods and different learning environments. Research into innovative schools shows that schools where staff are mutually supportive of each other's developing knowledge and skills are more likely to be successful in tackling these challenges than those where knowledge about computers and computing is seen to be the province of a select few.

As a profession, teachers need to find solutions to issues related to wider use of ICT such as ensuring the reliability of equipment, resourcing, training and the development of new pedagogic skills as well as ethical and health issues. Different schools are finding different ways of solving these problems. The learning curve for many teachers is very steep. But the challenge of changing practice must be faced if children are to be prepared properly to face life in the twenty-first century and not ghettoised from an early age into the 'information rich' and the 'information poor' sectors of society.

The ideas that are described in this book are recording what some teachers are doing now. New ways of teaching pupils are continually developing. As LEA and school intranets and handheld technologies develop and digital television becomes commonplace more changes will happen in classrooms.

The book is of course just a starting point for exploring the possibilities which ICT offers to the school and both teachers and pupils, but we hope we have provided enough ideas and thorough enough justification of these ideas to encourage those who are new to this area to embark on experimentation in their classrooms and schools with some confidence.

The ideas in this book have been tried and tested in innovative schools around the UK and abroad. The school in which you teach may not be able to offer you many of the opportunities which you read about here. However you may find that working through online communities of colleagues provides opportunities to extend your skills and knowledge in the area of ICT. We are committed to the notion of lifelong learning and hope this book provides you with opportunities for continuing professional development which we think is a professional responsibility we all need to undertake for the benefit of the education of our pupils.

The focus of this book is on pedagogy, on the application of new technologies in the classroom, not on requisite ICT skills. However the book is not a prescriptive guide about how to use ICT. It aims to present a framework for ICT use in subject teaching based on an understanding of theoretical issues, possible approaches, strategies and examples from practice. We include activities which are intended to act as an 'interface' between the experience of the authors of individual chapters and your own personal circumstances.

However, there are a number of major hurdles to effective use of ICT in schools which may yet limit the vision which the writers in this book hold. Three particular hurdles have been known about since the earliest experimentation in schools in the mid-1980s and were apparent in early research in this area. These are, first, the *lack of adequate technical support*, so that only the very keen teachers, who also have technical expertise, can use the software and hardware confidently with classes; second, the *ongoing costs* of connection, maintenance, hardware and software. If teachers can use the technology at home, then they are more likely to be able to keep abreast of new developments; and third, there is the need for continuing professional development in the field necessitated, among other things, by rapid developments in technology.

We believe that changes in the world around us present us with the moral obligation to prepare young people for an adult life which increasingly requires knowledge, skills and understanding other than those traditionally covered by school curricula, such as the capability to work effectively with technologies in order to be able to make a full contribution to tomorrow's society or critical media literacy to ensure that they are able to take part in social and entertainment activities not as passive recipients but as active and empowered participants.

We hope you share our vision.

Marilyn Leask and Norbert Pachler
July 2005

1 Using ICT in your Particular Subject

Marilyn Leask, David Litchfield and Sarah Younie

INTRODUCTION

All state maintained schools are expected to have plans in place to support the use of ICT in the specific subjects across the curriculum. Many schools have intranets which hold the shared teaching materials of the department including images, simulations, interactive worksheets and so on. Many schools and subject associations also have material openly available on their website which you will find valuable in developing your understanding about the use of ICT in your subject area . In Chapter 2 there are examples of ICT projects involving staff and departments across the school as well as whole year groups. In this chapter, we discuss projects which can be achieved with smaller groupings of staff and pupils and in particular projects which you can undertake in your own classroom. As using and developing multimedia with pupils is covered in Chapter 7, the focus in this chapter is on utilising the communicative potential of ICT through email and internet projects. Examples from specific subject areas will lead to a consideration of principles underlying good practice with ICT and you will be asked to plan for your own classroom. In considering the use of ICT, this chapter reflects the principle that ICT should be integrated into all curriculum areas. Some schools have video conferencing facilities. If this is the case in your school, then we suggest that you observe lessons where this equipment is used before trying it yourself.

There is a wide range of contexts in which teachers and pupils work and the provision for ICT is one of the most varied. Some schools are able to provide large numbers of high specification computers, whilst others are slowly developing their provision. School policies for the development of ICT reflect great differences in the knowledge and expertise of teachers and managers, as well as differences in funding. All these influences will have a considerable impact upon your own classroom.

As a starting point, you should be aware of the information and communication needs of your own subject area. The extent to which your subject requires the retrieval and processing of information and the communication of ideas and knowledge will determine the range of work you are likely to undertake. If you are working in England and Wales you should also be aware of the demands of the National Curriculum with regard to information technology and your own school's requirements for the delivery of skills in ICT. The case studies attempt to illustrate how ICT helps deliver the curriculum, but also forms part of the curriculum itself.

Detailed subject specific guidance is available in the other texts in this series (the Learning to Teach in a Secondary School series)[1] each of which has a chapter devoted to ICT. BECTA also provides advice and guidance on integrating ICT into classroom practice (<www.becta.org.uk>). In addition, your subject association in most cases will be able to provide advice or at least put you in touch with others interested in developing knowledge about ICT applications specific to your subject. The ITTE (Information Technology in Teacher Education) website has links to the subject associations (<www.itte.org.uk>). Also the Specialist Schools Trust website provides case studies of innovative ICT use in different subjects (<www.schoolnetwork.org.uk>). If you wish to use the internet to find information about your subject then we suggest you use websites specialising in providing information for teachers. The URLs included at the end of each chapter provide you with further contacts.

OBJECTIVES

By the end of this chapter you should have considered:

- ways of organising curriculum projects which utilise ICT and which involve schools and various partners;
- the aspects of the curriculum for your subject for which you might use ICT;
- the possibilities of ICT supporting extension work in your subject.

INTERNET AND EMAIL PROJECTS WITH OTHER SCHOOLS

Successful email projects can be undertaken with a class even if the school has only one point of connection to the internet. This is because messages can be written using a word processing package on any machine and then they can be 'cut and pasted' into an email message or attached as a file attachment. Email is not limited to text. Pictures can be sent in a variety of formats. However, you will need to check with your email partner that they can download your files successfully. If you cannot work out how to do any of the suggested activities, ask somebody more experienced to explain how to do it. As with so many of the options which networked computers bring us, 'just in time learning' is the best way to learn, i.e. when you have the problem is when you need the training. This is why we believe one of the most important factors in enabling staff to use ICT both in their professional development and in their teaching is the creation of a collaborative learning culture within the school. Within the school it must be okay to admit that you don't know and to ask for help.

The communicative element of ICT can facilitate collaborative learning cultures for both pupils and teachers. Leask and Younie (2001, p. 118) argue that the term 'communal constructivism' conveys a meaning which 'captures these specific elements of the additional value that various forms of ICT bring to modern-day learning environments specifically the different forms of virtual and real community building and operation as well as the different ways in which knowledge is constructed, shared and reconstructed, published and republished by both teachers and learners alike'.

Examples of successful types of projects are given in Table 1.1 and more examples can be found through the websites listed at the end in this chapter. Further examples, particularly those relevant to a younger age group are given in the companion to this text: *Learning to Teach with ICT in the Primary School*. But the limits are your imagination and the context in which you have to work.

Projects such as this need clearly established parameters. But undertaking such projects needs careful planning. Starting with projects that are focused, and achievable in the short term (a few weeks) is a good way to build up experience.

Various international sites allow you to post requests for project partners as well as providing a service for you by advertising projects, so ways of finding partners include the following:

- by using existing contacts, through exchanges for example or through the local community and teachers in the school;
- by emailing schools direct. Various sites provide lists of schools' emails, e.g. European Schoolnet (<http://www.eun.org>);
- by advertising your project, e.g. by registering it on a site such as those mentioned below;
- by searching sites listing school projects and finding projects which seem to fit with your curriculum goals.

Sites such as the Global School House in the USA,[2] OzteacherNet in Australia,[3] European Schoolnet, Internet Scuola in Italy,[4] provide all three options. The European School Net site provides access to sites supported by the ministries of education in a large number of European countries.

Task 1.1
Planning an email project

Explore some of the sites mentioned and identify a project in which you would like to take part. Using the planning checklist in Figure 1.1, consider the factors necessary to make the project a success. Fundamental to the success of a project is a clear setting of objectives at the beginning and deciding on the practical learning outcomes, so you know by the end whether you have achieved your goals. If possible, put your plans into action.

Table 1.1 Examples of projects with other schools

Project	Description
Dialogue partners	Partners in different locations undertake discussions in focused areas over a set period of time. The purpose is to increase 'critical literacy' skills. Spires *et al.* (1998) used outsiders in the world of work for this and they reported significant learning gains. However the activity was teacher intensive because of the effort required to find partners. This is a more structured version of traditional penpal exchanges. The immediacy of the 'conversation' compared with traditional forms of penpal communication is seen as an advantage.
Virtual field trips[1]	Pupils link in with expeditions which are being undertaken and those on the expedition report regularly to the pupils. Some pupils have been on virtual trips in space and to the Antarctic.
News desk	A school in one country hosts a 'newspaper' site and children from schools all over the world contribute.
Favourite poems	A poetry theme is chosen and participating schools are asked to send poems on the theme, from their culture, to the school hosting the site, where the poems are displayed.
Book rap[2]	Here a teacher or librarian takes responsibility for running a structured online discussion about a particular book, often involving the author, over a couple of weeks. Pupils are asked to read the book before the rap starts and then, over a period of a couple of weeks 'rap points' are posted which stimulate discussion and debate.
Ask an expert	Contact is made with an expert in the field the pupils are studying and the expert answers the pupils' questions over a set period. Netherhall School have extended this idea to create an 'expert panel' of parents who are prepared to answer questions from pupils, which are related to their work and specialist knowledge. With increasing numbers of businesses online many schools will find they are able to link into a wide range of experts in their local area. Care should be taken in establishing such projects that the experts participating are not inundated with emails from the school.
Developing secondary and primary liaison	Some schools run projects where primary school pupils who are at the stage of transition to secondary school, are able to email pupils in secondary school to ask questions about secondary school life.
Virtual art gallery	Pupils from different cultures display their art work in a common electronic space and perhaps communicate with the artists. (Note, there are possible copyright issues here as pupils' work can be downloaded from the web by others and potentially used in commercial designs.)
Surveys and research	Pupils from different schools collaborate to build a database of information on a particular subject. For example, pupils in Food Technology may wish to explore the different food groups represented in meals in different countries.

Notes
1 Virtual field trips: <http://www.field-guides.com/>.
2 OzTeacherNet <http://www.owl.qut.edu.au/oz-teachernet>.
  Projects are on <http:// www.owl.qut.edu.au/oz-teachernet/projects/projects.html>.

1	What learning objectives and learning outcomes do you want to achieve in terms of: knowledge/concepts, skills, attitudes?
2	What is the time scale of the project and how does that fit with school holidays and other events in the partner school?
3	What languages can you work in? (Don't forget that parents, other schools and the local community may be able to help here.)
4	What resources: staff, equipment, time are involved?
5	Does anyone need to give their permission?
6	How are you going to record and report the outcomes?
7	Do staff need training?
8	Can you sustain the project within the staff, time and material resources available to you?
9	What sorts of partners are you looking for?
10	How are you going to find the partners?
11	How are you going to evaluate the outcomes?

Figure 1.1 Checklist for planning ICT projects with other schools

Potential learning outcomes from email projects

Skills development is an obvious outcome of any ICT work. But in this context, we would like you to consider the possibilities in your subject area. Learning outcomes include access to relevant, up-to-date information (e.g. news[5] items for business studies pupils; in the case of BSE, pupils found nothing in their textbooks but found information from research centres posting their findings on the web; for MFL, news items in the target language), increased motivation and increased subject knowledge. Pupils must of course be taught to exercise their critical literacy skills. They need to evaluate the quality of information they are receiving – who is providing it (to what extent are they an expert?); why are they providing it (are they seeking to influence me?).

As well as subject knowledge, there will also be a whole range of outcomes from any projects, which the teacher may not have anticipated. In the final report of the Schools Online project (1998, p. 47) schools reported that pupils found the net very useful for studying topics that were currently in the news. They also kept up with ex-pupils, teachers on exchanges, and parents around world. In another project, a teacher reported that pupils (from a special school in the UK) were not sure what the Danish children with whom they were working on a maths project by email, might look like. Pupils for whom English is a second language find material on sites in their home language. Liaison with other schools, parents and experts in the community via email may support work in specific subjects as may the careers service, Connexions. The different time zones around the world take on real meaning, as does knowledge about environmental issues, climatic conditions, historical events and political, social and religious contexts. Some educators involved in this work openly express the hope that increased knowledge about others will increase understanding and tolerance and thus, perhaps lessen the tendency for conflict between nations.

OPPORTUNITIES WITHIN A SINGLE SCHOOL

Some teachers will find difficulties in developing projects with other schools. In some cases this may reflect the nature of the facilities available. You could consider how the communication element of ICT can be developed within your own school or even your own classroom.

For example, Drama classes within Year 7 working on a journey project, such as the Oregon Trail, may use an internal email system to send each other messages to develop the drama. If you have access to the internet, there are several sites which could act as models for this type of work.[6] You may come across the concept of 'rings on the internet'. Groups of people interested in similar things have a button labelled with the ring name (e.g. History Ring) on recommended sites which leads onto other sites of a similar nature. An example is provided on the Oregon Trail site. For example, for GNVQ Travel and Tourism pupils and business studies pupils, the various sites associated with airlines, railways and ferries may be of interest. Sites with railway timetables are extremely useful for travellers. Also booking online is often a cheaper option for travel (e.g. Eurostar) and hotel accommodation.

Within a single classroom, there is now the possibility of using infra-red connections to send messages from one laptop to another. For example, questionnaires could be sent between groups of pupils. In English or Drama, this could be used to reinforce concepts of audience and appropriate use of language. In Modern Foreign Languages, work on vocabulary could be extended by focusing on specific elements of a topic.

Any work you undertake should be based on a good knowledge of the facilities available in your school. ICT should be a part of the induction process for new staff and you should know which staff within your own subject area and within the school as a whole are both responsible for ICT development and available to support you.

In England, the National Curriculum in IT can be delivered through a wide variety of subject contexts. We recommend that you use the QCA and BECTA websites for subject specific guidance documents. As you read through the examples relevant to your context, we suggest you consider whether these ideas could apply in subjects and in schools in which you have experience. The core requirements for the National Curriculum at key stages three and four are as follows:

Pupils are expected to gain skills in:

- finding things out;
- developing ideas and making things happen;
- exchanging and sharing information;
- reviewing, modifying and evaluating work as it progresses.

Figure 1.2 provides examples of how these skills may be demonstrated in different subject areas.

Art and design

Finding things out	Surveys (e.g. consumer preferences), web galleries, online artist/movement profiles
Developing ideas	Spreadsheets to model design specs
Making things happen	Embroidery CAD/CAM
Exchanging and sharing information	Digital imagery CAD Multimedia for students' design portfolios
Reviewing, modifying and evaluating	Real world applications – e.g. commercial art

Business & commercial studies

Finding things out	Pay packages, databases, online profiling
Developing ideas	Business / financial modelling
Making things happen	Business simulation
Exchanging and sharing information	Business letters, web authoring, multimedia CVs, email
Reviewing, modifying and evaluating	Commercial packages, dot.com, admin. systems

Performing arts

Finding things out	Online information sources, surveys
Developing ideas	Planning performance / choreographing sequences
Making things happen	Lighting sequences, computer animation, MIDI, multimedia presentations
Exchanging and sharing information	Video, audio, digital video, web authoring, multimedia, animation, DTP posters / flyers / programmes, email
Reviewing, modifying and evaluating	Ticket booking, lighting control, recording / TV studios, theatre / film industry

Maths

Finding things out	Databases, surveys, statistics, graphing, calculators, graphical calculators, dynamic geometry, data logging / measurement (e.g. timing), web-based information (e.g. statistics / history of maths)
Developing ideas	Number patterns, modelling algebraic problems / probability
Making things happen	Programming e.g. LOGO turtle graphics
Exchanging and sharing information	Formulae / symbols, presenting investigation findings, multimedia
Reviewing, modifying and evaluating	Comparing solutions to those online, online modelling and information sources

Technology

Finding things out	Product surveys, consumer preferences, environmental data
Developing ideas	CAD, spreadsheet modelling
Making things happen	CAM, simulations (e.g. environmental modelling), textiles, embroidery, control
Exchanging and sharing information	Advertising, product design and realisation, multimedia / web presentation
Reviewing, modifying and evaluating	Industrial production, engineering / electronics

Physical Education

Finding things out	Recording / analysing performance, internet sources (e.g. records)
Developing ideas	Planning sequences / tactics
Making things happen	Modelling sequences / tactics, sporting simulations
Exchanging and sharing information	Reporting events, posters, flyers, web/multimedia authoring, video, digital video
Reviewing, modifying and evaluating	Website evaluation, presentation of performance statistics, event diaries, performance portfolios

English	
Finding things out	Surveys, efficient searching / keywords, information texts, online author profiles, readability analysis
Developing ideas	Authorship, desktop publishing (balancing text and images)
Making things happen	Interactive texts / multimedia / web authoring
Exchanging and sharing information	Exploring genres (e.g. writing frames), authoring tools, text / images, scripting, presenting, interviewing (audio / video)
Reviewing, modifying and evaluating	Website evaluation, online publishing, email projects

Humanities	
Finding things out	Surveys, databases, internet searching, monitoring environment (e.g. weather), census data
Developing ideas	Multimedia, DTP, modelling (spreadsheets / simulations)
Making things happen	Simulations, interactive multimedia / web authoring
Exchanging and sharing information	Web authoring, email projects
Reviewing, modifying and evaluating	Weather stations, satellite information, website / CD-ROM evaluation, archive information

Modern Foreign Languages	
Finding things out	Class surveys, topic databases, web searching / browsing
Developing ideas	Concordancing software, interactive video packages, DTP and word processing
Making things happen	Online translation tools, interactive multimedia
Exchanging and sharing information	Word processing, DTP, web / multimedia authoring, email projects, video / audio recording, digital video editing
Reviewing, modifying and evaluating	Internet communication, website / CD-ROM language teaching evaluation, translation software

Science	
Finding things out	Data recording and analysis, spreadsheets and graphing packages, internet searching (e.g. genetics info.)
Developing ideas	Modelling experiments / simulations
Making things happen	Datalogging, modelling experiments, simulations (what if....?)
Exchanging and sharing information	Communicating investigation findings (DTP, web / multimedia authoring, DV)
Reviewing, modifying and evaluating	Accessing information (evaluating for bias or issues (e.g. nuclear power)

Figure 1.2 How ICT skills may be demonstrated in different subject areas. Source: Based on: Leask and Pachler, 1999 (with thanks to Dave Maguire)

Task 1.2
Identifying ICT opportunities
across the curriculum

> Read through the curriculum documents for your subject area together with any relevant school documents. For example, in your school read the schemes of work for your subject as these should contain instances of how and where ICT can be incorporated into learning and teaching activities. Consider how ICT is integrated into the curriculum. Make notes about how you think ICT could be used to support teaching and learning in your subject area.
>
> Now consider other subject areas. What opportunities for cross-curricular work might arise between your subject area and other areas?

How the National Curriculum in IT is delivered depends on the schools' approach. In some schools the whole staff will be involved in delivering IT across the curriculum. Advice given by BECTA on the Virtual Teacher Centre makes the following points and suggests a series of options from which schools might choose:

> Achievement in IT capability will not happen by accident. Pupils need to be taught new techniques and offered opportunities to try them out and to compare the effectiveness of using IT with other methods of working. These opportunities need to be offered in a coherent manner. Pupils are unlikely to be given opportunities to use IT in all areas of the curriculum unless this is carefully planned and co-ordinated.
>
> The Order (relating to the National Curriculum for IT) makes no statement about how IT is to be taught: this is a decision for individual schools. There are three approaches to teaching IT commonly used in secondary schools:
>
> - entirely through a discrete IT course
> - entirely across the curriculum
> - using a mixture of course and cross-curricular work.
>
> There are schools which use the first or second method with great success, but there are dangers with either approach. IT courses can lead to thorough but sterile coverage of IT, while fully cross-curricular IT can lead to many pupils missing out on certain aspects of IT, or not making any progress beyond learning rudimentary skills. A way of avoiding these two extremes is to develop a carefully designed IT course together with appropriate consolidation across the curriculum to enhance learning in the other subjects ...
>
> (BECTA 1998, p. 1)

In this BECTA document five models of IT courses are defined:

> model A – courses based on IT competencies;
> model B – courses based on study skills;
> model C – courses based on topics;
> model D – courses based on demands of subjects;
> model E – IT coverage without a discrete course.

The document goes on to give advice about continuity, progression, differentiation, assessment, special educational needs and monitoring and review. We recommend that you visit the website where you will find this document and that you read the whole text. This example shows how the web can be used effectively to make ideas freely available. In the past, this advice would probably be disseminated by sending one copy to the school and the chance that many staff would get to see this would be small. Now the document is freely available to anyone with an interest in the area.

Clearly there many opportunities for developing pupils' ICT capabilities in a whole range of subject areas. How the school tackles this challenge is a responsibility of management and, without the support of the management, there are severe limitations as to what can be achieved.

EXTENSION WORK USING ICT

In the past, some teachers have been wary of ICT work produced by the pupils at home. Uncertainty about word-processed essays and projects has been generated by the possibility that the work is not genuinely that of the pupil. With a growing appreciation of the possibilities of ICT, you should be able to devise activities which extend pupils and enhance their skills, demonstrating capability rather than simply concentrating on production.

For example, in English, it is possible to promote the use of word and document processing packages at the same time as addressing skills of drafting. A series of lessons based on the published drafts of writers could be extended by homework which asks the pupil to draft and re-write their own piece. The finished assignment would *not* be a final version of the pupil's poem but a presentation of the drafts and finished poem showing the development of ideas. Such an activity would allow pupils with access to a computer to choose a suitable package, save the various drafts and consider appropriate forms of presentation.

Design Technology offers a number of opportunities to use the range of information sources available to pupils through ICT. Work on products could include a consideration of the influences on consumer choice and ways in which image is developed by manufacturers. Internet access could offer pupils the opportunity to make a critical analysis of the ways manufacturers present themselves to their audience and provide knowledge of current promotions. In particular, pupils could be asked to research a variety of manufacturers within a specific field. Pupils could use publishing packages to design their own web pages or magazine layouts, or to take on real activities such as the design of pages for school websites. Integrating activities of this nature into the curriculum, with a background of analysis, will promote for pupils a more critical awareness of the impact of ICT on their lives.

Access to CD-ROM in school and at home, could promote a more open approach to homework and extension work. In earth science and physical geography, work may be reinforced by directing pupils towards the reference and information material available. There is a considerable amount of material available on topics such as hurricanes, earthquakes and volcanoes, with information updated on a daily basis. By designing activities which demand interpretation rather than just gathering of information, concepts may be reinforced and learning extended.

Studies of bias in the media may be extended using access to news agency sites. By directing pupils to the different levels of reporting, it is possible to encourage a more thorough understanding of how news is developed for specific purposes and audiences. By examining the differences between newspapers and web-oriented news facilities, the nature of media devices may also be considered.

Websites may also be of use in subjects such as History. Increasingly, different factions and communities in conflict have used the internet to promote their own perspective of events. Such sites could be used as examples of historical sources that require evaluation and may be compared with the sources available from past conflicts.

In Drama, the use of a digital camera can allow pupils to take home files for further consideration. For example, a class using a digital camera to record 'freeze-frames' could be given the activity of writing a critique of the frame devised by their working group. Pupils could be offered the choice of a printed or disk copy of the picture. Some pupils may wish to word-process their work and illustrate this with the frame within the body of the text.

A similar technique taking pictures using digital cameras could be used to create a story board for an assignment in English, which may support SEN pupils. Digital video footage could be taken of pupils in PE lessons and played back for analysis in order to improve sporting skills.

Modern Foreign Languages can benefit from using the variety of sites available to reinforce specific topics. The weather, sport and regional topics would be well supported by existing sites. As the range and variety of sites grows in Europe and elsewhere, the material relevant to teachers of languages should grow accordingly.

In all curriculum areas the advance of ICT is likely to demand more open approaches to the work of individuals. It is desirable that teachers have a good knowledge of the technology available to their pupils, but it is unlikely that this will be exhaustive. More important is an approach to learning that allows pupils to explore the range of sources and types of information, to make choices about appropriate technologies, and to develop as autonomous learners.

As with any extension work, planning is vitally important. You will need to consider the objectives of the work, the possible learning outcomes, and the technical demands on yourself and your pupils.

Not all pupils will have access to computers at home. Activities need to allow alternatives that do not disadvantage pupils by requiring a level of technology unavailable to them. Where a minimum level of technology is required, teachers must consider how the school or college provides this through resource centres, homework and study clubs, or loan systems.

In developing ICT policies, schools will need to have increasing regard for the implications of homework and extension work. In setting up homework or supported study facilities, it will be increasingly necessary to have regard to the demands being made by subject areas for the use of technology.

Task 1.3
Extension work incorporating ICT

In your own subject area, plan a piece of extension work that invites pupils to explore and present information. You should attempt to devise an activity which promotes choices about information or communication and includes the requirement to demonstrate sources where necessary. (For example, it is necessary for referencing purposes to record the date on which the website was accessed.) The activity needs to require pupils to transform information rather than simply gather it.

What will you need to prepare in advance?

How can pupils present their sources as well as the information gained?

What preliminary work will help pupils understand possibilities of presentation?

SUMMARY

This chapter has outlined ways in which ICT could be incorporated into your subject through online projects, which specifically develop the communicative potential of ICT, alongside subject knowledge and skills. ICT also provides the opportunity to create extension work in your subject, as the examples illustrate.

ICT literacy and specifically network literacy is a form of literacy which is equipping pupils to deal with the life that faces them in the twenty-first century. In this chapter, the intention has been to highlight some of the exciting practice which is part of the curriculum experience of pupils in some schools and to provide ideas on which other teachers might build.

The disparity in the pupil experience in ICT in different schools in the UK has been unacceptably high and in some cases remains so. Experiential learning in ICT from a young age seems to enable users to develop problem-solving capabilities so that they are often able to use intuition to work their way around technical problems; others who are denied this opportunity may well struggle to keep up for the rest of their lives. You, in your role as a teacher, are responsible for providing these learning opportunities to your pupils.

NOTES

1   The texts in the Routledge series, *Learning to Teach [subject] in the Secondary School*, cover many of the subjects in the secondary school curriculum. Each text has a chapter on ICT.

2   Global School House. Online. Available HTTP: <http://www gsn.org/>. Projects are on <http://www gsn.org/pr/index.html>.

3   OzTeacherNet. Online. Available HTTP: <http://www.owl.qut.edu.au/oz-teachernet>. Projects are on <http://www.owl.qut.edu.au/oz-teachernet/projects/projects.html>.

4   Internet Scuola. Online. Available HTTP: <http://www. quipo.it/internetscuola/homeing.html>.

5   Searching through the news and media categories in Yahoo. Online. Available HTTP: <http://uk.yahoo.com> provides access to thousands of news sites around the world. Ones we use regularly

include <http://www.reuters.com>; <http://www.bigissue.com>; <http://www.telegraph.co.uk>; <http://www.guardian.co.uk>. The BBC news site is excellent. Online. Available HTTP: <http://www.bbc.co.uk. If you have Realplayer on your computer (available free. Online. Available HTTP: <http://www.realplayer.com>, the g2 version is best, Realplayer plus is better but costs) you can access radio and video news of the day.

6   Oregon trail. Online. Available HTTP: <www.teleport.com/~eotic/index.html>; <www.trails.kcmsd.k12.mo.us/>.

REFERENCES

All the subject-specific texts in the RoutledgeFalmer Learning to Teach in the Secondary School series have chapters about the use of ICT in the specific subject area.

The BECTA and QCA websites provide very useful materials. Online. Available HTTP: <http://www.becta.org.uk>; <http://www.qca.org.uk>.

BECTA (1998) *Approaches to IT Capability*, Coventry: British Educational Communications Technology Agency. Online. Available HTTP: <http://www.becta. org.uk>.

Leask, M., and Younie, S. (2001) 'Communal constructivist theory: pedagogy of information and communications technology and internationalisation of the curriculum', *Journal of Information Technology for Teacher Education*, 10(1–2), pp.117–34.

Spires, H. *et al.* (1998) 'Real life in virtual communities: the light side and the dark side', paper presented at the American Educational Research Association Conference, San Diego, April.

2 Using ICT for Professional Purposes

Sarah Younie and Tom Moore

INTRODUCTION

This chapter illustrates, by way of examples, how to use ICT to support your professional practice in addition to your subject integration of ICT (Chapter 1). It outlines in particular how to create an e-mark book, e-resources and e-portfolio, how to find e-support for yourself and how to develop your use of e-pedagogy.

As part of your teacher training you are required to know how to use ICT for subject teaching. However, beyond subject delivery there are many other ways you can deploy ICT to helpfully support your daily practices. For further information with regard to the integration of ICT into your subject teaching see the BECTA website (<http://www.becta.org.uk>).

The following suggestions are based on a case study undertaken in a school with advanced practice in ICT, of teachers' use of their laptops to enhance and facilitate their daily lives backed up by research from various sources. Research (EUN, 2000; OECD, 2001; Web@Classroom, 2002; Younie, in preparation) suggests that the use of ICT can save you time and enable greater coherence in the disparate jobs you have to juggle in your daily practice, from storing pupils' marks to recording your own professional development.

Five particularly useful uses of ICT to facilitate teachers' professional practice are as follows. An electronic mark book co-ordinates all pupil progression data in one place and enables analysis of such data. Second, an electronic resources webpage enables teachers to create a portal of all their teaching materials, to facilitate pupil learning and enable departmental resource development. Third, you can use an electronic portfolio to collate your professional development experiences and you can also capture and showcase your best practice. Fourth, a list of online contacts who can provide e-support gives you access to professional advice, and can be built up across the course of your career. Lastly there is developing an e-pedagogy, where we outline ways to use ICT for learning and teaching, which can easily be used to suit your subject area.

OBJECTIVES

By the end of this chapter you should know how to:

- create an e-mark book, e-resources and an e-portfolio;
- use ICT to provide professional e-support;
- develop an e-pedagogy.

Examples of each are provided, by Tom Moore of King Edward VII School in Melton Mowbray, to illustrate how to use ICT in a step-by-step way. Further examples can be found by visiting the school's website, which houses the examples used in this chapter (<http://www.learningat.ke7.org.uk>). The school's website also demonstrates many more uses of ICT, which can enhance your professional practice and teaching. Where URLs have been referenced for specific figures in the chapter, it is important to note that the URL pages may change as the school's intranet site develops; however, the school's homepage remains the same. Also look at the websites referred to in the other chapters and additional school websites referenced at the end of this chapter.

E-MARK BOOK

The rationale for developing an e-mark book is to empower you as a teacher with data that will inform your decisions about how to enhance individual pupils' achievement, which forms the core of your professional practice.

The most important use of data within schools is to enhance teaching and learning within the classroom. The key to achieving this is for you as a teacher to have an intimate knowledge of the strengths and weaknesses of each pupil and to use this knowledge to design learning activities that will engage and challenge all pupils within the classroom. This will undoubtedly lead to improved attainment. As a typical classroom teacher you may be responsible for hundreds of individual pupils, and the job of keeping track of pupils' data and more importantly using the data to inform your classroom practice is often left to the humble paper-based teacher mark book. If you, as a classroom teacher, invest time and energy in developing a bespoke electronic mark book for your use, many advantages are gained over the traditional paper-based mark book.

Advantages of an e-mark book include:

- New data can be added, deleted or inserted between existing data easily.
- Data can be filtered and sorted for particular purposes.
- Routine tasks such as calculating averages, percentages and converting marks to grades can be automated, thus reducing staff workload.

- A mark book can be duplicated or backed up easily to provide additional security and/or an archive. No more stressed teachers searching for lost mark books!
- Data can easily be shared with other interested parties e.g. subject leaders, parents.
- If the mark book is held on a network, the possibility of two teachers modifying entries in one mark book is achievable, allowing, for example, a student teacher and regular classroom teacher to share the same mark book.

The rest of this section is concerned with getting you started with the formation of a simple e-mark book.

How can teachers make a simple electronic mark book?

A classroom teacher can easily use the functions of a spreadsheet such as MS Excel to create a simple mark book to record and monitor pupil progress.

This section will cover the following:

- how to input data;
- how to calculate percentages;
- how to calculate averages;
- how to assign grades to percentages;
- how to use conditional formatting;
- how to produce class summaries;
- how to use lookup tables.

Task 2.1
Developing your e-mark book

Talk to other teachers about how they record pupil grades and what else they might include in their mark books.

Following the advice in this section, build and use an e-mark book for one of your classes so that you become familiar with using your electronic mark book.

Develop ways of backing up and archiving your data and then extend the approach to cover all of your classes. As you become familiar with this way of recording pupil information, you will find other ways of using ICT to support your recording of pupil information. Make sure you check with your school about what storage of data is permitted under the Data Protection Act.

How to input data

Copy the data in Figure 2.1 into Excel and then add your own data (at least 10 pupils) – leave the blank columns blank – see Figure 2.2.

	A	B	C	D	E	F	G	H	I	J
1	Surname	First Name	TG	Tutor	Test 1/25	Test 1 %	Test 2/38	Test 2 %	Avg score	Pred Grade
2	Apple	Alison	1105		23		27			

Figure 2.1 Column headings for your electronic mark book

How to calculate percentages

To calculate the Test 1 percentage (column F in Figure 2.2), type =E2/25 into cell F2 then click the % icon. You can alter the number of decimal places using the increase and decrease decimal icons.

Copy the formula down the column by selecting cell F2 then hovering over the bottom right corner of the cell. Click and drag the formula down the column.

Use a similar formula to calculate the Test 2 percentage in column H in Figure 2.2.

Figure 2.3 shows what your results should look like.

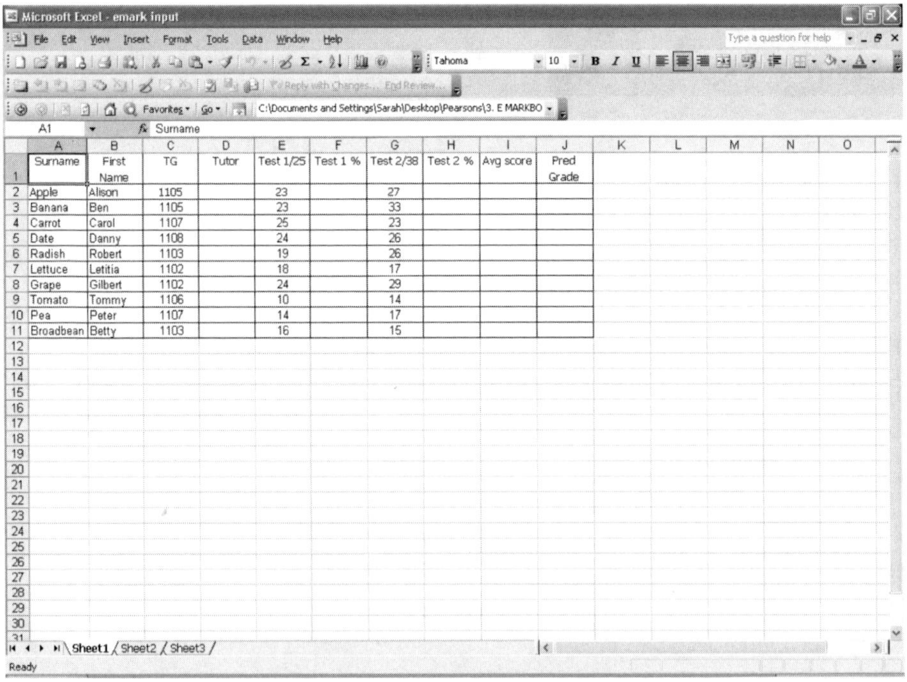

	A	B	C	D	E	F	G	H	I	J
1	Surname	First Name	TG	Tutor	Test 1/25	Test 1 %	Test 2/38	Test 2 %	Avg score	Pred Grade
2	Apple	Alison	1105		23		27			
3	Banana	Ben	1105		23		33			
4	Carrot	Carol	1107		25		23			
5	Date	Danny	1108		24		26			
6	Radish	Robert	1103		19		26			
7	Lettuce	Letitia	1102		18		17			
8	Grape	Gilbert	1102		24		29			
9	Tomato	Tommy	1106		10		14			
10	Pea	Peter	1107		14		17			
11	Broadbean	Betty	1103		16		15			

Figure 2.2 Setting up your electronic mark book

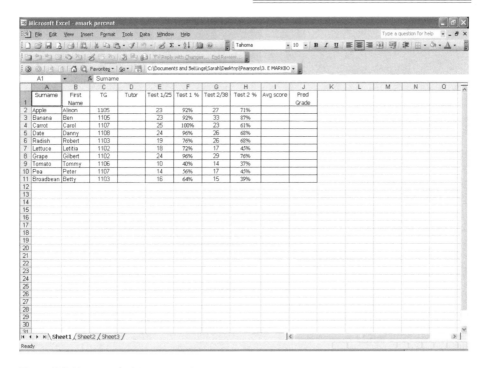

Figure 2.3 How to calculate a percentage

How to calculate an average

To calculate an average percentage test score for each pupil, type =AVERAGE(F2,H2) into cell I2.

This will average the contents of cells F2 and H2.

Again copy this formula down the column.

To calculate the average Test 1 score of the whole class, select the cell at the bottom of your list. In the example, the formula would be =AVERAGE(E2:E11); this will average ALL the cells between E2 and E11 – in other words the whole of column E. See Figure 2.4.

How to assign grades

First you need to assign some grade boundaries. In the example they are:

> 70%	A
> 60%	B
> 50%	C
> 40%	D
< 40%	U

So, 70% is needed for an 'A' grade, 60% for a 'B', 50% for a 'C', 40% for a 'D' and any less than 40% results in a 'U' grade.

The formula for this looks complicated but actually has four sections (look for the brackets!). What the formula does is the following – if cell I2 is greater than 0.7 (70%) then it will put an 'A' in the cell. Then if I2 is greater than 0.6 (60%) it puts a 'B', then if I2

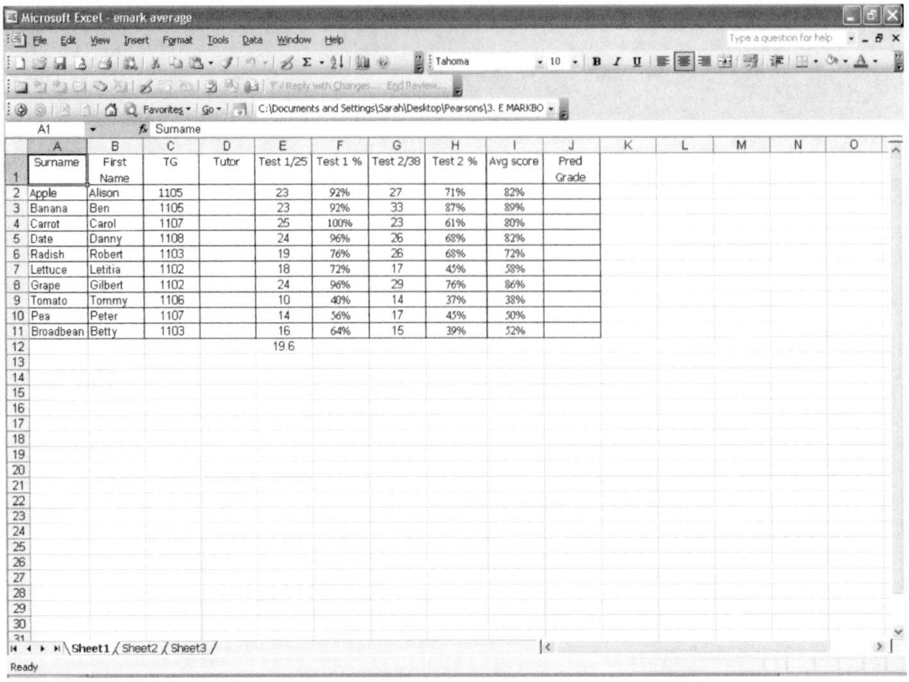

	A	B	C	D	E	F	G	H	I	J
1	Surname	First Name	TG	Tutor	Test 1/25	Test 1 %	Test 2/38	Test 2 %	Avg score	Pred Grade
2	Apple	Alison	1105		23	92%	27	71%	82%	
3	Banana	Ben	1105		23	92%	33	87%	89%	
4	Carrot	Carol	1107		25	100%	23	61%	80%	
5	Date	Danny	1108		24	96%	26	68%	82%	
6	Radish	Robert	1103		19	76%	26	68%	72%	
7	Lettuce	Letitia	1102		18	72%	17	45%	58%	
8	Grape	Gilbert	1102		24	96%	29	76%	86%	
9	Tomato	Tommy	1106		10	40%	14	37%	38%	
10	Pea	Peter	1107		14	56%	17	45%	50%	
11	Broadbean	Betty	1103		16	64%	15	39%	52%	
12					19.6					

Figure 2.4 Calculating averages

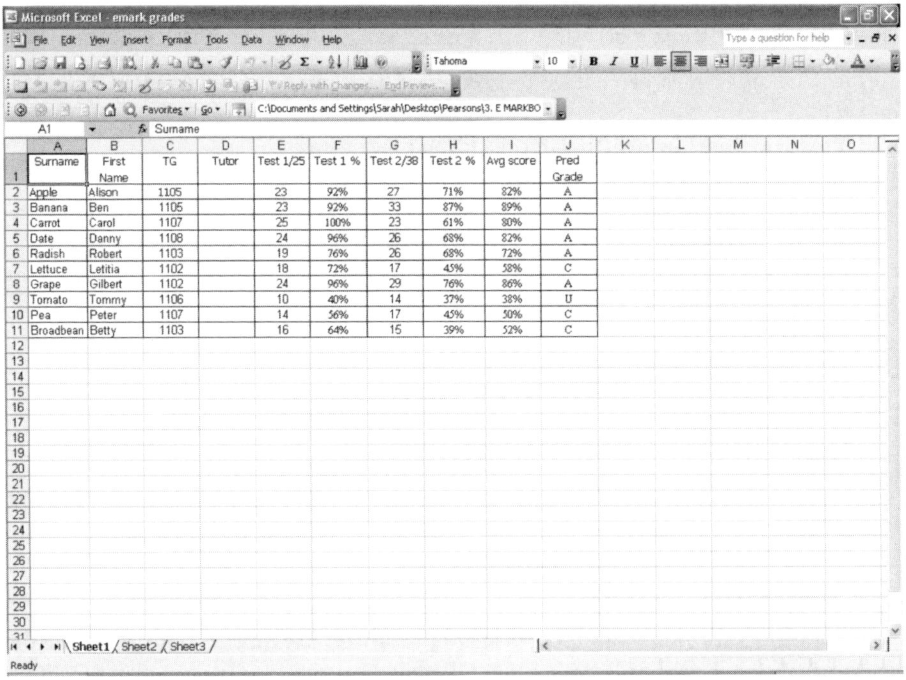

	A	B	C	D	E	F	G	H	I	J
1	Surname	First Name	TG	Tutor	Test 1/25	Test 1 %	Test 2/38	Test 2 %	Avg score	Pred Grade
2	Apple	Alison	1105		23	92%	27	71%	82%	A
3	Banana	Ben	1105		23	92%	33	87%	89%	A
4	Carrot	Carol	1107		25	100%	23	61%	80%	A
5	Date	Danny	1108		24	96%	26	68%	82%	A
6	Radish	Robert	1103		19	76%	26	68%	72%	A
7	Lettuce	Letitia	1102		18	72%	17	45%	58%	C
8	Grape	Gilbert	1102		24	96%	29	76%	86%	A
9	Tomato	Tommy	1106		10	40%	14	37%	38%	U
10	Pea	Peter	1107		14	56%	17	45%	50%	C
11	Broadbean	Betty	1103		16	64%	15	39%	52%	C

Figure 2.5 Assigning grades using grade boundaries

is greater than 0.5 (50%) it puts a 'C'. Finally if I2 is greater than 0.4 (40%) a 'D' is entered. If the number is not greater than 0.4 then a 'U' is included. The formula is

=IF(I2>0.7, "A", IF(I2>0.6, "B", IF(I2>0.5, "C", IF(I2>0.4, "D", "U"))))

See Figure 2.5.

How to use conditional formatting

Conditional formatting is used to pick out certain numbers to make them obvious.

In the example we are looking at the predicted grades for the pupils. You may wish to be alerted to pupils whose performance is below C. So if the cell is 'A', 'B' or 'C' (i.e. a grade between 'A' and 'C') then you might choose to colour the cell green i.e. not of concern. However, if the predicted grade is a 'D' then the cell could be coloured orange to alert you and if the predicted grade is a 'U', then the cell could be coloured red.

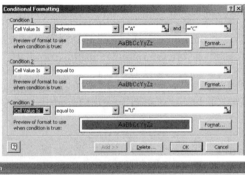

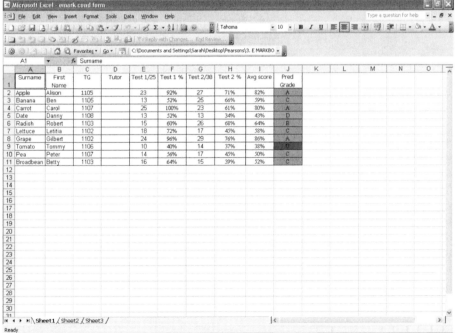

Figure 2.6 Using conditional formatting to highlight pupil underperformance

To do this, select cell J2 (the top of the predicted grade column) and choose FORMAT – CONDITIONAL FORMATTING. Add the following formats by typing in the conditions and then choosing FORMAT to choose the colour from the PATTERNS tab. You can also choose font styles, sizes and borders if you wish. Click ADD after each condition to add another. The maximum number of conditions allowed is three! Click OK when finished. This is illustrated in Figure 2.6.

How to summarise the number of grades for each class

To do this we use the COUNTIF function to create a small table on the same worksheet to summarise how many A, B, C, D and U predicted grades there are in the group.

Pick a blank part of the worksheet and list the grades A, B, C, D and U down the column. In Figure 2.7 this list starts in I13. In the cell next to the A (cell J13 in the example) type the formula =COUNTIF(J2:J11, "A") This simply counts how many cells between cell J2 and cell J11 contain an 'A'. Do this for each grade B, C, D and U in turn. You cannot copy down the formula in this case so you need to type out the formula for each cell. Do a quick check to make sure the counts are correct.

It is quite simple to total the number of grades as a way of checking that all the pupils are included. Select the cell below the numbers in this summary table (cell J22 in the example) and click the Sum icon. This 'has a guess' at what you would like to add up. In this case it should choose cells J13 to J20. Hit return for the formula to work out the total. Using the Sum icon is a quick way of entering the formula =SUM(J13:J20).

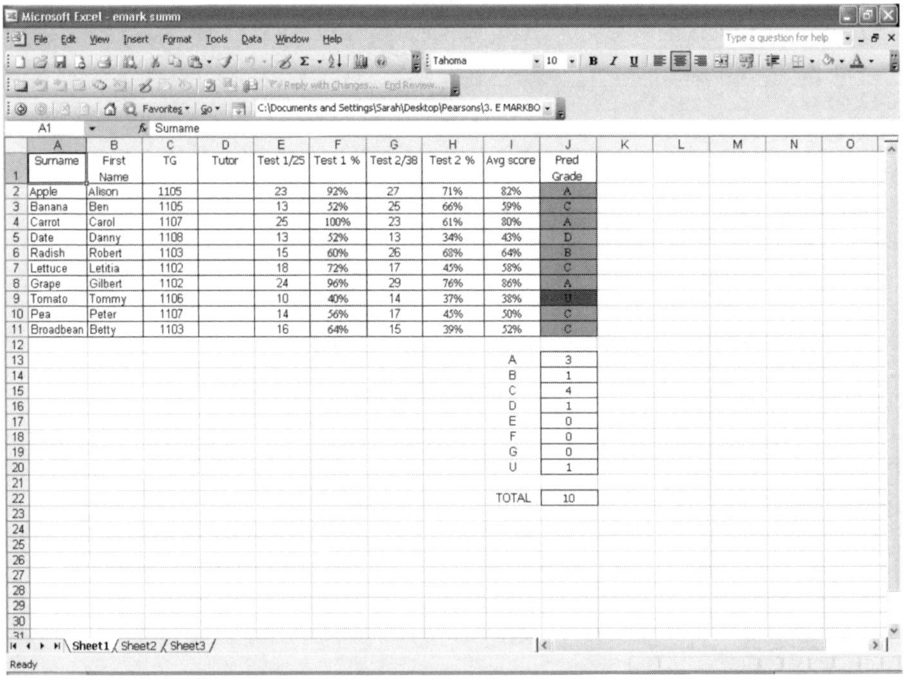

Figure 2.7 Summarising the grades in the class

How to use lookup tables

This function is useful to look up the value of a certain item in a table. For example, if you wish to change SAT Levels into point scores. First create a table where the data will be 'looked up'. This can be somewhere on the same worksheet or can be on a different worksheet.

Figure 2.8 illustrates this. In cell H2, type:

=VLOOKUP(G2,$C$14:$D$21,2,FALSE)

The formula has four sections separated by commas. So the above example means that the formula reads what is in cell G2, then looks in the table that goes from C14:D21. When it finds a match it goes to the 2nd column and then inputs the value it finds into cell H2. The FALSE means that an error message appears if a match is not found (try it! – this can be a useful check). If TRUE is used then the formula returns what it thinks is closest!

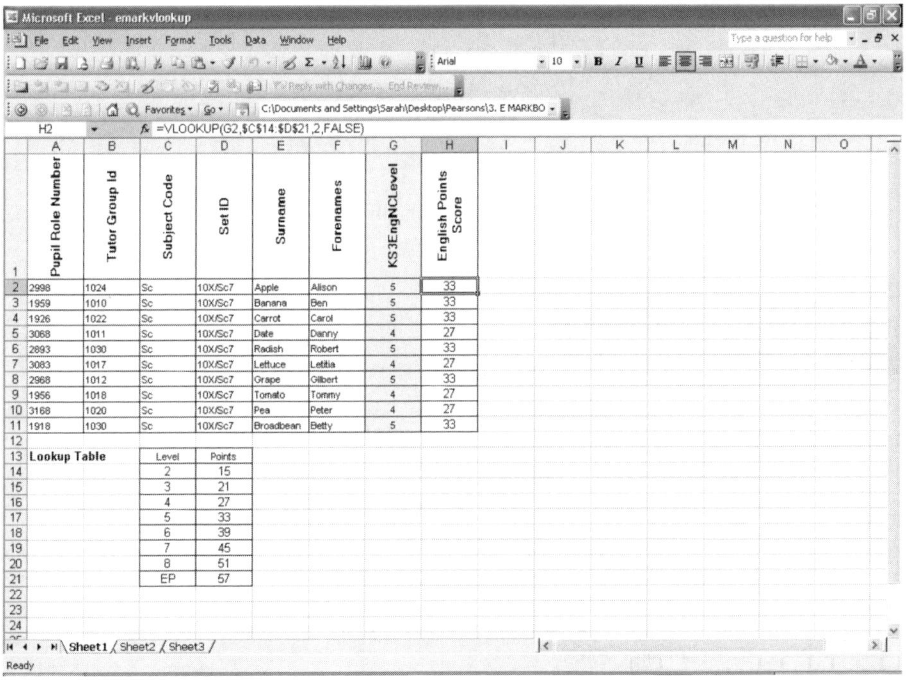

	A	B	C	D	E	F	G	H
1	Pupil Role Number	Tutor Group Id	Subject Code	Set ID	Surname	Forenames	KS3EngNCLevel	English Points Score
2	2998	1024	Sc	10X/Sc7	Apple	Alison	5	33
3	1959	1010	Sc	10X/Sc7	Banana	Ben	5	33
4	1926	1022	Sc	10X/Sc7	Carrot	Carol	5	33
5	3068	1011	Sc	10X/Sc7	Date	Danny	4	27
6	2893	1030	Sc	10X/Sc7	Radish	Robert	5	33
7	3083	1017	Sc	10X/Sc7	Lettuce	Letitia	4	27
8	2968	1012	Sc	10X/Sc7	Grape	Gilbert	5	33
9	1956	1018	Sc	10X/Sc7	Tomato	Tommy	4	27
10	3168	1020	Sc	10X/Sc7	Pea	Peter	4	27
11	1918	1030	Sc	10X/Sc7	Broadbean	Betty	5	33
12								
13	Lookup Table		Level	Points				
14			2	15				
15			3	21				
16			4	27				
17			5	33				
18			6	39				
19			7	45				
20			8	51				
21			EP	57				

Figure 2.8 Using lookup tables

Figure 2.9 Incorporating school produced baseline data on pupils

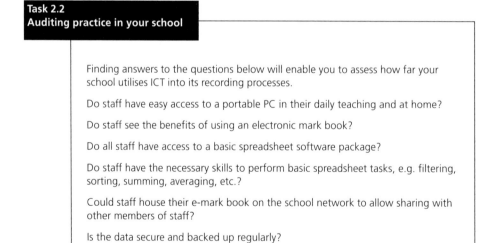

Task 2.2
Auditing practice in your school

Finding answers to the questions below will enable you to assess how far your school utilises ICT into its recording processes.

Do staff have easy access to a portable PC in their daily teaching and at home?

Do staff see the benefits of using an electronic mark book?

Do all staff have access to a basic spreadsheet software package?

Do staff have the necessary skills to perform basic spreadsheet tasks, e.g. filtering, sorting, summing, averaging, etc.?

Could staff house their e-mark book on the school network to allow sharing with other members of staff?

Is the data secure and backed up regularly?

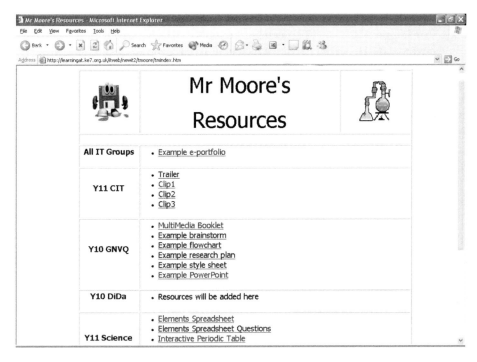

Figure 2.10 Your e-resources for your class

Combining baseline data into the mark book

Of course, if a baseline data file is made available to staff, for example key stage test results, a more sophisticated and useful mark book can be produced, like the one shown in Figure 2.9.

E-RESOURCES

E-resources are an online resource bank of teaching materials, created by the teacher and stored in one place, accessible online. Figure 2.10 shows the front page of one teacher's e-resource area.

Instead of writing paper-based worksheets and booklets, which necessitate photo-copying, you can make your resources available to pupils online from your teacher resource page. This is a web page that contains your classroom teaching resources in an electronic format. For example, your worksheets can become interactive and have links to relevant websites.

The advantage is that the online resources are always available to pupils, either from home or school at any time of the day, throughout the school year, which is particularly useful for re-visiting during revision periods, or if pupils have missed lessons. Teachers report that pupils with particular special needs find it helpful to be able to go through lesson material in advance of the lesson as well as being able to go through the material again afterwards, thus reinforcing their learning.

Similarly if more than one teacher from the same subject area creates resources on a topic, then it is possible to build up a range of resources, which may offer differentiation, could cater to different learning styles, which in turn can create greater access to the topic for pupils to enhance their learning.

Also developing e-resources amongst teachers creates a culture of sharing and support for staff, as it models good practice. If other teachers' e-resources are accessible to you, you can then adapt these to your teaching needs. In a culture of mutual exchange and adaptability, it is possible to build up a bank of e-resources quite quickly.

Advantages of developing e-resources include that they are:

- instantly available, to pupils and other teachers;
- more interactive, because you can develop hyperlinks in the resources, which creates more choice and learning paths, for example you could refer to three websites relevant to the topic under review, which could be differentiated;
- pupils can download the e-resources to their own work area, which saves time and tedium for pupils copying out questions or work from the board or books.

Task 2.3
Building your e-resources

For more examples of e-resources visit the King Edward VII website and the websites of a selection of schools (use a search engine or websites listed at the end of this chapter to find schools of interest). Start creating your own e-resources building on the examples you find.

The King Edward VII site is well fleshed-out with teachers' resources due to the deployment of Learning Resource Assistants (LRAs) who receive teachers' resources and upload them onto the internet. LRAs take an active role by re-designing and enhancing the resources for e-learning where appropriate. Not all schools provide this support for teachers.

E-PORTFOLIO – CPD&T

The aim of an e-portfolio is to provide you with a record of your continuing professional development and training in an online format. Your e-portfolio can contain sections which you update throughout your teaching career. You may house this as a webpage. Your e-portfolio may have a section for a short CV, a section for the inset courses and training you have received, and inset you have delivered. The sections may be put as links across the top of the webpage, which contains a photo of yourself.

You may want to capture and store examples of your teaching, chosen by you, to reflect your best practice, through video or screen shots of lesson activities, examples of pupils' work, examples of pedagogical activities, or a link to your e-resources page. You are the author and selector of the evidence that you feel best reflects your professional practice and development.

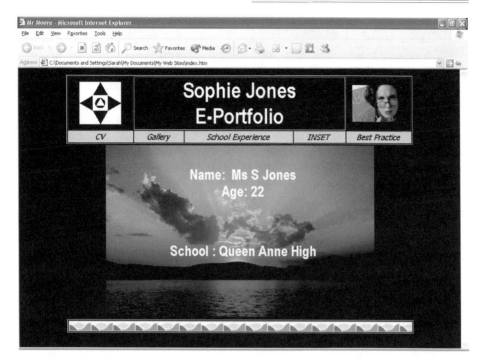

Figure 2.11 Example of the structure of an e-portfolio

Your e-portfolio may also contain a list of URLs that you find most useful in your daily professional practice, for example educational websites.

Pupils can also create an online portfolio, for their school work, as a place to record their learning and achievements too. Figure 2.11 is an example which can be adapted to your needs across your career.

Some advantages of an e-portfolio are:

- Your e-portfolio is a showcase of your best practice and work, you can contain it on one CD-ROM, or put it online. You can then send this to prospective employers, which clearly indicates your level of ICT literacy and differentiates you from other candidates presenting paper-based information.

Task 2.4
Developing your e-portfolio

Some countries are developing a national e-portfolio framework, and some schools already have a set format. Ask colleagues in the school where you are conducting your teaching practice whether e-portfolios are used. If they are, compare their approach to the one outlined in this chapter.

- Your e-portfolio is a multimedia showcase of your professional practice, which may be better represented than by paper, for example video capture of your teaching, with the examples chosen by you. Also by authoring the portfolio and selecting the best evidence of your work, for example which pupils' work and pedagogical activities to include, you can present yourself in your best light.

E-SUPPORT

As part of your professional development you may want to develop e-support links on your web browser.

To support your professional practice you can list links to websites, online communities and contacts that offer information and advice. For example, you can bookmark educational websites – subject associations and/or government education sites such as TTA, DfES, QCA, BECTA, TeacherNet, SENCO, etc.

You can make links to educational electronic forums and discussions, which offer the opportunity to pose questions and obtain answers from a range of teachers in the field, with experience and expertise of teaching your subject for many years. This enables you to be in contact with a community of practice that offers insights and support in your particular field.

There are also links to online advice and newsletters, for example the BECTA 'teachers online ICT advice', which come into your email inbox when you sign up; visit the BECTA website for more details (<http://www.becta.org.uk>). BECTA have also produced a pack of information on how to use ICT for learning and teaching, including CD-ROMs on effective practice with ICT in the classroom. Details can be found on the website. Your subject association website will also provide invaluable support.

The Information Technology in Teacher Education (ITTE) website includes links to all the subject associations, and promotes the use of ICT in initial teacher training and teachers' continuing professional development. Similarly the Specialist Schools Trust website also has case studies and news articles on innovative use of ICT.

The advantages of using e-support are:

- keeping up to date with developments in your subject;
- keeping up to date with government initiatives, etc.;
- accessing advice and support from experienced colleagues;
- accessing ideas for new practice.

Task 2.5
Building your own e-support resources

Examples of useful URLs are listed at the end of this chapter and the other chapters in the text. Review sites relevant to you and begin to build your own e-support resources.

Build your own email address book, listing key contacts to support your professional practice and test out these support networks.

E-PEDAGOGY

E-pedagogy is the term used to describe the ways in which you integrate ICT into your teaching and the learning experiences you provide in your classroom.

Advantages of the use of ICT in your classroom are addressed in a number of chapters in this book. In particular, teachers report that integrating ICT use into your teaching can increase pupil motivation and interest and mean pupils use their time more effectively rather than spending time in copying out materials. What follows here are ideas for how you can maximise these advantages for the pupils you teach.

Step 1 – Information giving: upgrading your written teaching materials into an electronic format

As an easy example of how to use ICT to develop your teaching, your first step could be to upgrade your written materials into an electronic format, and then to upload these onto the school network. For example, any information booklets or paper-based worksheets can be put online, alongside any PowerPoint presentations that you have delivered in class. This will locate all your teaching aids and information for pupils in one place, available online. The advantages of this are: if pupils are absent or lose their notes, the pupils can easily retrieve a replacement copy of the information. Second, by having your teaching information available electronically, this relieves you of the responsibility for printing and photocopying duplicate sets. Also, the resources are accessible for pupils at other times, such as revision and recap sessions. This empowers the pupils by giving them autonomy to manage their own learning, as they no longer need to rely on the teacher for the information, as it is available beyond the teacher contact of the classroom. See Figure 2.12 for an example.

Step 2 – Providing online templates and writing frames for pupils to download and work with or edit

A second step could be to give a resource to pupils to download and work with, for example, for pupils to edit, to add answers to, or to solve a problem. For example, the screen shot in Figure 2.12 is of a task that requires pupils to analyse two presentations, which contains specific guidelines on how to complete the task.

You could also provide online templates and writing frames for pupils to work on. For example, the pupils save the worksheet (from Step 1, you have turned this into an electronic format and put on the school network), the pupils can then download the worksheet into their network area and then complete the template or writing frame. You can make resources available for pupils to edit or work directly on, as in the case of writing frames.

The advantage is that it saves pupils duplicating the worksheet questions, or copying out the outline of the writing frame. In short, this removes the 'dead-time fillers'; instead the pupils are focusing on writing the answers, solving the problem, or completing the writing frame.

Figure 2.13 provides an example of an online template for pupils to complete.

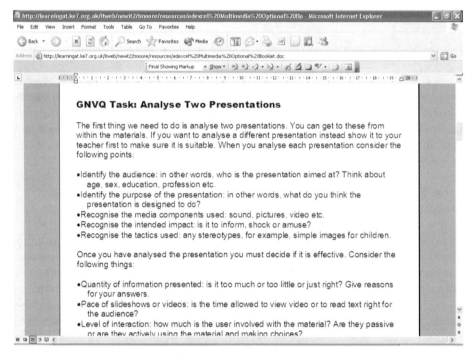

Figure 2.12 Upgrading your written materials into electronic format

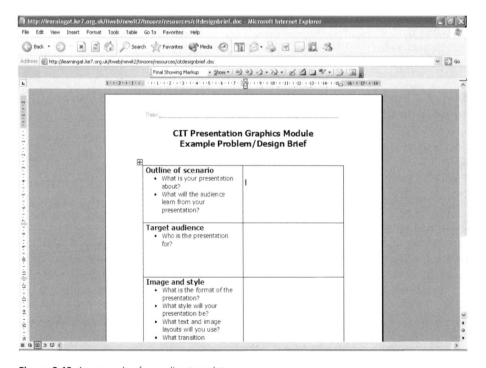

Figure 2.13 An example of an online template

Step 3 – Developing pupil interactivity with the online resources by inserting hyperlinks

As a next step, you can combine your online resources with links to relevant websites.

For example, Figure 2.14 shows a worksheet containing a link to an external website, which contains activities that pupils can then complete.

The pupils can access the worksheet online and save this to their area on the network and then follow the hyperlinks.

The first screen shot in Figure 2.14 contains the link to the website and the second screen shot is of the external website. In this example, the website contains an interactive periodic table, so pupils can engage with the external website (e.g. in this case an interactive model of the periodic table). Another example could be to access a pro-abortion website and an anti-abortion website to compare the use of evidence. Selection of relevant websites is the pedagogical choice of the teacher.

Pupils are guided directly to the websites selected by you for the topic under investigation. By providing a direct link you are ensuring that pupils go straight to the site you want; this saves time as pupils do not have to type in a URL from a paper worksheet, which creates room for error with misspellings, also it prevents pupils from being distracted by other sites if they were to do a general search.

The purpose of adding hyperlinks into your e-resources is to generate pupil interactivity as an aid to learning.

Step 4 – Developing more interactivity with online resources

Once you are comfortable with creating online worksheets and hyperlinks, then you can make the learning more interactive by downloading free software programs to generate word searches, crossword puzzles, interactive quizzes, or mix-and-match exercises, such as 'hot potatoes'. (See http://web.uvic.ca/hrd/halfbaked/ These tools for making quizzes are free of charge to educational institutions who then make their pages available free of charge on the web.)

Using free software you can create interactive tests containing multiple choice questions, which pupils complete and are marked, giving pupils a score. Pupils can then revisit and complete again, enabling them to monitor their own progression by revisiting the interactive tests during revision to see improvements.

Figure 2.15 provides examples of online interactive learning tools:

- interactive word searches;
- multiple choice quizzes/tests;
- interactive crosswords;
- diagram labelling exercises using drop-down boxes;
- Cloze exercises using drop-down boxes;
- mix-and-match exercises.

These illustrate the kind of interactive exercise you could develop for your subject.

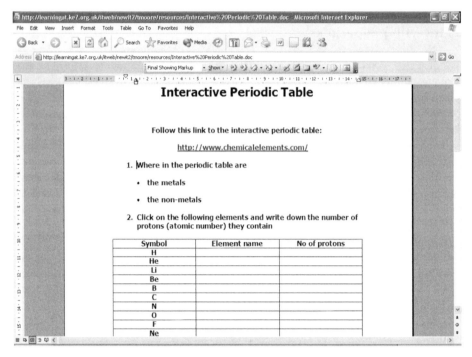

Figure 2.14a Example of online interactive learning tools: link to the website

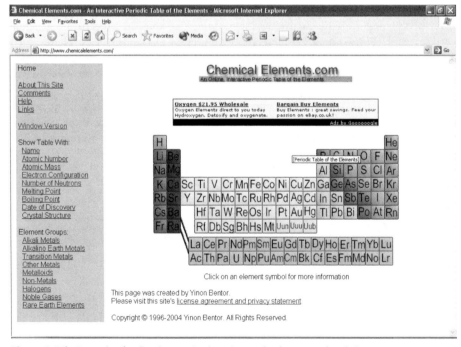

Figure 2.14b Example of online interactive learning tools: the external website

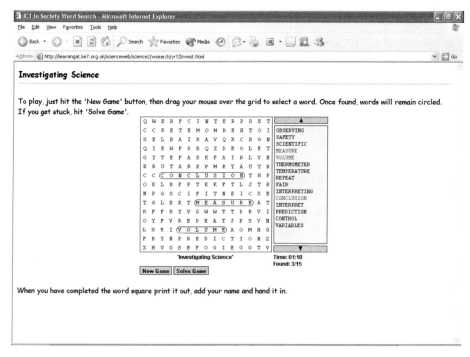

Figure 2.15a Example of online interactive learning tools: interactive crossword

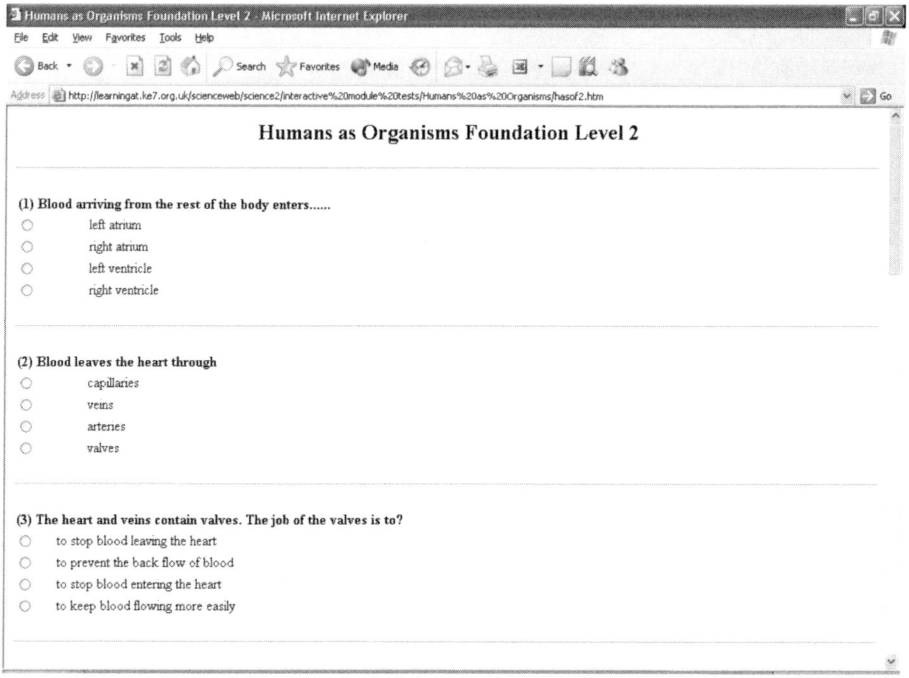

Figure 2.15b Example of online interactive learning tools: multiple choice test

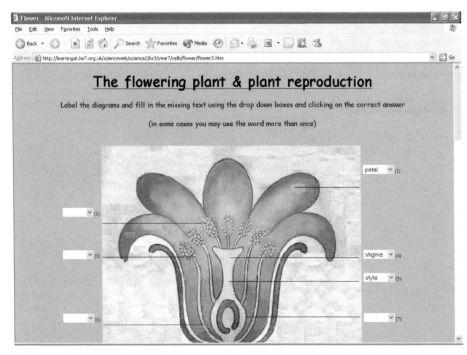

Figure 2.15c Example of online interactive learning tools: diagram labelling exercises using drop-down boxes

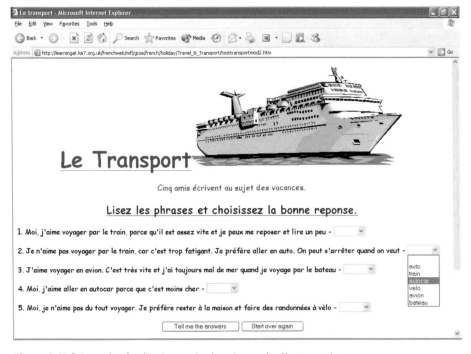

Figure 2.15d Example of online interactive learning tools: Cloze exercise

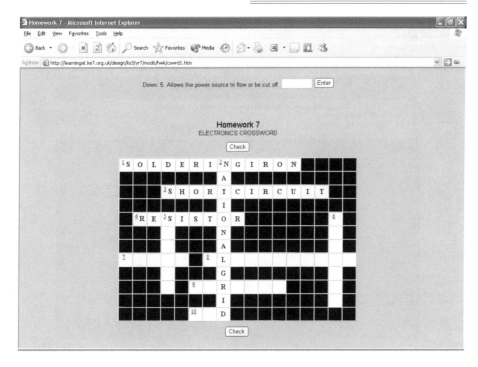

Figure 2.15e Example of online interactive learning tools: interactive crossword

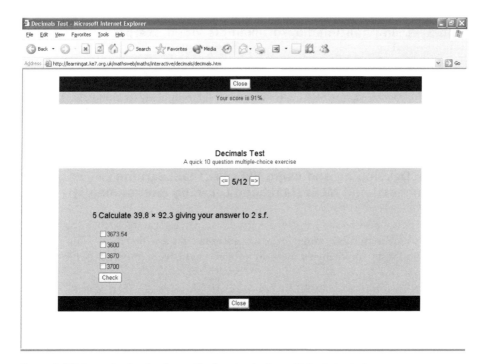

Figure 2.15f Example of online interactive learning tools: multiple choice test

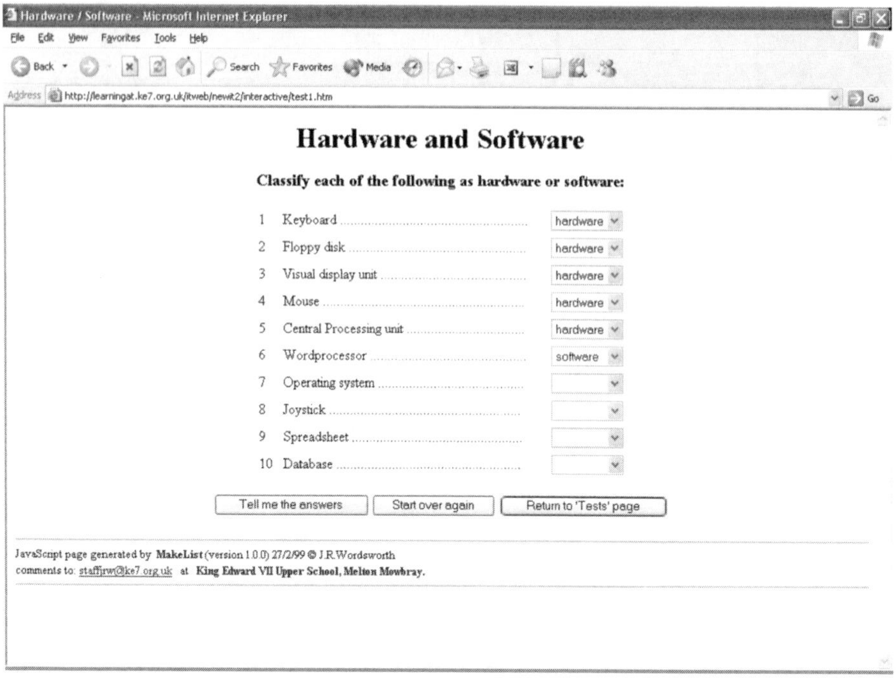

Figure 2.15g Example of online interactive learning tools: multiple choice test

Step 5 – Using multimedia, for example video exerpts

Further developments could include capturing lesson demonstrations, such as science experiments, on short video clips for pupils to revisit after the lesson. Other examples could include video capture of activities showing food technology techniques, or painting techniques. Many animations illustrating key concepts are available on the web for teachers to use. The BBC website provides some examples (<http://www.bbc.co.uk>).

Step 6 – Developing and using VLEs (Virtual Learning Environments) and MLEs (Managed Learning Environments)

You could develop VLEs and MLEs for yourself using free software, such as the MySQL database, which is available online for you to adapt to your teaching needs. This requires technological skills; alternatively there are products available to purchase, which can be adapted.

For further information on VLEs and MLEs see the 'BECTA ICT Advice Technical Paper', accessible on <www.ictadvice.org.uk> and Chapter 5 in this book.

SUMMARY

This chapter has outlined how ICT can support professional activities that you will need to do as a teacher, such as recording, monitoring and evaluating pupils' attainment.

This chapter provides strategies demonstrating how to use ICT to support your professional practice in addition to your use of ICT to teach your subject. These ICT strategies provide effective ways to co-ordinate and conduct the key jobs teachers need to do. By developing electronic versions of your mark book, teaching resources, lesson activities, and examples of your best practice, you can administer and enhance your professional development. Through ease of access and updating of materials, you will find that ICT provides invaluable support in managing the range of different jobs teachers have to perform in their daily practice/ professional lives.

ACKNOWLEDGEMENT

The authors would like to thank the staff at King Edward VII School for permission to reproduce the resources within this chapter.

REFERENCES

EUN (European Schoolnet Multi Media Project) (2000) 'Researching effective practice with ICT in schools across Europe'. Funded by European Commission, Socrates Programme (MM1010) and 23 Ministries of Education.

OECD (2001) *ICT and Whole-School Improvement*, a project within the ICT and Quality of Learning Programme. Case studies of innovative schools around the world can be found on <http://www.oecd.org/home/>. Searching the site for 'ICT and whole-school improvement' brings up the studies.

Web@Classroom Project (2002) 'Integrating ICT into the curriculum: investigating teaching and learning outcomes in the permanently connected classroom'. Funded by European Commission, Socrates Programme.

Younie, S. (in preparation) 'Integrating ICT into teachers' professional practice', PhD thesis, De Montfort University.

Relevant websites

BBC. Online. Available HTTP: <http://www.bbc.co.uk>. The BBC website provides a wide range of support materials including simulations and revision questions.

Beauchamp Community College Leicestershire. Online. Available HTTP: <http://www.beauchamp.leics.sch.uk>.

BECTA. Online. Available HTTP: <http://www.becta.org.uk>. BECTA has been set up by government to provide advice and support to schools and teachers on issues related to ICT.

Cornwallis School. Online. Available HTTP: <http://www.cornwallis.kent.sch.uk>.

Hot Potatoes. Online. Available HTTP: <http://web.uvic.ca/hrd/halfbaked/> This site provides tools for making quizzes. The software is free to educational institutions if they make public the pages using the software.

Information Technology in Teacher Education (ITTE). Online. Available HTTP: <http://www.itte.org.uk>. The ITTE association promotes ICT in Initial Teacher Training and the continual professional development of teachers with ICT; the website includes links to all the subject associations.

King Edward VII School Melton Mowbray website. Online. Available HTTP: <http://www.learningat.ke7.org.uk>.

Specialist Schools Trust. Online. Available HTTP: <http://www.schoolnetwork.org.uk>. The website provides case studies of innovative ICT use. For further information contact the Subject Leader for ICT, Paul Hynes, email: paulh@specialistschools.org.uk.

Teachernet. Online. Available HTTP: <http://www.teachernet.gov.uk>. The Teachernet website provides information on professional development.

3 ICT and Classroom Management

Mary E. Webb

INTRODUCTION

Experienced teachers using ICT to support pupils' learning have found that using ICT can make classroom management easier because it enables teachers to prepare interesting and challenging materials and it increases pupil motivation (Cox and Webb, 2004). However, classroom management issues associated with the use of ICT are complex because different types of ICT provide new and varied opportunities for learning and there are many interacting factors to consider when planning and managing their use. Hence when you make significant use of ICT, classroom management presents different challenges from when you are using other resources.

The Department for Education and Skills defines classroom management as:

> the management of student behaviour and learning activities by teachers by, for example, designing learning activities in ways that structure relationships to support learning, the use of rewards and sanctions and negotiating classroom 'rules' or codes of conduct.
>
> (<http://www.standards.dfes.gov.uk/research/glossary>)

The Elton Report (DES, 1989) commissioned by the government is still a seminal document which schools use when drawing up their own behaviour policies and codes of conduct. The report recommended addressing the issue of behaviour management in a positive and planned way by encouraging good behaviour rather than simply punishing bad behaviour. The report established connections with the curriculum and overall classroom management and organisation and recognised that the quality of teaching and learning has a significant impact on pupils' behaviour.

ICT has a range of roles in teaching and the curriculum, for example, in a recent study teachers agreed on the following.

1   ICT can help teachers make the lesson more interesting.
2   ICT helps teachers explain things more clearly to learners.
3   ICT can be used in most curriculum subjects.
4   ICT encourages teachers to vary the ways in which they organise the pupils in their lessons, e.g. computer partners, pairs, larger groups.
5   Teachers can prepare for relevant activities beforehand, e.g. selecting suitable websites or preparing a folder of images.
6   An important activity for the teacher is to prepare tasks requiring pupils to demonstrate their knowledge.

(Cox and Webb, 2004, p. 82)

ICT is often used as a blanket term but in fact it encompasses many different types of technology that can be used in many different ways to support different learning goals. The type of ICT used, the way it is used and the purposes for which it is used will determine the classroom management issues that arise. For example, the computers available for classroom use include desktop PCs that are generally fixed and have a major impact on the physical classroom environment as well as laptop computers and palm-top devices that are portable and may 'fit in' better to a range of different classroom configurations. In addition there are a range of display devices including interactive whiteboards that can have a significant effect on how the teacher and class interact.

In this chapter you will be encouraged to think about the issues for classroom management associated with using different types of ICT in different ways.

OBJECTIVES

By the end of this chapter you should have considered:

- how classroom management may be affected by the use of a range of types of ICT;
- the management issues involved when you have one or several machines in the classroom;
- managing lessons in a computer room;
- using portable computing;
- classroom management issues in using networks and the Internet.

ICT AND MOTIVATION

A review of the research literature on ICT and attainment found many reports over a number of years of pupils using ICT 'staying longer on the task, increasing their commitment to learning, achieving more through the use of computers and of being enthusiastic about using computers in their lessons' (Cox and Abbott, 2004, p. 39). Thus the use of ICT may reduce discipline problems.

Furthermore, the ImpaCT2 project measured the motivation of pupils through 15 case studies. Researchers found that 'not only was ICT perceived to encourage pupils to become more focused on the task, but it was also seen by some teachers to enhance both the performance and cognitive functioning of those who had hitherto been on the margins of classroom activity, or traditionally had performed poorly' (Comber *et al.*, 2002, p. 9).

ICT AND CHANGING PEDAGOGY

Studies suggest that the use of ICT is associated with a decrease in teacher direction and an increase in pupil control, self-regulation and collaboration (Hennessy *et al.*, 2003; Pedretti *et al.*, 1998; Kozma, 2003; Waxman and Huang, 1996; Hudson, 1997; Ruthven and Hennessy, 2002). Many writers have also suggested that developments in ICT provide very different learning opportunities and a need to design a new 'integrated pedagogy' has been identified (Cornu, 1995). This has implications for teachers' roles as well as their classroom practices. For example, McLoughlin and Oliver (1999) define pedagogic roles for teachers in a technology supported classroom which include setting joint tasks, rotating roles, promoting pupil self-management, supporting metacognition, fostering multiple perspectives and scaffolding learning.

Hennessey *et al.* (2003) found that using ICT was associated with a decrease in teacher direction and exposition, a corresponding increase in pupil control and self-regulation, and more pupil collaboration. Moseley *et al.* (1999) found that teachers who favoured ICT were likely to value collaborative working, enquiry and decision-making by pupils. In other studies, for example Jarvis *et al.* (1997), teachers have found difficulty in understanding their new role. Thus ICT may be enabling teachers who want to adopt a more pupil-centred model to make this change more easily but the use that teachers make of ICT depends on the resources available to them and the attitudes of the teachers towards ICT and its value in education (Cox, 1997).

In a science programme that made extensive use of ICT, pupils discussed how the self-pacing enabled by ICT required them to monitor their own learning, and contributed to their time management and organisational skills, fostering a kind of self-regulation and direction extending beyond the immediate use of technologies (Pedretti *et al.*, 1998).

The role of the teacher in classroom interaction may change alongside the integration of ICT use into the curriculum.

In ICT-based science classrooms teachers facilitated learning by working with small groups of pupils, directing them to useful resources, and helping with problem-solving activities (Mayer-Smith *et al.*, 2000). They still used whole-class teaching for short introductions to new units, revisiting concepts that pupils found challenging, and end-of-unit summaries.

As ICT becomes more extensive and integrated into learning we may expect pedagogy to change with resultant effects on classroom management. During the transition period a wide range of pedagogical approaches are likely to be used in lessons incorporating ICT, resulting in a range of classroom management issues.

EFFECTIVE CLASSROOM MANAGERS AND ICT

One of the first large-scale, systematic studies of classroom management was done by Jacob Kounin (1970). Kounin's findings are still often referred to in advice on classroom management techniques. Kounin identified several critical dimensions of effective classroom management including the following:

- 'withitness': teachers know what each pupil is doing; they have 'eyes in the back of their heads' so are able to pay attention to several things at the same time;
- letting pupils know what behaviour is expected of them at any given point in time;
- smoothness: teachers are able to guide pupil behaviour verbally or non-verbally without having to interrupt teaching;
- maintaining group focus and interest.

Using ICT can influence teachers' behaviours within these dimensions. Their 'withitness' can be affected if they become engrossed with a computer program and fail to keep an eye on what is happening elsewhere in the classroom. A way of avoiding this is to refrain from taking over the mouse or keyboard and stand back a little letting the pupils manipulate the software while you question or instruct them. In so doing you can keep one eye on the rest of the class. This also has the pedagogical advantage that the pupils are more likely to remember what to do next time. If you can direct them by careful questioning to find the solutions to the problems themselves this will be even more beneficial for encouraging independent learning.

Pupils need a set of routines to regulate their behaviour at particular points in the lesson. For a lesson in a computer room they may be expected to line up outside until the teacher arrives and then when they enter the room to log on to the network straight away while the teacher takes the register. It is important to manage the logging on process as it can take several minutes for the whole class to log on. If pupils need to move around during the lesson, for example to come closer to the board, you need to establish safe practices to manage these transitions as they present opportunities for misbehaviour. At the end of the lesson pupils will need to save their work and perhaps to print some of it. You need to manage the printing of documents and the procedures for collecting printouts otherwise there may be large quantities of unnamed printouts or crowds of pupils around the printer. A printer will also not be able to print thirty documents in five minutes at the end of a lesson.

Effective teachers are able to guide pupil behaviour verbally or non-verbally without having to interrupt teaching and for this they usually depend on being able to achieve eye contact with all the pupils. This may be difficult if some pupils are able to 'hide behind' computer monitors or become engrossed in using the keyboards. Where there is space in a computer suite for the pupils to move to a discussion area near the display facility and away from the computers this can greatly facilitate the management of a whole-class discussion although you will have to manage the movement of pupils and probably of their chairs.

It has long been recognised that visual aids are very helpful for maintaining the focus and interest during a class discussion. A computer with a large display device attached enables a wide range of visual and aural stimuli.

Task 3.1
How and why is ICT being used?

Over a period of about a week observe the way ICT is being used in lessons. Note:

- the number of computers being used;
- the number of pupils working at each computer;
- the types of software and the electronic materials being used;
- how the lessons are structured;
- the way the teacher interacts with pupils during whole-class discussions;
- the way the teacher interacts with pupils working at computers;
- any rules and procedures for computer use.

In what ways do you think the ICT is supporting pupils' learning?

In what ways do you think the teacher has had to adopt and adapt different classroom management techniques as a result of using computers?

TEACHERS' ICT SKILLS AND UNDERSTANDING

In a review of research into ICT and pedagogy we identified the following ICT skills and understanding that are needed by teachers in order to make effective use of ICT.

- Teachers need to understand the relationship between a range of ICT resources and the concepts, processes and skills in their subject.
- Teachers need to use their subject expertise to obtain and select appropriate ICT resources which will help them meet the learning objectives of a particular lesson. Resources include subject-specific software as well as more generic resources.
- Teachers need knowledge of the potential of ICT resources, not only in terms of their contribution to pupils' presentation skills but in terms of their facilities for challenging pupils' thinking and extending pupils' learning in a subject.
- Teachers need confidence in using a range of ICT resources, which can only be achieved through frequent practice with more than one or two uses of ICT.
- Teachers need to understand that some uses of ICT will change the nature and representations of knowledge and the way the subject is presented to and engages the pupils.

(Cox and Webb, 2004, p. 7)

The list may seem daunting but the way to start is to try out one approach focusing on your learning objectives for your pupils with one piece of software. Then you can gradually expand your experience through observing other teachers, reading about good practice and experimenting in your own lessons. You also have to accept that it is impossible to know all of the different facilities in a software application as most packages now have many different features. You do need to think about how the use of the ICT is supporting your learning objectives when you plan your lessons.

PUPILS' ICT SKILLS AND UNDERSTANDING

It is likely that some pupils in your class will know more than you about the software you plan to use but this should not be a concern, indeed you can make use of their expertise. The range of ICT skills and understanding of the pupils in any particular class may be very varied. It is worth finding out as far as possible what skills the pupils have with the software and hardware you plan to use by asking the ICT coordinator and other teachers. You then need to decide what ICT skills they may need to learn and devise a strategy for teaching and supporting these. The following are some possible strategies that you could combine in various ways:

- at the start of the lesson, demonstrate the key features of the software that they will need;
- allow some time for pupils to explore and experiment with a new piece of software so that they can find out its capabilities;
- encourage pupils to use the help facility in the software;
- bring the class together at key points to demonstrate new features of the software that they will need;
- use a help sheet that you or another teacher have written to support pupils in using the software;
- arrange pupils in groups such that each group has a range of ICT expertise and encourage the pupils to work together to find their own way with the software;
- use pupils with better ICT skills as experts to support other pupils;
- train a few pupils to use the software so that they can act as 'experts';
- use a structured worksheet with software instructions as well as task instructions to guide them.

Some points to bear in mind when deciding on your strategy are:

- pupils need time to become familiar with a new piece of software before they can use it effectively;
- most pupils enjoy being 'experts' but if they spend too much time helping others this may hinder their own progress;
- pupils should be encouraged to become independent learners;
- the help text for some programs that are often used in schools is designed for adults and may be difficult for younger pupils.

ICT AND THE PHYSICAL CLASSROOM ENVIRONMENT

You can incorporate ICT into your teaching by taking your pupils to a computer room or by having computers in your own classroom. The option that you choose for a particular lesson will depend on your learning objectives for the lesson and the resources that are available. The following are some of the different arrangements of computer hardware and each will present different classroom management opportunities and issues:

- a computer room with sufficient computers for each pupil to work individually;
- a computer room where pairs of pupils need to share computers;
- an ordinary classroom with one computer connected to a large display device;
- an ordinary classroom with one or two computers in a corner;

- a cluster of computers situated in a shared area between classrooms;
- a set of portable computers that can be used in a normal classroom.

Classroom management in a computer room

In a computer room the computers dominate the physical environment and you will not necessarily have access to all the other resources for your subject. Hence linking the work in the computer room to other subject work may be difficult. Nevertheless taking your class to a computer suite can be very productive in developing pupils' ICT skills and giving them an opportunity for intensive use of particular software packages.

In a computer room the computers are usually connected to a network which introduces additional classroom management issues as will be discussed in a later section.

Most computer suites in schools now have a large display device connected to one or more of the computers. This is important for introducing the tasks, demonstrating software and for plenaries that may review what pupils have achieved and what they have learnt. In order to focus pupils' attention during these whole-class discussions you need to be able to maintain eye contact with all the pupils, perhaps by moving them closer to the display device as discussed earlier and to reduce the distraction from the computers. You need to establish a climate for whole-class discussion in which everyone shows that they value each others' contributions by listening attentively. Some tips for managing these discussions are:

- make the pupils turn off their monitors – make sure they press the button on the monitor only rather than switching off the computer;
- make sure they have all turned their chairs to face you or the centre of the discussion;
- use one of the pupils to manipulate the mouse and keyboard so that you can watch the class.

Task 3.2
Designing a computer room

This activity is intended to encourage you to think about how the physical layout of the room may affect classroom management. Unfortunately in reality you are not likely to have much control over the physical arrangement in the rooms in which you teach but if you have thought about how the pupils may be affected by the physical environment you may be able to anticipate and mitigate these effects.

Produce a design layout for a computer room which will facilitate classroom management. Think about how it will facilitate:

- whole-class discussion;
- demonstration of software;
- individual work;
- group work.

Where would you organise the pupils for different types of activities?
What are the limitations of your design?
How would you manage those limitations?
What routines would you establish for movement about the room, storing pupils' bags, printing etc.?

Task 3.3
Lesson observation focusing on
physical factors in a computer
room

While you observe a lesson in a computer room, draw the layout of the room and list problems that do result or may result from the physical arrangement of the ICT resources. Note how the teacher prevents or overcomes potential problems.

One or two computers in a classroom

In addition to the usual considerations for lesson planning with ICT discussed earlier, when one or two computers are available in your classroom you need to think about how to schedule their use so that work done on the computers links to and complements other work in the classroom and each pupil has an appropriate share of time on the computer(s). In an ideal world where computers are fully integrated into classroom use and pupils understand their potential for supporting their work, it may be possible for the pupils themselves to decide when to use a computer, for example to process data from an experiment or to find some information that they need for a report. However, at present in most schools one or two computers in a classroom are unlikely to be used effectively unless the teacher plans and schedules their use. Two possible approaches to managing one or two computers in a room are as follows:

- for a lesson, plan a circus of activities, one of which uses the computers, for example for exploring a simulation or logging data for an experiment;
- over a series of lessons pairs of pupils work at the computers on an activity that addresses some of the learning objectives for the current unit of work.

If a large display facility is available, one computer may be used by the teacher to support teaching of a group or the whole class.

Task 3.4
Lesson observation of using
computers in a standard
classroom

List the things you would look out for where you were focusing on classroom management in a lesson observation where one or two computers are used in a classroom.

What questions might you want to ask the teacher?

PORTABLE COMPUTING

Martin (1995) compared the use of portable computers in a classroom with desktop computers in a computer room and identified the following advantages of portables:

- the structure of the learning experiences set up by the teacher can be maintained;
- the image is less threatening. Pupils felt better working with computers in their own classroom;
- the computers were smaller so pupils were able to talk to each other over the machines.

Portable computers have become more popular in schools in recent years as they have become more powerful, reliable and affordable so that they compare favourably with desktops. In addition the recent improvements in wireless networking mean that it is now possible for a class of pupils to use portables even to access multimedia applications over a wireless network. Networks will be discussed in the next section but note that if your school does have a wireless network you should check with the network manager in your school where the wireless network is available rather than assuming that the same facilities are available throughout the school.

Many teachers now own a portable computer and use it to prepare material which they can then use in class by plugging into a data projector. If you intend to do this, do check well before the lesson so that any technical problems with hardware or software incompatibility can be overcome. It is usually a matter of just pressing a function key to make the display show on both the computer screen and the projected image, but this is not always the case.

Portable computers for pupil use may be managed in two main ways:

- pupils may be issued with their own computers which they bring to lessons and take responsibility for;
- sets of portable computers may be maintained in a classroom, department or central store for loan for use in lessons.

Two main issues with managing portable computers are reliability and security. You will need to check the school's policy and procedures for managing the security of portable computers. Reliability of portable computers has improved but there may still be problems with battery life. You should check what the procedures are for ensuring that batteries are recharged and whether all laptops could be plugged into the mains in the classroom if necessary.

USING NETWORKS, THE INTERNET AND DATA STORAGE

Most schools use an intranet that is managed within the school to link some or all of the computers in the school. This enables computer programs to be stored on a central server rather than on each individual computer and also provides storage for pupils' work. In order to use the intranet most schools now provide each pupil with their own login and data storage area. Generally the school intranet will also be linked to the internet but access may be restricted for security reasons. The school may be using wireless technology for all or part of its network, in which case there will be wireless hubs around the building and portables with wireless network cards.

Network facilities are becoming increasingly sophisticated and integrated so that data may be shared between schools, with the local education authority and with parents and pupils in their homes. Under the UK government's national grid for learning (NGfL) initiative Regional Broadband Consortia (RBCs) were set up in England to procure broadband internet access for schools in the local education authorities (LEAs) in their region. These RBCs are non-profit making organisations that now provide a range of services including data storage, electronic learning materials, video conferencing and management of network security as well as broadband. Schools vary over the extent to which these services are now managed by the school itself, the LEA, the RBC or in some cases commercial organisations. You may not need to understand the technical arrangements but in order to plan for pupils to have access to electronic resources and to be able to store, retrieve and view their work you need to find out the answers to the questions in Figure 3.1 by consulting school documents and talking to the network manager or other teachers.

USING THE WORLD WIDE WEB

In our study of experienced teachers' pedagogies with ICT, teachers agreed that pupils needed a structure to focus research tasks in order to use the Web effectively, and they needed to consider the following:

- the purpose and learning objectives for using the Web;
- many sites had too advanced language for young learners;
- sites which had more graphics helped interpretation for pupils;
- there is only a finite amount of time for pupils to complete the task in a lesson or lessons;
- even at A-level, pupils can meander unproductively when conducting research (Cox and Webb, 2004, p. 83).

- Where can teachers store materials on the network so that a particular class can use them in a lesson?
- Where do pupils store their work electronically?
- What software and materials are available on the network?
- Are the same software packages and materials available on all the computers in the school? So, for example, could pupils continue their work in lunch hours on library computers?
- Are teachers and pupils able to access the software and learning materials from home?
- What is the school's policy on Internet access?
- What is the school's behaviour policy relating to Internet use and email?

Figure 3.1 Questions to ask about data storage and access

Methods for scaffolding pupils' work on the Web include:

- downloading websites on to the school intranet;
- providing a set of web-links or 'bookmarks';
- starting with a class discussion to decide on keywords to use in searching.

INTERACTIVE WHITEBOARDS AND OTHER DISPLAY DEVICES

Large display devices such as data projectors that project the computer display on to a large screen enable the teacher or pupils to present material to the class. Teachers can prepare interesting materials incorporating pictures, diagrams, video, sound etc. and they can use and re-use them in a flexible way; for example, they can adjust the order of presenting material depending on how the pupils respond. Initially the preparation of material may be time-consuming but teachers gradually build up a bank of resources. The use of a range of sights and sounds can increase pupils' attention and interest and hence facilitate management of a whole-class discussion.

Interactive whiteboards (IWBs), as their name suggests, can support interactions between the teacher, pupils and computer software as well as enabling presentation of material. IWBs are large touch-sensitive boards that are connected to a data projector and a computer. The user can interact with the computer software by touching the board either with a finger or with a special pen. The potential uses of an IWB over a data projector alone include:

- handwriting on the board may be converted to text by handwriting recognition software;
- saving notes made on the board during the lesson;
- annotating diagrams and text;
- moving objects around by dragging on the board.

In addition some IWBs support sets of graphics tablets that enable pupils to interact with the board without leaving their seats.

Some basic practical considerations for managing IWB use include the following:

- Ensure that the material on the board is large enough for all pupils to see. Although the boards are quite large, text and icons can be difficult to see from the far side of the classroom. You may need to bring the pupils closer to the board.
- When you are interacting with the board you need to stand to one side as far as possible so that you and your shadow do not obscure the pupils' view of the board and you do not have the projector beam in your eyes.
- Make sure that the pens are available with the boards.
- Make sure that sunlight and other light reflections do not reduce the visibility of the board.

Glover and Miller (2001) identified three levels of IWB use:

- to increase efficiency, enabling teachers to draw upon a variety of ICT-based resources without disruption or loss of pace;
- to extend learning, using more engaging materials to explain concepts;

- to transform learning, creating new learning styles stimulated by interaction with the whiteboard.

IWBs (see Chapter 6) are now in widespread use in schools but early research has shown that few teachers make good use of the facilities to enable the range of interactions that is possible and that can benefit learning (BECTA, 2003). The intention of the teacher for whole-class or group interaction should be to encourage dialogue between the teacher and pupils and between pupils. An IWB can support teachers in developing this dialogue, for example by:

- providing a stimulus for discussion, e.g. from an image, piece of text, video clip etc.;
- enabling the teacher to pose a more complex question by displaying it on the IWB;
- enabling the teacher to ask 'what if?' questions when reviewing a model, simulation or scenario on the IWB and following a discussion to allow pupils or groups of pupils to test their ideas on the IWB.

An alternative solution for providing interactivity for a whole class with a computer is a data projector with a TabletPC and wireless or infra-red connectivity. The TabletPC can be used without wires anywhere in the classroom by the teacher or a pupil. The TabletPC screen is projected onto the big screen. The TabletPC supports handwriting recognition as well as being a fully functioning computer.

One other display technology is software that enables the teacher to view and control the screens of all the computers in a room from the teacher's computer. This enables the teacher to demonstrate software techniques or present ideas to the class who follow the presentations on their own screens. It does not support interactive teaching so well and it is not so easy for the teacher to watch what the class is doing while the teacher is manipulating the software. On the other hand, it does encourage pupils to watch the demonstration and prevents them from continuing their own work on the computers while the teacher is instructing the class.

MANAGING WHOLE-CLASS INTERACTIVE TEACHING

Technologies such as the IWB described in the previous section support whole-class teaching as well as group work. A study by Hennessey *et al.* (2003) with teachers who were developing and evaluating their practice with ICT showed that mediating interactions between pupils and technology through whole-class interactive teaching, modelling and discussion were under-developed, suggesting that these aspects of teachers' practice are not developed easily. This may be because teachers find the management of this difficult and/or because the questioning techniques are difficult to acquire. Black *et al.* (2002) discuss research that found that generally 'many teachers do not plan and conduct classroom dialogue in ways that might help pupils to learn' (p. 5). From their research with teachers, they suggested the following actions to promote useful dialogue through whole-class discussion that I suggest can be supported by using a computer with a large display device.

- Think carefully about framing questions that are worth asking, i.e. questions that explore issues that are critical to the development of pupils' understanding. The questions could be prepared in advance on a computer and presented on an IWB or other large display. A question could be supported by a picture, diagram or graph if this would help to make the question clear.

- Increase the time you wait for an answer (wait time) to at least several seconds in order to give pupils time to think. Having the question displayed on the screen ensures that all the pupils can review the question while they think of their answers.

- Expect everyone to have an answer and to contribute to the discussion and encourage pupils to value all responses as important for learning. Then all answers, right or wrong, can contribute to the discussion. The aim is thoughtful improvement rather than getting it right first time. If you have a set of graphics tablets, you could ask pupils to write the answers and then display them on the screen. Alternatively you could write the answers as the pupils say them. The advantage of doing this on an IWB is that you can easily come back to them at the end of the lesson or after several lessons.

Task 3.5
Planning classroom dialogue

For a lesson that you are planning, think of a set of questions that you will use in a class discussion. Ensure that the questions relate to your learning objectives and are worth asking.

Frame the questions carefully and decide whether any graphics would help to make them clear.

Try to predict the range of possible answers that pupils might give.

Decide how you will gather the pupils' answers and whether you will want to revisit the answers later in the lesson or series of lessons. Do you have access to ICT facilities that will support this?

How will you establish a classroom climate that will make all pupils feel comfortable about contributing?

MANAGING GROUP WORK WITH ICT

Studies of pupils using ICT suggest that effective pupil collaboration for learning is not easily achieved (Crook, 1998). In a three-year project in Australia, Goos *et al.* (2003), who studied mathematics learning using ICT, found that technology can facilitate collaborative enquiry in small group conversations. Their report highlights the vital role of the teacher in encouraging pupils to think and to use more powerful ways of working with technology. A teacher in the Computers as Learning Partners (CLP) project, where computer use was designed to be integrated into the science curriculum, described his role as:

> I'm kind of a catalyst. I try to not take part in the interaction between kids but to throw in some ideas that will stimulate a group discussion or introduce pivotal cases.[1] I probe kids to think. Then I let them take it from there.
>
> (Linn and Hsi, 2000, p. 132)

As for all collaborative work, group work with computers needs to be planned carefully and pupils need to be taught how to collaborate. They also need to understand what they are expected to learn as well as what they are aiming to produce otherwise they may become purely product focused. The ICT resources can provide a stimulus, focus for learning and various tools to support the group work but the teacher needs to plan and facilitate it. Therefore the teacher's role in planning and managing the lesson is crucial.

LESSON STRUCTURE IN LESSONS USING ICT

There is no good pedagogical reason why the use of ICT should determine the lesson structure but there has been a tendency for teachers who are using a computer room to neglect the whole-class introduction and the plenary in order to maximise the time that pupils spend working on the computers. This is now changing and indeed the Key Stage 3 ICT Strategy published by the DfES (2002) emphasises the importance of the 'three-part' lesson with an introduction and plenary. Since many lessons using ICT are quite long they are likely to be 'multi-part' with a range of different activities.

ICT AND PITFALLS FOR TEACHERS

The various types of ICT use discussed in this chapter provide useful and varied learning and teaching opportunities. However, there are a number of potential technical problems that can wreck a lesson for an unprepared teacher. It is best to work on the assumption that what can go wrong will go wrong sooner or later and this will usually happen at the worst possible time. You should also assume that no ICT devices are failsafe so you should have contingency plans. Pupils can become upset and difficult to manage if you don't cope with technical problems quickly.

Most teachers who use ICT a lot have some general non-ICT-based lesson plans that they can adapt to use if all the computers go out of action. However, if there is a strong chance of breakdown or the lesson is very important, for example if you are being observed, you should consider producing a 'plan B' that is clearly focused on the learning objectives for the lesson.

Figure 3.2 shows a set of technical problems that have happened to me or to trainee teachers that I have observed.

- The network goes down so you are teaching in a computer room with no working computers.
- You book a computer room with enough computers for your pupils to work individually but find that only two-thirds of them are working.
- The Internet connection goes down or works extremely slowly while pupils are searching for material for their projects.
- Some pupils can't log on to the network because they have forgotten their passwords.
- You prepare some work for your pupils and store it on a shared network area but then find that the computers in the room that you have booked are on a different network so you cannot access the work.
- The data projector overheats and will not work.
- The laptop screen will not display through the data projector.
- The document or spreadsheet that you have prepared will not load because it was developed in a different version of the word-processing or spreadsheet software.
- A computer crashes so a pupil loses all the work that he spent the last forty minutes on.
- The network is infected by a virus and your class's work cannot be accessed. The network manager is hoping to restore most of it by tomorrow but the class are waiting for you to teach them now.
- The printer jams so pupils cannot print out their work at the end of the lesson.

Figure 3.2 Some potential technical problems with ICT

Task 3.6
Coping with technical problems

For each of the technical problems in Figure 3.2, consider what steps you could take to avoid it and what contingency plans you would need to cope with it.

ICT AND PUPIL MISBEHAVIOUR

For the few pupils who are intent on disrupting classes or upsetting other people and for other pupils who just like to experiment, ICT does provide some opportunities. The equipment may be damaged by removing mice, removing balls from mice, sticky substances on keyboards, etc. Pupils who are very skilled ICT users may hack into the school network. You also need to be aware of the potential for email bullying. You can help to improve behaviour by knowing and implementing the school's policy and practices for computer use as well as being aware of potential opportunities for misbehaviour. Misdemeanours are usually dealt with by following the school's behaviour policy and practices as with any other bad behaviour.

Using ICT also provides opportunities for pupils to be off-task by surfing the Web or playing computer games. In some rooms, e.g. where computers are arranged in a horseshoe, you can check what pupils are doing by scanning round the screens. In many rooms however you cannot see all the screens at once so you need to circulate frequently to check that pupils are on task as well as to support their learning. Some pupils become very adept at keeping one eye on you and quickly flicking between programs when you approach so you need to notice what other programs, that they should not be working on, they have opened and minimised or hidden on the screen.

PLANNING LESSONS THAT USE ICT

Good planning is a pre-requisite for effective classroom management as well as effective teaching. When you plan lessons you work from your learning objectives and identify activities that will enable pupils to achieve these objectives. When planning to incorporate ICT into your lesson you need to consider what ICT resources are available and how they can be used to support these objectives. You can then think about how to structure the lesson and how to organise the pupils to optimise learning and make best of the resources available, e.g. will they work in groups? and how will you arrange the groups? You also need to consider what interventions the pupils at the computers are likely to need from you in order to learn effectively. Sometimes teachers assume that pupils will learn with ICT without intervention from the teacher but very few software packages are intended to take the place of the teacher.

Using ICT introduces some additional planning issues including:

- booking equipment;
- preparing electronic resources, e.g. a spreadsheet model that you want pupils to develop further;
- ensuring that you know how to access the hardware and software, e.g. you can't assume that all computers in the school provide access to the same software;
- consideration of pupils' ICT skills and understanding.

Throughout much of this chapter we have been looking at how to manage resources and the pupils in their interactions with the ICT hardware. However there are also different types of software that can be used in different ways and on the different types of hardware platforms such as desktops, portables and IWBs. Figure 3.3 shows a range of different scenarios for different types of ICT use reported by teachers who were experienced ICT users (Cox and Webb, 2004).

1   In small groups, pupils role-play a story or episode from fact or fiction which they video. They then edit the video to produce a film or multimedia presentation, for a particular audience.

2   The whole class brainstorm about a topic to produce a mind-map on the interactive whiteboard.

3   Pupils use a modelling environment to challenge their own misconceptions and build steps in a model.

4   The teacher leads a question and answer session with the whole class based on a simulation, animation or problem-solving activity on the interactive whiteboard.

5   Pupils work at a cluster of computers in the classroom on a data-logging or problem-solving task that focuses on some specific learning objectives for the current topic while the rest of the class work on other activities.

6   Pupils work collaboratively in groups during lessons to research a topic from the Web, obtain material and develop a multimedia presentation, poster, or newspaper.

7   The teacher develops a Web-based multimedia resource that functions as a set of notes and learning activities. The teacher refers to it in the lesson and sets homework based on the resource.

8   Pupils work individually to research a topic from an Internet, intranet or CD-ROM based resource prepared or selected by the teacher and produce notes or answers to specific questions.

9   Pupils research a topic individually by conducting their own Web searches and making notes.

10 Pupils construct models to investigate the relationship between variables in a process.

11 Pupils search a specialised database to find answers to questions

Figure 3.3 Scenarios for different types of ICT use (Cox and Webb, 2004, pp. 122–3)

Task 3.7
Planning for using ICT

Choose one of the scenarios from Figure 3.3 that you think might be useful in your own teaching.

If you used this approach in your subject, what might it enable pupils to learn?

List the resources, both ICT and other types, that would be needed.

What ICT skills and understanding would the pupils need?

How would you structure the lesson and/or series of lessons?

How would you organise the pupils?

How would you organise the resources?

What technical problems might occur and what would be your contingency plans?

SUMMARY

In this chapter you have been encouraged to think about the issues for classroom management associated with using different types of ICT hardware and software in different settings and for different purposes. There are many ways of using ICT to enhance learning and teaching and different approaches create different issues for classroom management.

When you are planning a lesson in which ICT will be used, you need to think first about your learning objectives and whether the ICT resources available to you will support pupils in achieving those objectives or whether it would be better to use a different approach. Then you need to think about exactly what software and other ICT facilities you will need and book them if necessary.

You will need to plan how you will manage the equipment, organise the pupils and encourage and facilitate suitable interactions that will promote learning. In doing so you need to consider the pupils' ICT skills and understanding, their ability to collaborate, what support they will need and how it will be provided. You should also try to anticipate any potential problems and devise contingency plans.

Remember that the ICT equipment and resources can provide a stimulus and a focus for learning and a range of tools to support interactive class discussions and group work but it is still how the teacher plans and manages the learning that makes the greatest impact.

NOTE

1   Pivotal cases are concepts or models that motivate rethinking or reorganising of scientific views.

REFERENCES

Becta (2003) 'What the research says about interactive whiteboards'. Online. Available HTTP: <http://www. becta.org.uk/page_documents/research/wtrs_whiteboards.pdf>. Accessed 24/03/05.

Black, P., Harrison, C., Lee, C., Marshall, B. and Wiliam, D. (2002) *Working Inside the Black Box: Assessment for Learning in the Classroom*, London: King's College, London, Department of Education and Professional Studies.

Comber, C., Watling, R., Lawson, T., Cavendish, S., McEune, R. and Paterson, F. (2002) *Learning at Home and School. Case Studies: A report to the DfES*. ICT in Schools Research and Evaluation Series – No. 8, London and Coventry: British Educational Communications and Technology Agency and the Department for Education and Skills.

Cornu, B. (1995) 'New technologies: integration into education', in D. Watson and D. Tinsley (eds) *Integrating Information Technology into Education*, London: Chapman and Hall.

Cox, M.J. (1997) 'Identification of the changes in attitude and pedagogical practices needed to enable teachers to use information technology in the school curriculum', in D. Passey and B. Samways (eds) *IFIP: Information Technology: Supporting Change through Teacher Education*, London: Chapman and Hall.

Cox, M.J. and Abbott, C. (2004) *ICT and Attainment: A Review of the Research Literature*, Coventry and London: British Educational Communications and Technology Agency/ Department for Education and Skills.

Cox, M.J. and Webb, M.E. (2004) *ICT and Pedagogy: A Review of the Research Literature*, Coventry and London: British Educational Communications and Technology Agency/ Department for Education and Skills.

Crook, C. (1998) 'Children as computer users: the case of collaborative learning', *Computers & Education*, **30**: 237–47.

DES (1989) *Discipline in School* (The Elton Report), London: HMSO.

DfES (2002) *Key Stage 3 National Strategy Framework for teaching ICT capability: Years 7, 8 and 9*. DfES Publications. Online. Available HTTP: <http://www.standards.dfes.gov.uk/ keystage3/subjects/ict/>.

Glover, D. and Miller, D. (2001) 'Running with technology: the pedagogic impact of the large-scale introduction of interactive whiteboards in one secondary school', *Journal of Information Technology for Teacher Education*, **10**: 257–78.

Goos, M., Galbraith, P., Renshaw, P. and Geiger, V. (2003) 'Perspectives on technology mediated learning in secondary school mathematics classrooms', *Journal of Mathematical Behavior*, **22**: 73–89.

Hennessy, S., Deaney, R. and Ruthven, K. (2003) *Pedagogic Strategies for Using ICT to Support Subject Teaching and Learning: An Analysis Across 15 Case Studies*, Research Report 03/1, Cambridge: University of Cambridge.

Hudson, B. (1997) 'Group work with multimedia', *MicroMath*, **13**, 15–20.

Jarvis, T., Hargreaves, L. and Comber, C. (1997) 'An evaluation of the role of email in promoting science investigative skills in primary rural schools in England', *Research in Science Education*, **27**: 223–36.

Kounin, J.S. (1970) *Discipline and Group Management in Classrooms*, New York: Holt, Rinehart and Winston.

Kozma, R.B.E. (ed.) (2003) *Technology, Innovation, and Educational Change: A Global Perspective*, Washington, DC: International Society for Educational Technology (ISTE).

Linn, M.C. and Hsi, S. (2000) *Computers, Teachers, Peers: Science Learning Partners*, London: Erlbaum.

Martin, A. (1995) 'Portability as a catalyst for cross-curricular information technology permeation', *World Conference on Computers in Education*, London: Chapman and Hall.

Mayer-Smith, J., Pedretti, E. and Woodrow, J. (2000) 'Closing of the gender gap in technology enriched science education: a case study', *Computers & Education*, **35**: 51–63.

McLoughlin, C. and Oliver, R. (1999) 'Pedagogic roles and dynamics in telematics environments', in M. Sellinger and J. Pearson (eds) *Telematics in Education: Trends and Issues*, Oxford: Elsevier Science.

Moseley, D., Higgins, S., Bramald, R., Hardman, F., Miller, J., Mroz, M., Tse, H., Newton, D., Thompson, I., Williamson, J., Halligan, J., Bramald, S., Newton, L., Tymms, P., Henderson, B. and Stout, J. (1999) *Effective Pedagogy using ICT for Literacy and Numeracy in Primary Schools*, Newcastle: University of Newcastle.

Pedretti, J.E., Mayer-Smith, J. and Woodrow, J. (1998) 'Technology, text, and talk: students' perspectives on teaching and learning in a technology-enhanced secondary science classroom', *Science Education*, **82**: 569–90.

Ruthven, K. and Hennessy, S. (2002) 'A practitioner model of the use of computer-based tools and resources to support mathematics teaching and learning', *Educational Studies in Mathematics*, **49**: 47–88.

Waxman, H.C. and Huang, S.-Y. L. (1996) 'Classroom instruction differences by level of technology use in middle school mathematics', *Journal of Educational Computing Research*, **14**: 157–69.

4 Whole-school Approaches: Integrating ICT Across the Curriculum

Marilyn Leask and Lawrence Williams

INTRODUCTION

Many of the chapters in this book focus on what you, as a teacher, might do in your classroom. However, research (OECD, 2001; Kington *et al.*, 2001, 2002) into the role of ICT in whole-school improvement illustrates the value gained for pupils and teachers when there is a whole-school integrated approach to the use of ICT. This chapter provides examples of such approaches.

The pace of technological development is such that the world many children face outside school, demands ICT competence. E-commerce (electronic commerce) is growing, with business transactions on the web and jobs related to this form of technology rapidly increasing. The distinction between the TV and the computer is increasingly blurred as both items offer both functions. Network literacy, i.e. the capacity to use information and communication technologies appropriately to communicate and to access information, is an important basic competence for all young people. We suggest that network literacy is a vital extension of the ability to read and write.

In 1998, a survey carried out by the Specialist Schools Trust (Gillmon, 1998, p. 7) indicated that 'there are approximately 450,000 serving teachers in the UK whose initial professional training did not include IT. This phenomenon has occurred within their teaching lifetime, and for the most part they have been expected to take it on board and integrate it into their teaching on the back of minimal training. Small wonder that the level of confidence is low'. Increasingly, teachers are competent in the use of ICT in their subject but given the range of possibilities for creating different learning opportunities using different forms of ICT, a planned whole-school approach offers both an integrated experience to pupils but also supports teachers in becoming familiar with the forms of ICT most appropriate for their subject, knowing that other teachers will be offering pupils other complementary experiences.

Some teachers who can see the potential of ICT to support teaching and learning are in schools where much of what we discuss in this chapter, seems impossible to achieve in their school. Attitudes of staff may appear set and apparently unchangeable, and indeed in some schools, change is very slow. We predict that it will be many years before the knowledge recorded and presented in this book, is embedded in the professional knowledge of the majority of teachers in the UK. It is of course not just attitudes which need to change. In the introduction, we discuss some of the hurdles which have to be overcome if we are to integrate ICT use into the curriculum.

Where staff work together, supporting one another in experimentation and change, the acquisition of skills and knowledge is easier. In this chapter, we chart the progress of development in one school over a four-year period.

The projects described in this chapter, involving as they do staff from departments across the school, provide opportunities for teachers to learn together about the various technologies and to build new practices together. We suggest that undertaking such activities promotes attitudinal change and training through an experiential model which is coupled with just-in-time learning, i.e. you learn just what you need to achieve your current goal, rather than undertaking a block of training in which you try to learn everything at once.

OBJECTIVES

By the end of this chapter you should have considered:

- how the school ethos and the school's philosophy of learning can support the development of ICT across the curriculum;
- possible learning outcomes for pupils and staff where a number of departments collaborate in undertaking cross-curricular ICT projects;
- whether ICT projects involving staff from a range of departments are feasible in your context.

SCHOOL ETHOS AND CHANGE

In a US-based study of a group of 'networked schools' where ICT use permeated the curriculum, school administration and the professional lives of teachers, Wasser *et al.* identify the importance of a supportive, collaborative school ethos. They define three major features in 'truly networked schools' as:

1 networked work space combined with a defined set of common software tools and peripherals;
2 electronic mail internal electronic communications;
3 internet (email to the outside and web activities).

(Wasser *et al.*, 1998, p. 2)

The schools in which Wasser *et al.* worked offered teachers and pupils access to work space both public and private on the school server (the computer directing the network).

Software was also available to allow users to combine text with images and sound. The electronic mail in schools in the study allowed schools within the cluster to improve communications. They found, however, that collaborative work between staff was crucial:

> What is important about a networked school, as we have defined here, is that EVERYONE is engaged in this process of coming to grips with the notion of the network and its organisation. In pre-networked schools, it is typical that only a few teachers are engaged in this process, meaning that there are far fewer opportunities for discussion about the network and experience with technology to convey the environment.
>
> (Wasser *et al.*, 1998, p. 7)

Research into the integration of IT into whole-school practice reported by Deryn Watson (1997) showed that staff in schools where one person was seen to be the holder of knowledge about IT, delegated their professional responsibilities in this area to the individual. Consequently, there was no shared body of professional knowledge about the use of IT and when the individual left, the knowledge left with them. Schools can no longer afford to allow this concentration of knowledge to happen.

Task 4.1
Is the ethos in your school supportive of change?

We suggest you undertake a self-appraisal of your 'network literacy', testing your knowledge and understanding of ICT tools against those outlined as necessary in Chapters 1, 2 and 5. Now we ask you to consider the ethos in your school. To what extent are the staff working together in considering the role ICT can play in the experience of pupils at the school?

Teachers in schools need to be provided with technical support to enable them to be confident that the technology will work in the lesson. Otherwise, the teacher is faced with having to have two lessons prepared, one for if the technology works and the other for if it doesn't. The quality of technical support has been found in early ICT projects (Leask and Wilder, 1996; Leask, 2002) to be a critical factor in aiding or hindering whole-school development. Schools are solving this in different ways. Schools with large budgets are employing technicians and teaching assistants to support teachers' use of the technology (see Chapter 2). Other schools in a cluster may be able to share the costs of employing one person for the cluster. Companies also provide managed services for schools.

Task 4.2
How is technical support provided?

Investigate technical support in your school. How are hardware and software problems solved? How is the current set-up enabling or hindering the teaching and learning process? Discuss the issue of training and costs with staff. Consider the effectiveness of current strategies and provision.

There is a variety of solutions to these very real problems which schools are solving in different ways. Working with ICT across the school does provide a supportive framework for staff working within these constraints. In the case study which follows, you will see how at Holy Cross Convent School, staff skills and expertise were built up over a period of years through collaborative work across departments.

In the section which follows, Lawrence Williams, the Director of Studies from Holy Cross Convent School in Surrey describes how the school's philosophy of learning has supported the development of a whole-school approach to the use of information communications technology which took place over a period of several years and emerged from practice in several projects. In the first part of his contribution he looks briefly at what sort of curriculum we need for the twenty-first century and how we prepare pupils to become active participants in a highly technological world.

The model of cross-curricular projects supported by ICT, developed from a project embracing English and Dance, which widened to include Music and Drama, and eventually covered every aspect of the school curriculum, through the Caribbean Project. Further projects allowed staff to refine and develop their skills still more.

KNOWLEDGE AS A SEAMLESS FABRIC: DEVELOPING A MODEL OF AN INTEGRATED CURRICULUM SUPPORTED BY ICT

This section has three main aims:

First, to show how one school made a steady and continuous development in its use of ICT across the curriculum. Second, to outline some specific examples of our practice. Third, to suggest a cross-curricular model of working which not only uses ICT to support all aspects of the curriculum, but attempts to unify that curriculum, by opening windows between subjects, while retaining the integrity of individual subject specialisms. Other examples of schools' incremental development of ICT across the curriculum are available through the publications of the OECD ICT and whole-school improvement project where case studies of the role of ICT in whole-school improvement were undertaken across countries and across types of schools (OECD, 2001; Kington et al., 2001, 2002).

The school's philosophy of learning

Here Lawrence Williams is describing the work done in his own school. The model which was developed at Holy Cross is based on a philosophical position which regards knowledge as a seamless fabric, a belief written into the Mission Statement. It made no sense to the school to abandon the excellent, integrated approach of the local Primary schools (ages 5 to 11 years) in order to deliver the National Curriculum, so that, to parody the secondary curriculum only slightly: 'History never happened anywhere, that's Geography. Places don't have a history, that's a separate subject.' And worst of all, as far as our examination system is concerned: 'Shakespeare didn't write English, he wrote English Literature, and you must not confuse the two!'

Alan Cribb in the 'Philosophy of Education' makes the following point:

> We do not experience the world separated into ingredients. If we want to under-
> stand or change it, we must be able to integrate different forms of knowledge.
> (Cribb, 1995, pp. 78–81)

How else can we ensure that our children emerge equipped to participate as active members in a highly technological world?

Holy Cross School started, then, from this belief that children learn better when links are made between different subjects, and that the computer provides teachers with an immensely powerful set of tools, which enable teachers to develop a model of learning which serves this purpose.

The model developed in response to a number of challenges which faced the school over a period of years, and by adopting a positive stance in each case, the staff was able to turn problems into solutions, and thereby advance the learning of the pupils.

The first problem concerned the restricting effect which the English National Curriculum was having on the development of Expressive Arts in the school. Dance and Drama were reduced in curriculum time to a risible amount. The second problem was how to teach a programme of English Literature designed by a government committee. I'm sure you can imagine the result! Accordingly, staff devised the following system (see Figure 4.1).

The second project was also the solution to two problems:

- How do you teach a Shakespeare play meaningfully to thirteen-year-olds?
- How do you develop the use of the new digital camera which we had purchased as a result of the success of the Dance Project?

The solution was to unite the two, see Figure 4.2.

The next problem arose out of a school inspection. The school was highly praised for its work, and was named as one of the most improved in the UK, but (and there is always a 'but') the inspectors suggested that we should more actively celebrate the cultural diversity of the pupils. We took this challenge seriously, and embarked on what was to prove to be a turning point in the academic success of the school, the Caribbean Project, see Figure 4.3.

Such was the impact of the Caribbean Project across a variety of learning outcomes, that we decided to take a further step. There were two faults in the Caribbean Project work. One was that too many children had a tendency to produce work which contained elements that though well researched and stunningly presented, were copied from books or down-loaded from CD-ROM, with little evidence of some of it having actually passed through the brain. Secondly, scientific work was poorly represented.

So, the next project was designed to solve these two problems. I realised that I had, in fact, created the curriculum model inside out. However, by restructuring the model, these

Dance and Drama were concentrated into useful, practical blocks of time. Then, in English, we studied the particular literary extracts, highlighting the metaphors and similes in the text. Next, we went to the Dance Studio and explored how these images could be set to music, illustrating the effects which Shakespeare and other writers had created. We recorded these dance performances onto video tape, exported digitised still images into our desk-top publishing program, and word-processed articles about the performances, in the role of newspaper reporters. The quality of the finished work was astonishing. By using the desk-top environment to unite English and Dance, new standards of achievement were set.

As pupils' commented:

'When I first heard that we were going to have dance lessons during English, I thought to myself, "What has dance to do with English?" Now I can see that dance is another way of expressing yourself. It also becomes useful in explaining the poem and making it become alive.'

'Putting the poem into dance helped the poem actually come alive. It wasn't a poem to me – it was a real situation.' and

'I learnt things in dance that I had never thought about before.'

I find these perceptions astonishing for pupils aged thirteen.

The computer had led us to a new way of approaching learning. This was an exciting beginning.

Figure 4.1 Project 1 – Integrating Dance, Drama and English through the use of ICT

Our main aim was to develop an understanding of 'Romeo and Juliet', as was required for a national test. This would then expand into a study of 'West Side Story' and Prokofiev's 'Romeo and Juliet', so that we could build on the earlier dance work. We planned to produce a dance assessment, a drama assessment and a word-processed English Literature assessment, as well as developing our understanding of how the digital camera could be usefully deployed as a supporting tool for drama.

The advantage of the digital camera is that images can be fed directly into a monitor and viewed instantly. This has obvious applications in drama. The pupils prepared the text, chose a scene to dramatise, and then selected a moment from their performances to 'freeze frame'. Two images were taken with the camera, and these two images could be discussed immediately in class with regards to their visual effectiveness. By moving from, say picture three to four, and then back again, a useful and otherwise impossible comparison could be made. Of course, since the image was digitised, it could now be imported back into the desk-top, and word-processed text could be added. This was done with a prepared page of four frames, available on the school network – to save time and effort – a quotation was added below the picture, a summary of the scene followed this, and an in-role response finished the assignment. Once again, the response of the pupils was staggering. The sensitivity of the writing was amazing, and it was clearly the integration of the various elements of the process which had brought this about. This marked another step in our journey. (Chapter 7 provides detailed guidance about the use of digital video in your classroom.)

Figure 4.2 Project 2 – Romeo and Juliet: integrating Music, Drama, Dance and English through the use of ICT

This was to be a detailed study of every aspect of Caribbean life, studied across the whole curriculum, and using as many IT tools as possible (to develop skills) – word-processing, desk-top publishing, spreadsheets, databases, clip art, scanned images, digital camera work, draw files, graphics packages – and would be completed in a single school term by all of the lower school (some 400 pupils). Each Department contributed ideas appropriate to its own needs in meeting the requirements of the National Curriculum, and the pupils moved from subject to subject, building on their knowledge of the topic.

It is important to note that there was no pressure for Departments to contribute particular amounts of time or resources, only that which arises naturally out of existing schemes of work. Looking back at the scale of this project, it was clearly complete madness on my part, and my only defence is that the pupils and staff made it completely successful in every way. I was grateful for this. The creative energy which it released was colossal. **The learning outcomes went far beyond what we expected.** Pupils visited libraries, consulted CD-ROMs, searched the internet, went to travel agents for brochures, telephoned Trinidad (I was relieved to learn that they had parental permission to do this). They danced to the music which they had recorded onto audio tape, took photographs of the dances with the digital camera, imported the images into the desk-top, and added word-processed comment. They used their IT lessons (once a week), time before school, lunch time, time after school (often until 6 o'clock), their computers at home, where possible, and simply poured information into their project folders. An outline of aims was given, but this was completely ignored as they sailed graciously past every assessment marker devised. The finished folders were of such a high standard, displaying knowledge, skill and creative energy that colleagues from colleges and universities in the UK and the USA asked to borrow them. They were used to support a Race Relations Conference, because of the harmonious multi-cultural dimension they gave to the school. Again, the use of computers to create the folders had proved a triumph.

Figure 4.3 Project 3 – the Caribbean project: using ICT to unite subjects across the curriculum around a theme

two problems could be solved simultaneously. Instead of an Expressive Arts based project, with science and technology added on, as it were, we would start, instead, with solid scientific content and ensure that the pupils word-processed their own experiments, undertaken in the laboratories, and create the Light Project, see Figure 4.4.

Clearly a wide variety of learning outcomes were being achieved. Grades achieved by pupils were higher than expected.

Next steps at Holy Cross School

From this success, we decided to develop another project, centred this time on Japan, for our Year 9 pupils, and drawing together all of the experience outlined here. Each Department would contribute as much as is appropriate to the topic, as shown on the curriculum model used for the Light Project. We aimed to use the model this time, however, to target specific teaching Departments, so that staff training needs could be met. For example, Science teachers wished to develop their skills in data-logging, and the Art Department wanted to use a new graphics package for computer-controlled calligraphy work. I wanted to experiment with sending music files in midi format to Japan, so that the accuracy of our attempts to write Japanese music could be monitored at source! The model

The project was therefore initiated by the Science Department with Year 8. The topics covered would have cropped up in the syllabus later in the year, but they were brought together in the Autumn Term. The topics included the following:

- The eclipse of the sun and the partial eclipse
- How to view a partial eclipse with a pin-hole camera
- Colour and colour chemistry
- Fibre optic light and cable
- Neon lighting and gas discharge lamps
- Holograms
- Shadows / shadow theatres
- Camouflage
- Radiation
- Reflection
- Refraction
- Lenses
- Photosynthesis
- Fuels
- The changing seasons
- Light detectors

In Drama, by now a familiar partner in all our work, the pupils improvised short scenes on the theme of good and evil (light and darkness). The Drama teacher used the digital camera to take a picture of a freeze-frame from the play, which the pupils then imported into the computer. They then wrote up what the play was about underneath the picture. Although the picture would only be printed in black and white in their project folders (colour printing is horribly expensive!) the pupils discussed what colour of light could be used in the staging of their performances. Red was seen as an appropriate colour for evil and anger, and white or blue was thought to represent goodness and 'calmness'. Some pupils word-processed a play to go with their Science Shadow Theatre. The moral dimension of the characters in the plays was broadened in the Religious Studies lessons into moral and spiritual aspects of good and evil. The symbolism of light and dark recurs throughout the Bible and the liturgy, so the pupils studied this, too, and presented attractive work as part of the Light Project.

When the Art Department started working on the project the pupils already had a far greater understanding of colour, light and shadow than would normally be expected. The subject was infinite when it came to painting and drawing. In English, they spent two double periods in the computer room. They scanned through a slide-show of 100 high-quality images installed on the network, and chose the one they most liked to write a poem about light on. They then printed the poem together with the picture. A student teacher was helping with this lesson, and was amazed to see how easy they found it to write something which would have been quite abstract as a normal classroom task. Obviously the finished product gave them a great deal of satisfaction, and they proudly showed her their work the following day. They also used a graphics package to create decorative 'light' vocabulary, and explored the uses of the thesaurus to find more words. Some groups did the same in French.

Later in the term, the new music software 'Sibelius' was deployed on the school network, a music keyboard was added (for faster input), and the pupils were soon able to write both the words and the music for some Christmas songs to do with light, using the pentatonic scale – required for the National Curriculum in Music.

In Mathematics, they studied enlargement, reflection, and mirror images. In Technology, they made circuits, created stained glass mirror effects, and used computer-aided design to make T-shirts with computer-embroidered candles on them. In Geography, they studied the sun, the seasons, and starlight using CD-ROMS. A group that went to Germany returned and wrote about the Christmas lights they had seen there. The project culminated in a beautiful Advent Service in the Church, with carols, dance, and drama, all linked to the theme of Light, and a fitting conclusion to a busy and successful term's work.

Pupils' comments included the following:

'I like using computers. It gives me more confidence.'

continued...

'It made me go to the library more than I normally do … I didn't use to stay in the computer room after school, but now I do.'

'I could use a lot of resources on the computer. Talk to other people.'

'I really understand science better now, and enjoy it more.'

'I enjoyed doing this project, and I find the research to be fun, as there are so many different sources of information, and it was inspiring.'

'It showed how different subjects can be linked up.'

Figure 4.4 Project 4 – the Light Project: using ICT to unite subjects across the curriculum around concepts from the science curriculum

for integrating the curriculum and ICT outlined above, can thus be used as a professional development tool, as well as for inspiring the pupils, see Figure 4.5.

Mrs Watson, the Head Teacher commented, 'We see our many international links as small steps towards world peace. If our children can grow up with an understanding of people from different cultures across the world, they will find no need to engage in conflict with them, when they are older. We see the Internet, used creatively, as a powerful tool for spreading peace and harmony in the world. Today marks one more step forward towards that goal.'

Spurred on by this success, the next move was to see if Music could be added as another dimension to our work over the Internet. Accordingly, the school set out to collaborate with a school in Japan – Ikeda Junior High School, Osaka. Coupled into a whole Year Group project (Year 9) using IT across the curriculum, and incorporating an Open Day with Performing Arts productions (integrating music, dance, drama and IT) the school sent Ikeda JHS some simple specifications for music to be performed on the actual day. This was accompanied by explorations of the technical difficulties of collaborating in this way.

Having thus established a successful pattern of working, the students at Ikeda JHS set about writing some Japanese-style fanfares to introduce the Open Day.

The whole project brought Holy Cross staff and pupils, and the work of Ikeda pupils together in a day of vibrant collaboration. On the Open Day, the school welcomed a small Japanese vocal group, who sang a number of Japanese songs, and performed a traditional dance. The girls from Year 9 then took up the theme in a series of integrated music/dance/drama/martial arts performances, in which they explored various aspects of Japanese life and culture.

This was all carried out against a colourful background of art, textile, and pottery displays, and included a range of Project Folders produced during Information Technology lessons, which showed the girls of the school using and integrating up to sixteen different IT tools. These included desk-top publishing programs, word-processors, databases and spreadsheets, flat-bed scanners, clip art, digital cameras, CD-ROMS, files from the Internet, files from the school's intranet, art packages, graphics programs, and music software.

Figure 4.5 Project 5 – Japan Project: using email, image files, and music files to support pupil learning

CONCLUSIONS FROM THESE PROJECTS

We have found that the stimulus of using ICT to develop our curriculum has had a quite astonishing effect on the motivation of pupils across the whole school. There is a real sense of purpose to all of the related curricular activities. Our belief is that, like any new technology, ICT is neither intrinsically useful nor interesting. However, our experience shows us very clearly that, used creatively, ICT tools open up new audiences, bring together new partners in learning, and stimulate pupils to reach ever-increasing high standards in their work. We owe it to our students, therefore, to approach these opportunities with all of our skill and imagination.

GUIDELINES FOR THOSE WANTING TO DEVELOP WHOLE-SCHOOL APPROACHES

On the basis of the experience at Holy Cross, the following points may provide useful guidance to others following in our steps.

- **Confidence** Approach this model of work with confidence. The model works extremely effectively, and has considerable educational research supporting it.
- **Enthusiasm** No-one will follow you if you are half-hearted in your leadership.
- **Build a team** Begin by working in small ways with people who share your vision. This might, at first, be just one colleague in a different subject area. Expand the team as your success grows. This may take months or years. Be sensible in your expectations concerning change. At Holy Cross this process took nearly three years.
- **Keep others informed** If you want more equipment, resources or time, then let people know of early successes, so that they are encouraged to support your work.
- **Display good work** Publish your pupils' success by displaying their work prominently everywhere (not just in the computer rooms). Give copies to your Senior Management Team.
- **Work within the right framework** Don't do ANYTHING which distorts good practice, or which distracts others from their own responsibilities. Let others work with you to develop their own skills, and meet their own agendas, within your over-all framework.
- **The framework** Create a framework (an outline, a set of goals, a set of tasks) and then let the pupils have freedom to explore for themselves. They will ALWAYS surprise you by exceeding your most ambitious expectations!
- **Above all keep focused** on the learning outcomes to be achieved by the pupils. Ask yourself WHY you are using a computer. If the answer is not convincing, use a pencil!

The work undertaken at Holy Cross provides examples of the learning outcomes, the constraints and the excitement engendered in pupils by integrated ICT projects. In the following activity, we suggest you consider the approach taken by Holy Cross and think about whether it would work in your context.

Clearly there are many opportunities for developing pupils' ICT capabilities in a whole range of subject areas. How the school tackles this challenge is a responsibility of management and teachers wishing to work across curriculum will no doubt need to convince appropriate managers within the school.

Task 4.3
Identifying ICT opportunities
across the curriculum

Consider how ICT is integrated into the curriculum in your current school. Read through the curriculum documents for your subject area together with any relevant school documents to identify how ICT relates to your specific area. Make notes about how you feel that ICT could be used to support teaching and learning in your subject area. Now consider other subject areas. What opportunities for cross-curricular work might arise between your subject area and other areas? If appropriate, discuss these ideas with other colleagues and perhaps start with planning small projects.

SUMMARY

There are a number of other projects and initiatives integrating the use of ICT into a range of curriculum areas and in which groups of teachers from different subject areas are working together. Building the resources on the school intranet is an important way of drawing on the varied expertise of staff and creating an environment where planning time can be reduced. Staff interviewed for the English case studies in the OECD ICT and Whole School Improvement project (Kington *et al.*, 2001) said that considerable time was saved by such shared working and once all staff had their own laptops which gave them access to the network and resources when they were planning. The BECTA site gives extensive examples of good practice in the use of ICT in classrooms. It is recommended that you spend some hours reviewing the material made available for you through BECTA.

The school-to-school link which Lawrence describes above can be used for a whole range of purposes and projects. Teachers with whom we work have explored the possibilities of virtual field trips and virtual factory tours (in preparation for work experience) and in collaboration with colleagues in other countries. Clearly, opportunities to extract more learning outcomes from school exchanges exist. Aspects of school exchanges which could be included are pre-visit preparation, communications during a visit, e.g. letters home, and post-visit review. Building in a multimedia presentation of the visit for pressing as a CD-ROM for those who attended is another option. (CD-ROM writers can be bought relatively cheaply.) These three opportunities apply as much to the teachers organising such trips and integrating the work into the curriculum as to the pupils who are undergoing the experience.

Developing content for the school website provides opportunities for collaborative, integrated work across subject areas and not just between teachers. Different year groups, for example, could be given responsibility for maintaining aspects of the school site (e.g. the annual drama production) and this responsibility could be passed on year after year. This work could involve tasks focused around particular sets of learning outcomes. (Care should be taken not to publish details about pupils which make them easy to identify, in areas of the website which are publicly accessible.) Files containing video clips and pictures can be quite large. It is worth knowing that files can be compressed using 'zip' software.[1] You can expect to find help in creating webpages within your school. Otherwise approach your local education authority or BECTA.

These sorts of possibilities highlight the need for a school to adopt policies covering the use of the internet. Examples are provided on the National Association for Co-ordinators of IT (ACITT) website.[2] The documents there include an example of a parental permission letter, guidelines for pupil use and sanctions.

NOTES

1   Free software for compressing large files, e.g. for transfer between machines. Online. Available HTTP: <http://www.winzip.com>.
2   The parental permission and school policy advice from ACITT. Online. Available HTTP: <http://www.acitt.org.uk>.

REFERENCES

Cribb, A. (1995) 'Philosophy of education: a few questions', *Educational Issues: A Reader*, London: Kings College.

Gillmon, E. (1998) *Building Teachers' ICT Skills: The Problem and a Framework for the Solution*, London: Technology Colleges Trust.

Kington, A., Harris, S. and Leask, M. (2002) 'Innovative practice using ICT in schools: findings from two case studies', *Management in Education*, 16(1): 31–5.

Kington, A., Harris, S., Lee, B. and Leask, M. (2001) 'Information and communications technology and whole school improvement: case studies of organisational change', paper reporting outcomes of the UK case studies for the OECD ICT and Whole School Improvement research project. BERA, September.

Leask, M. (2002) *The New Opportunities Fund ICT Training for Teachers and School Librarians: Progress Review and Lessons Learned Through the Central Quality Assurance Process in England*, London: Teacher Training Agency. Online. Available HTTP: <http://www.teach-ttaa.gov.uk>.

Leask M. and Wilder, P. (1996) 'Project Connect evaluation report', Bedford: De Montfort University.

OECD (2001) Case studies of innovative schools use of ICT are listed on the OECD website. Online. Available HTTP: <http://www.oecd.org/home/>. Searching the site for 'ICT and whole-school improvement' brings up the studies.

Wasser, J., McNamara, E. and Grant, C. (1998) 'Electronic networks and systemic school reform: understanding the diverse roles and functions of telecommunications in a changing school environment', paper presented at the American Educational Research Association Conference, San Diego, USA, April (available on the AERA 1998

Conference website. Online. Available HTTP: <http://www.scre.ac.uk/bera> via the web links button).

Watson, D. (1997) 'A positional good: change and IT', paper presented at the British Educational Research Association Conference, York, September.

5 ICT Tools and Applications

Michelle Selinger

INTRODUCTION

This chapter explores the extent to which a range of ICT tools and Internet connectivity can be used to transform the learning environment. The answer to real educational transformation and improving student achievement using ICT is not simply providing access to content, but using the full range of tools available for students to seek the answers to authentic (relevant to the student's life experience) questions in a supported environment where well-constructed resources are just one part of the equation and where critical thinking and problem-solving skills are key. My background as a teacher, a teacher educator, a researcher and now working for an IT company as an education adviser, has enabled me to visit classrooms across Europe, the Middle East and Africa and be involved in observing and advising on the use of ICT for teaching and learning. This chapter is based on the experience I have gained and explains how these tools can justify the use of ICT alongside or instead of traditional text-based resources; the possibilities the tools open up for individualisation and personalisation; the potential for learning to be collaborative and to be supported and accessed anytime and anywhere; and the opening up of the classroom through access to other teachers, experts and students in other schools nationally and internationally.

Each section describes and explains the uses of a wide range of tools; firstly content development tools are explored, namely virtual learning environments (VLEs) and associated managed learning environments (MLEs); then a range of tools to engage and motivate learners, to offer remediation through revisiting a previous learning experience or being offered an alternative; and to provide a virtual lab environment. There is a section on collaboration and communication tools and finally a section on the devices available to receive the learning resources with a discussion on the pros and cons of each tool.

Each section provides ideas about how and when to make use of the tools and should leave you with a greater appreciation of the potential that ICT has to enhance the teaching and learning experience for every student and every teacher.

OBJECTIVES

By the end of this chapter you should:

* know about a wide range of tools and applications that can be used for teaching and learning with ICT;
* understand the potential they have for you as a teacher;
* be able to make informed decisions about which tools and devices are most appropriate for the subject and topics you will be teaching.

TECHNOLOGY AND EDUCATION

You will have read earlier in this book that there is clear evidence that ICT can improve the quality of education. The use of learner management systems and administration tools can bring increased transparency to procedures, ensuring that funds are channelled to where they are most needed and are accounted for. This can free up resources for new educational projects such as new schools, professional development for teachers or increased facilities within schools. Data can be transmitted through the Internet using centralised administration processes and can avoid duplication of cost and effort.

Through a range of Internet-based applications and services all learners with some level of connectivity to the Internet can, in theory, access high-quality content and receive an education that is relevant and applicable, and taught by well-qualified teachers from both within their country and outside. Students can work at their own pace, pursuing their own interests and developing the skills for employment, society and lifelong learning.

Any educational vision for ICT use is premised on a number of factors including access to content-delivery tools that will enable content to be delivered to the desktop for teachers to use in their whole-class teaching using one PC/laptop and large screen, or for students to work on in groups or for individual study. Teachers' understanding of how to make best use of the new tools including the adaptation of their role to a range of technology-based learning environments is also critical in this development. Bringing the Internet to schools can provide you with a whole range of tools and applications that will enhance students' understanding. Most of the tools that are available are used under the umbrella heading of 'e-learning' and this chapter will illustrate how this word has become a catch-all term for any learning with or through ICT and represents a multitude of ways of working.

For example, in a response to the European Union's (EU) e-Europe 2005 Action Plan, which presents a vision for the use of ICT in education and training across Europe, key features of e-learning were described:

- enhanced computer-based training and computer-assisted learning using interactive tools;
- the ability to provide learners with authentic data and real-life situations within which to study;
- the ability to offer an increased variety of learner experiences, providing the learner with flexibility in choice and personalised experience based on learning style and personal situations;
- an enhanced learning process building upon traditional learning methodologies;
- the reality of scaling exponentially to meet the needs of the growing learning community;
- being able to update content in real-time as compared to revising traditional text-based content;
- an increased range of choices for developers to find the most appropriate medium and teaching situations for explanation and discussion on a topic (eLIG, 2003, p. 9).

VIRTUAL AND MANAGED LEARNING ENVIRONMENTS

There is often confusion surrounding the meanings of the terms Managed Learning Environments and Virtual Learning Environments, but there has recently been some clarification offered by the JISC MLE steering group (JISC, 2003) as to what each term represents: a Virtual Learning Environment (VLE) refers to the 'online' interactions of various kinds which take place between learners and teachers, while a Managed Learning Environment (MLE) includes the whole range of information systems and processes of a school (including its VLE if it has one) that contribute directly, or indirectly, to learning and the management of that learning. The components of a VLE could include the following (Becta, 2003, p. 6):

- notice-board/bulletin board;
- course outline (course structure, assignments, assessment dates);
- email facility;
- conferencing tools (asynchronous conferencing or discussion groups);
- student home pages;
- metadata (ability to catalogue resources electronically);
- assignments (ability for tutor to create assignments);
- assessments;
- synchronous collaboration tools (such as whiteboards, chat and video conferencing);
- multimedia resources (accessing, storing and creation);
- file upload area (ability for students to upload their resources to a shared area);
- calendar.

A VLE will sit inside an MLE and can interact with the MLE in a number of ways:

- controlled access to the curriculum, which has been mapped to elements that can be separately assessed and recorded;
- tracking of student activity and achievement against these elements, using simple processes for teachers to define and set up a course with accompanying materials and activities to direct, guide and monitor learner progress;

- support of online learning, including access to learning resources, assessment and guidance; the learning resources might be self-developed or professionally authored and purchased, and can be imported and made available for use by learners;
- communications between the learner, the teacher and other learning support staff to provide direct support and feedback for learners, as well as peer-group communications that build a sense of group identity and a community of interest;
- links to other administrative systems, both in house and externally.

Figure 5.1 shows that a VLE sits inside an MLE and operates with an integrated management system (IMS) within it.

The market for VLEs and MLEs in schools is relatively new. However, schools have been running management information systems for many years, but until now they have not been linked to learning systems. A number of pilots for various commercial VLEs are in progress (Becta, 2003, p. 16). The benefits for students and teachers are seen as the teacher having more time for working alongside individual or groups of students, with greater personalisation and individualisation of learning if learning materials are more easily created and shared. Also students are able to take more responsibility for their learning and can have access to resources from anywhere in the school, at home or from a community centre and they are able to work collaboratively online as well as in the classroom.

The resources held on a VLE are made available to students through an intranet which is a closed environment that is password protected and which may or may not have links to the wider Internet. This prevents access to students' work by the general public and protects students' identity as well as the intellectual property of the teachers posting

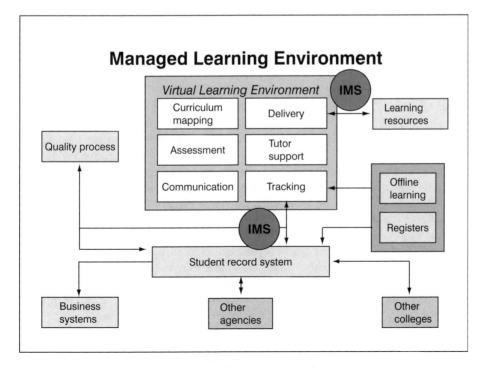

Figure 5.1 Links between a VLE and an MLE (Source: JISC, 2003)

materials for students to use. Students and teachers can usually access their school's intranet from outside the school using their password. Many local education authorities have set up intranets for teachers and students to access resources. In the case of Northern Ireland, the whole country has an intranet, known as Classroom 2000 and the whole ICT provision is linked into this structure with a managed service for all schools (for more details see Anderson and Stewart, 2004).

Task 5.1
Finding out about the VLEs and MLEs used in your school or recommended by the LEA

Why was it selected and how is it being used? If one is not yet in use, talk to the IT coordinator and find out what his or her thoughts are about MLEs.

TOOLS FOR E-LEARNING CONTENT AND RESOURCES

Content provided through the Internet can be used directly with students; it can be imported into a local intranet and/or a virtual learning environment, or developed or modified by teachers for their students. The Internet provides opportunities to access resources that are up to date rather than in outdated textbooks; it is not limited by the knowledge of the teacher, and it allows students to pursue their individual interests. Teachers are also able to work together to design and adapt e-content and produce relevant web-based learning experiences for students that are suitable for local needs and are culturally sensitive and pedagogically relevant.

Hard decisions need to be made about what static text and images will really be enhanced by digitisation. The relative costs of production are significantly higher for good-quality digital media than books, although the content of books cannot be readily changed. Decisions have to be taken about the presentation of the content if digitisation is being considered. For example, the contents of a biology book with images of different body parts and systems could be significantly enhanced through digitisation by offering virtual models and simulations of the blood and nervous systems and 3D models of the human body that can be rotated and manipulated virtually. Such enhancements can significantly improve conceptual understanding by providing a more relational understanding to students.

Large databases of images, slides enlarged via an electronic microscope, as well as digitised artefacts, can be stored so that they are easily searchable and accessible even when there are constraints on bandwidth. One example, seen at a conference organised by Microsoft for their Innovative Teachers programme in Europe, was demonstrated by a Swedish teacher. He used horrific images and sounds from the First World War to provide the atmosphere and setting for students to empathise with the soldiers. After observing the images and hearing the digitised sounds of war, the teacher told his students to imagine they were a soldier in the trenches about to go 'over the top'. He then asked them to write a letter home to their mothers. The quality of the writing and the emotion displayed in the letters illustrated the power of digital media in motivating students, and providing them with the empathy necessary to write such moving letters. This example demonstrates that content does not have to be pre-packaged into complete courses to be of value or involve high levels of sophistication, but it must be easily accessible and teachers must know where to find it if they are to put it to good use.

In geography the development of graphic animation through computer modelling has meant that contours, for example, can be shown by taking a picture of an area, looking at it from a bird's eye view and then drawing in contours.

In science lessons, students need to both observe and undertake experiments themselves in order to understand the inaccuracy of results, and to develop the notions of experimentation including the need to keep all except one factor constant so as to observe the effects of increasing or decreasing one variable at a time. Computer simulations can augment and enhance the students' understanding of experimentation. Through these media, students are able to observe experiments that are either too dangerous or too expensive to carry out themselves, that would take too long, or perhaps have ethical implications. However, it is not to say that these should replace all practical work because simulations can reflect a simplified version of reality and mask the complexities of experimentation. It is the teacher's role to consider which experiments will be attempted in class and which will be simulations in the same way that they decide to demonstrate an experiment or let the class undertake it themselves.

Virtual labs are now available, such as the Virtual Bacterial Identification Lab (<http://www.hhmi.org/biointeractive>). The purpose of the lab is to familiarise students with the science and techniques used to identify different types of bacteria based on their DNA sequence. As such processes are time consuming as well as expensive to perform, the opportunity to undertake a simulation in a virtual lab means that time can be speeded up. What is important, however, is that a teacher is available to ensure the students are not just clicking their way through without taking any note of the procedures. This can be done in a whole-class demonstration on an interactive whiteboard or a large monitor or by a teacher setting tasks on the way so that students really engage fully with the simulation.

Visiting speakers can record their presentations, as well as teachers recording key or introductory lessons for reviewing by students who attended or for students who may have missed a lesson. The lecturer's 'talking head' is synchronised with their slides, the text of their talk, an animation, a simulation or with video footage, and the resulting product, known as video on demand (VOD), can be accessed at any time by students. The talking head gives some personalisation to the presentation and learners can download the audio and presentation to use whenever they need to review material previously taught.

Task 5.2
Developing e-resources to support your teaching

Visit Curriculum Online (<http://www.curriculumonline.gov.uk>) and search for some resource related to a topic you have to teach. Find out more about one resource and also find out if it has been reviewed on the TEEM site (<http://www.teem.org.uk>) where teachers post reviews of educational software. Now find out if your department uses any particular software to teach that topic and either review the software, if they do, or discuss with them the reasons why they do not use any software.

COLLABORATION AND COMMUNICATION TOOLS

E-learning, just like all forms of learning, is not just about one-way transmission of content or interactive simulations; it is also about collaboration and communication with others. Many of the tools for developing educationally sound content support a constructivist view of learning and a belief that students learn best by enquiry and action. Social constructivism views collaboration as an important element in developing robust understanding.

Collaboration tools can be either synchronous (in real time), like instant messaging and chat forums, or asynchronous, like email and collaboration tools where messages are left for others to respond to when they next log in. Asynchronous tools do not require users to be online at the same time. You may well have used these tools yourself for communication with friends and family or in your own learning. Each tool has a role to play in learning. Instant messaging allows real-time collaboration or immediate responses to a query. Help desks often work that way.

Asynchronous communication provides learners with time to consider a view or a question posed by others and to respond later and support those who do not feel able to participate fully in face-to-face or synchronous discussions. This benefits learners who take more time to think and who therefore tend to respond more slowly than others in a class. In an asynchronous discussion these learners can take their time and thus they are more able to participate in the discussion and to have their voice heard.

The first online asynchronous collaboration tools were all text based in the form of computer-mediated communication tools. These tools opened up the classroom by giving teachers and learners the opportunity to communicate with other teachers, an expert other than a teacher or a group of other learners in the same class or school, in other classes or schools within the country or across the world, by posting responses to thought and views about a topic of mutual interest. The BBC has recently launched a site where people can post their stories of living in the Second World War and these will soon be categorised and held in a searchable database as part of a living history project (BBC, 2004). (This is also another area where content is created through a community.) The National College for School Leadership (<http://www.ncsl.org.uk>), for example, hosts a number of forums for head teachers and aspiring school leaders as part of its professional development programme, and school twinning programmes use email, purpose-built collaboration tools like FirstClass, or web forums like Yahoo groups or those built into a virtual learning environment like Blackboard.

There are also virtual project environments such as Sitescape (<http://www.sitescape. com>) which provide a space to work on a collaborative project and where documents can be posted and shared. Users are notified by email if they so wish each time some new posting appears on the site. Document sharing can also be facilitated through tools like Net Meeting which allow users to connect in real time and work on a document together by sharing a document or even a desk-top remotely.

Online communities, like any other, need a number of elements to be sustainable; for example, there needs to be a sense of purpose, a sense of ownership of the content of the discussion forums and a sense of who the audience might be. In addition, the system needs to have ease of use; it needs to be easy to access in both place and time; and there needs to be shared aims, goals and interests amongst the participants (Selinger, 1998, p. 25).

Newer collaboration tools involve the use of phone and video over the Internet and improve the potential of earlier video-conferencing which required dedicated bandwidth usually provided over an expensive ISDN line to a fixed point in one room in a school. These systems required other users to have a compatible system at the other end and to be timetabled to be in their video-conferencing suites at the same time. Now a webcam connected to any PC can be used using free tools like Yahoo Messenger, Net Meeting or iSite. Issues of compatibility between Apple and Windows has recently been resolved across most of these systems.

Voice over Internet Protocol (VoIP) has allowed institutions to place telephones in every classroom with no additional wiring, because the phones can share an existing data port with a PC. IP telephones operate like traditional telephones but offer cheaper or free phone calls because the data traffic goes across the Internet. An IP telephone can act as a terminal for class registration, provide a fast method for locating staff and students through an online timetable, and give access to email. Coursework help can be introduced by using intelligent call-handling software so that on-duty teachers could be contacted no matter where they are, and data on student attendance can be collated and sent to the management information system with minimum effort and error. You can invite visitors remotely into the classroom; for example, grandparents can talk to your class about their experiences of going to school when they were the age of their grandchildren through the speaker-phone capability built into the phone, and conference calls can be set up between classrooms so one external expert can communicate with several classes at the same time.

Softphone is similar, but the 'phone' is in fact software that sits on a PC and allows PC-to-PC interaction over the Internet free of charge or at a low cost if calls need to be made to another phone. The ability to combine an IP telephone with a webcam means that video telephony is going to be widely available relatively cheaply. IP telephony uses bandwidth detection devices to ensure the quality of sound is not compromised by reducing the refresh rate on video images. Teachers from anywhere in the world will be able to work with you and your class, and students at home for any reason will be able to keep up with the lesson. These technologies will start to challenge the location of 'school' and provide part-time learning opportunities to a myriad of people in a way that traditional distance learning could not. It will provide students with a way of staying on in education that does not compromise their financial situation by allowing them to study when it suits them yet still have access to the scaffolding a teacher can bring, albeit virtually.

The calls on an IP telephony service are carried across the data network to the limit of the network and to the nearest node to the telephone then a local call charge is incurred to the point of contact.

IP/TV enables broadcast-quality real-time video to be sent to all desktops within a network. The head teacher of your school could broadcast a welcome message to all the students each term, for example and this tool could be especially useful where schools do not have large enough halls to house all students simultaneously. This broadcast can be recorded and replayed at scheduled times. Later it can be saved as a VOD and accessed by those who missed it, or as required. IP/TV solutions have an additional advantage over traditional television transmission – they support interactivity. Viewers can type in questions and the speaker can relay answers, so students can ask questions of the head during these sessions by keying in a question which the head can read.

Virtual classroom software is also available and is increasingly being provided as a component of a VLE. This software enables traditional teaching to take place over the web with learners or tutors dispersed. Tutors and learners log in to the same website, and they can listen through either their PC or a separate telephone connection. This solution can be used in a variety of situations, for example, where:

- all learners are based in different locations;
- the teacher is in a different location from the class;
- a guest tutor or expert is invited to speak to the group but is unable to travel to the institution;
- a group of learners are located at another school; they have no specialist in that subject and are unable to travel to the location of the teacher.

Virtual classroom software means that minority subjects can be offered to students who might otherwise have had to transfer to another school for their post-16 studies.

In a virtual classroom you can show a presentation, whiteboard or web page to learners, and surveys are also possible so that you can check for understanding or gain immediate feedback on your lecture or seminar. The range of tools available with this software emulates the traditional teaching environment. A successful example of the use of virtual classroom software is the Nisai-Iris partnership in Warwickshire, which has meant that students who are unable to attend school have been able to join in lessons with their classmates as part of a package of resources to support them while absent from school (Nisai-Iris, 2004).

Task 5.3
Auditing your experience with ICT tools

List the communication and collaboration tools you have used yourself and the different purpose you have used them for. What is the value of each tool you have used? Does your school use any of them and if so, how are they used? If not, why not and what is school policy and justification? Interview the IT coordinator and a member of your department to find out whether they use them for teaching and learning and how. Do any of the staff use professional development online communities? If so, what have been the benefits and how have they made use of these forums (e.g. reading and making use of the content of messages, offering advice or posting questions)?

DEVICES FOR E-LEARNING

There are several potential models for the ideal computer specification for schools and with funding in the UK increasing with a further £700m to be spent by 2006, schools are beginning to rethink the computer lab and are experimenting with new ways of deploying PCs. All classrooms will need to have with one Internet-enabled computer per room with some projection facility: either a data projector or an interactive whiteboard so a whole class can take part in a web safari, or work together on some interactive media. This solution also provides opportunities for a small group to work with the computer during other times of the day. The computers or the school server need to have the capability of caching large amounts of resources so that the bandwidth limitations for Internet traffic coming into the school is not a factor in determining whether a planned lesson can go ahead or not.

Clusters of PCs outside a group of 2–3 classrooms are helpful in allowing fuller integration of ICT into all subject areas. These PCs might be also on trolleys so they can be wheeled between classrooms or a set of laptops connected by wireless to the Internet if possible, provides another flexible resource. Computer labs for computer studies / IT skills / Internet research projects or language teaching, as well as a library study or open learning area also essential resources.

Wireless access technology is highly recommended as it provides for flexibility and enables the computer lab to be brought to students and eliminates the need for new cabling. It also allows for cheaper security procedures as laptops on a wireless trolley could be locked in a secure cupboard overnight. However, the advantages and disadvantages of choosing laptops over PCs first need to be considered.

For laptops:

- they can be taken into different classrooms and students do not need to move to a lab;
- a set of laptops can be divided up between classes for a session, whereas fixed PCs could lie idle;
- they can be taken on field trips or outside the school grounds for data collection including the attachment of data-logging peripherals or webcams;
- students can borrow laptops to take home overnight or in the school vacation;
- data access points need to be in every classroom for Internet access rather than just in computer rooms (although wireless access can overcome wiring issues);
- linked to a large TV screen, a plasma screen, an interactive whiteboard or a digital projector, the laptop provides an opportunity for small-group or whole-class teaching using interactive media. In essence this is no different to having PC in a room, but if there are insufficient to provide each teacher or classroom with a PC, then a laptop may make sharing of resources a good deal easier.

Against laptops:

- they are more expensive than PCs and less robust;
- screens are small so it is harder for students to work collaboratively on a computer-based activity;
- theft is easier as laptops are smaller and more portable than PCs.

One of the greatest benefits of computers is the ability for students to capture their thoughts and to demonstrate their understanding in a number of ways using different media. Therefore access to web cameras and digital cameras as well as digital audio recording facilities, such as portable digital recorders will provide students with a range of means for capturing and recording data that they can later develop into multimedia presentations and web pages. For students who are unable to express themselves clearly through text, these audio and video tools provide a way into their thinking that was previously much harder to capture, and opens them up to possibilities that were previously only available to their more literate peers for whom expressing themselves through the written word comes more naturally. In the same way, graphics design and drawing packages allow those who are less artistic to express themselves though graphic media more easily.

The introduction of computers, however, does not negate the need for TVs and radio. There are still many opportunities where students can learn a considerable amount from a video or a DVD, or from a radio programme, and in many cases using a computer may be an unnecessary alternative.

E-books are dedicated machines that have come to be relatively inexpensive alternatives to textbooks and computers. Students and teachers can download lessons, notes, and books from the web thus saving money on expensive textbooks and reference books, and ensuring that students have up-to-date and relevant information. Students hook up their e-books to a centrally based computer connected to the Internet or having Internet connectivity at certain times of the day and with large data storage capacity.

Hand-held computer devices are now merging with mobile telephony and the educational applications for them are developing. They have not really taken off as a pedagogical tool except perhaps as a data-logging device for field trips, but do provide a management tool for teachers and learners.

Task 5.4
The school ICT inventory

Discuss with the ICT coordinator the inventory of technology provision in the school, future plans and strategy. How visionary is it? Does it take into account the full range of technologies available? How aware is the ICT co-ordinator of the range of tools available? What are the main challenges the school faces in implementing the school plan?

SUMMARY

The introduction of ICT is now beginning to have an impact on the nature of education and the relationship between teachers and learners. The emergence of networked computers and the Internet has opened up increased access to information and opportunities to collaborate and communicate with teachers and learners beyond the classroom and school, and marks a significant development in educational opportunities, yet they are not always exploited to their full potential.

Views of teaching have been changing. The teacher's role has developed over time and ICT can have a huge impact on perceptions of this role. Teachers can now move from a position in which they are the fount of knowledge, and in which they control the flow of information to 'give' knowledge to students, to one in which teachers are seen as expert learners working with novice learners in a problem-solving situation. Because of the introduction of Internet technology, students are exposed to and interact with other expert learners and other novice learners in order to develop their understanding and to further their knowledge. They do not have to rely on the limitations of one teacher; they can interact with peers and other experts to make sense of new information and to deepen their knowledge base. However, a teacher has a strong role in their students' development through helping them to question sources, making sense of new information and knowing how to go about finding new knowledge. Learning takes place within a community that can be as large or as small as the learner wishes to make it and the teacher permits.

The Internet has caused an explosion in the amount of information readily accessible, and it is no longer possible (or necessary) to remember everything. What is important, however, is knowing where and how to find and access this information and then how to process it. This means students need a whole new set of skills and as a teacher you have a role in teaching students how to acquire the information-handling skills essential for a knowledge society and making sensible use of the tools that have been discussed above as they are introduced into your school.

REFERENCES

Anderson, J. and Stewart, J. (2004) 'Relevant, reliable and risk free', in M. Selinger (ed.) *Connected Schools*, London: Premium Publishing.

BBC (2004) 'WW2 People's War'. Online. Available HTTP: <http://www.bbc.co.uk/dna/ww2/>.

Becta (2003) 'A review of the research literature on the use of managed learning environments and virtual learning environments in education, and a consideration of the implications for schools in the United Kingdom', Coventry: Becta.

eLIG (2003) *Contribution of the eLearninq Industry Group (eLIG) to the Implementation of the eEurope 2005 Action Plan: An Information Society for All*, Brussels: eLIG.

JISC (2003) 'Briefing paper 1: VLEs and MLEs explained'. Online. Available HTTP: <http://www.jisc. ac.uk/index.cfm?name=mle_briefings_1>.

Nisai-Iris (2004) 'Case study of using the Nisai Virtual Classroom for tutoring children out of school'. Online. Available HTTP: <http://www.nisai-iris.com/casestudies/warwickshire_ cs2.htm>.

Selinger, M. (1998) 'Forming a critical community through telematics', *Computers and Education*, 30(1/2): 23–30.

Selinger, M. (ed.) (2004) *Connected Schools*, London: Premium Publishing.

6 Teaching and Learning with Interactive Whiteboards

Ros J. Walker

INTRODUCTION

The first interactive whiteboards were developed in the early 1990s but it took some time before their potential use in classrooms was realised. Initially the cost of the boards placed them out of the reach of most schools and so the slant in the sales was more towards business than a school environment. As developers became more aware of the possible application of such technology within education, the UK government also began a drive to increase the amount of ICT hardware in schools and to improve the effective use of computers in teaching and learning. Some teachers had already discovered that they could plug their computers into a large-screen television, but the visual images were not good enough to make this a regular tool in teaching. Using a data projector with a computer was being tried in many schools from 1997, but with just one projector in most schools, its use was still a 'treat' rather than a regular event. Substantial ongoing investment has changed this. The years 1999–2004 saw a huge rise in the amount of technology used in the classroom, with the interactive whiteboard now being one of the most sought-after items of technology for the classroom. This chapter investigates the way in which interactive whiteboard technology is currently being used, looks at some of the criteria for effective use and examines the positive and negative aspects of this technology.

OBJECTIVES

By the end of this chapter you should be able to:

- give a brief explanation of what an interactive whiteboard is and how it works;
- explain ways you could organise your classroom to enhance the use of the interactive whiteboard;
- discuss at which stage of a lesson you would use an interactive whiteboard and for which tasks;
- give details of resources that you could use with your interactive whiteboard;
- explain when an interactive whiteboard is particularly beneficial in the teaching and learning process for you and for your pupils.

WHAT IS AN INTERACTIVE WHITEBOARD AND HOW DOES IT WORK?

Although there are several different brands of interactive whiteboard, they all carry out essentially the same function – namely, to enable the teacher or a pupil to control the computer from the board itself. The computer can also still be controlled using the keyboard and mouse. Figure 6.1 illustrates the usual set-up.

1   The computer screen has an image, which is sent to the projector.
2   The projector shines this image onto the interactive whiteboard.
3   The whiteboard is touch sensitive, either to a pen or a finger. There are two types of technology which make whiteboards touch sensitive. The first type is 'magnetic technology'. These boards always require a special pen and they are 'hard' when you touch them. The second type use 'resistive technology'. These boards have a membrane over the front and they can respond either to a pen or any other type of stylus – including a finger. They are often called 'soft boards'.

     As the board is touched, it will send a message back to the computer and the computer will interpret this touch in the same way as it would understand a mouse

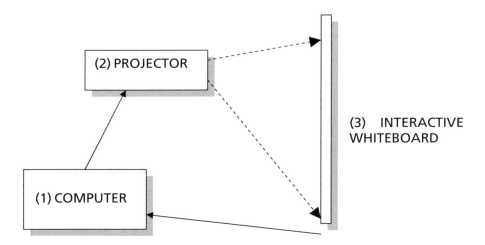

Figure 6.1 The set-up for an interactive whiteboard

click on screen. Some teachers say that it helps them to use their whiteboard if they think of their whiteboard pen or finger as being a mouse.

You may be wondering why you need to know all this. There are two reasons:

- As you are teaching with an interactive whiteboard, it helps to understand that EVERYTHING that is on the computer can be displayed on a whiteboard. This has some real advantages as we will see when we look at resources.
- If you have some technical problem as you are teaching, you may be able to solve it quickly and easily yourself, simply by checking the leads and connections to the board.

HOW CAN A CLASSROOM BE ORGANISED TO MAKE BEST USE OF A WHITEBOARD?

The position of the whiteboard in a classroom is very important as this has an influence on the way that the board is used. The following points should be taken into consideration:

- The board should be in a central location, visible from all parts of the classroom.
- There should be clear access to the board and items such as bookshelves, chairs and cupboards should be removed from the area where the board is situated. You and your pupils should be able to move freely from one side of the board to the other and stand to one side (see Figure 6.2).
- The board should be fixed at a height where the top can be reached by the teacher and pupils should be able to reach at least half way up. The teacher should be able to reach the top because the menus and buttons for many programs are situated at the top of the page. This is not a problem on a small screen but would be quite a reach if the top of the board were 6 feet from the ground. Pupils will also come and use the board and they should be able to undertake tasks comfortably without having to reach too far. You should never let a pupil stand on a chair.
- Look at the wiring for the whiteboard. All wires should be stored in trunking, so that they do not pose a trip hazard for yourself or your pupils. There should be no wires trailing or hanging loose.
- Look also at the lighting. How visible is the board? Can images and writing be seen clearly from the back of the classroom? Will the light in this room change over the day or in different seasons of the year? Blinds may be required for some classrooms.
- You should also think about where pupils will sit. Seating younger pupils on a carpeted area near the board can work well. Older pupils should be able to turn their chairs to see the board easily.

It may seem that there are a lot of details to consider, but this will be one of the main tools used in your teaching. It is important that both you and your pupils are happy and comfortable working with the interactive whiteboard.

| An interactive whiteboard with plenty of space to move around | A whiteboard where movement is restricted by boxes of folders |

Figure 6.2 Leaving space around the interactive whiteboard

Task 6.1
Setting up a whiteboard ready to use

Locate an interactive whiteboard in school. If you do not have one in your school, arrange to visit a school which does have one or look for one in your teacher training institution.

- What type of board is it – resistive or magnetic? Look carefully at all the connections and ask a member of staff to show you how to switch the board on and off correctly.
- Look at the layout of the classroom around the board. Do you think that this is appropriate? Note any changes that you would make in a classroom of your own and think about why.
- Look at the health and safety aspects of the board. Are wires safely stored in trunking? Are electrical points in a sensible location? Is the lighting suitable?

RESOURCES

As already discussed, you can display content from your computer on an interactive whiteboard. This means that all the resources on your computer can be used from the board itself. These resources could include:

- CD-ROMs;
- presentation packages (such as MS PowerPoint);
- word-processing packages (such as MS Word);
- spreadsheets (such as MS Excel);
- internet pages and websites;
- audio-visual materials including simulations;
- specialist software for your subject area.

In addition to this, most whiteboards come with their own software. The most commonly used packages are ACTIVstudio (ACTIVboards), Notebook (Smartboards), and Hitachi Starboard software. There are also software packages designed for use on any type of interactive whiteboard, irrespective of the brand, for example Easiteach studio.

Whichever type of whiteboard software you use, all the packages have one main function in common. Namely, they provide a 'toolbox' with various electronic 'tools' such as:

- pens in different colours;
- highlighter pens;
- tools which draw shapes on screen (line, circle, rectangle, etc.);
- camera tool to take screenshots (part or whole of the screen);
- eraser (to remove marks made with the pen tool);
- select tool (which allows you to select items and move them around the screen or resize them).

These 'tools' can be used:

- with blank pages (provided within the whiteboard software) which can be prepared before a lesson or started from scratch during a lesson;
- with other software, for example, writing comments over the top of an internet page.

A further area to consider when looking at resources for the interactive whiteboard is peripheral devices. The most commonly used devices, which are almost essential, are speakers and a video player (which can be wired through the projector). This allows the interactive whiteboard to be used with software that contains sound and existing VHS video cassettes. However, you may also want to look at items such as data-logging equipment, electronic microscopes, a gyro-mouse, remote keyboard, handheld device to control the board from anywhere in the classroom or voting devices. Images from these can be displayed directly onto the board so pupils can watch the progress of an investigation on the large screen.

Once you are aware of the resources available for you to use, you can begin to make decisions about how they can be used most effectively with an interactive whiteboard.

Task 6.2
Observing lessons using an
interactive whiteboard

Over a week, observe the use of an interactive whiteboard by at least three different teachers in three different lessons. Note:

- The software and resources used. In particular, look at what has been pre-prepared and what is done during the lesson.
- The way in which the teacher interacts between the board and the pupils. You may want to note down some of the questions that are asked.
- How often pupils come to the board and how much time the teacher spends at the board. How much time does the teacher spend talking and how much time do the pupils spend talking?

You can photocopy and use the form in Figure 6.3 to help you with your observation.

After each observation, think about the following questions and make notes on the back of your sheet:

- Were the aims and objectives of the lesson fulfilled?
- What were the main uses of the interactive whiteboard?
- What techniques did the teacher use to create interactivity and promote discussion?
- Did the use of the whiteboard help the teacher and the pupils to fulfil the lesson objectives?
- In which stages of the lesson was the whiteboard most useful?
- Were there any good ideas that I could use in my lessons?
- Was there any useful software that I would like for my teaching?
- If I didn't have an interactive whiteboard, could I achieve the same effect by using traditional methods?

LESSON STRUCTURE

There are four phases in a lesson when a whiteboard is most used.

- **Presentation:** During this phase, the teacher introduces the main teaching point for the lesson. New ideas or concepts are presented using materials at the board. Delivery of material at the interactive whiteboard is ideal for this phase. Many resources available now use colour, movement and video clips, which can help pupils to see and understand ideas more clearly. For example, think about an ordinary whiteboard with a picture of a cross-section of a heart (all in black) and lines showing the movement of the blood through the heart. Now, think about a large colour cross-section of the heart with oxygenated blood in red and deoxygenated blood in blue. As a button is pressed, the whole heart begins to move – valves open and close, the heart expands and contracts and blood is seen to move through the heart.[2]

  This is an example of the type of resource which is now available to teach Science. Similar resources are available for many subject areas. Even at a basic level, finding suitable images on the internet for teaching (<http://images.google.com>) is now much easier. Pictures to support almost every subject and topic taught in schools are readily available for use in lessons.

  However, the presentation does not simply evolve around the choice of visual materials for a lesson. Whilst these can be stimulating, it is the discussion of these items that assists with full comprehension. Learning to ask the right questions is very important. Closed questions, such as 'Which is it, A or B?', will allow pupils to make a choice, informed or otherwise, but will not demonstrate comprehension. Asking open questions, such as 'Which one would you choose and why?' provokes discussion within the classroom and leads to a deeper level of understanding.

  One teacher said that she had noted her pupils wrote much less in their books since having the interactive whiteboard in the classroom and yet their end of unit scores were better than they had been previously. She came to the conclusion that many pupils used to copy work from the blackboard or a textbook, without really understanding the topic. She felt that the discussion in class since the arrival of the interactive whiteboard had led to real understanding of the topics taught.

Teacher's name: _____

Lesson: _____

Aims and objectives of the lesson:

When was the board used during the lesson:

(tick all 5 min. segments when IWB is used)

5	10	15	20	25	30	35	40	45	50	55	60

Software resources used:

(write P against anything that was pre-prepared by the teacher)

Note whether any of these were used at the same time – for example, whiteboard software being used with an internet page.

Questions asked by the teacher:

Pupils and teacher at the board – comments:

Figure 6.3 Observation of a lesson using an interactive whiteboard

- **Closed practice:** This is where pupils begin to work on the ideas or practise the techniques which have been presented. The teacher is able to prepare the class for work that they will continue doing on their own. For example, in a maths lesson the teacher may bring up a series of exercises which have been pre-prepared and the class will begin to work through them together. In an English lesson, the teacher may show some examples of writing which the pupils will use as a model for their own work. As the class works together, the teacher is able to see who can cope well with the task and who may need more support. If a majority need support, then the teacher may use the whiteboard facilities to go back to the presentation materials and recap on the key points or present the information in a slightly different way. If the majority of pupils are happy with the work they will be doing, then the class can move on to the next section.

  Two techniques which are widely used in both Presentation and Closed practice are:
  - Drag and drop: On an interactive whiteboard, an item can be 'picked up' (either with a pen or finger) and dragged across the page in order to move it. This allows for a wealth of activities: matching, re-ordering, labelling and grouping.
  - Rub out to reveal: On most whiteboards, it is possible to cover pre-prepared text or pictures with a layer of 'virtual ink'. This can be 'erased' to reveal the words or pictures underneath. Pupils enjoy tasks using this technique as it allows them to guess answers and then immediately check to see if they are right.

  There are, of course, many other techniques and ideas, but these have been particularly successful using interactive whiteboard technology as they are difficult to recreate with traditional methods.

- **Open practice:** Pupils continue to work on the task but now on their own. This does not necessarily mean that the whiteboard is redundant. What is displayed on the board? It could be details of the task that the students are undertaking; it could be support materials, such as a graph, key words or references; it could be that pupils will be able to go to the board and access previous pages from the lesson to remind themselves of what they have been studying. If there is no useful or relevant information to display, then the board should be switched off to avoid it proving to be a distraction.

- **Plenary:** Teachers use the whiteboard at the end of a lesson to draw things together. This could be as simple as asking pupils to recap on what has been done and what has been learnt. However, a plenary can take pupils much further. Using the whiteboard allows you to ask some quick-fire questions, turning pages on a flipchart rapidly, using an interactive game or, if available, using voting devices. Pupils can test their knowledge and reinforce the content of the lesson at the same time. A further use is to show pupils how they can take the topic further, maybe by opening up a website with more information or resources on the topic or using pictures to stimulate further thought and questions.

Saving your lesson: At the end of a lesson using an interactive whiteboard, materials can be saved. This can be useful for you as a teacher, because you can recap on what has been covered. This is useful for your records, but it also means that you can open work again in a later lesson to remind pupils of key points. It also helps you as a reflective practitioner because you can add notes to the end of a presentation to remind you what went well and what could be improved in future lessons. This will be useful when you come to teach it again at a later stage. Saving your work to an area which can be accessed by pupils means that your pupils can open and review work from the lesson. This may be useful for homework and for pupils who have been absent from a class.

Task 6.3
Planning to use an interactive whiteboard in a lesson

Think about a lesson that you will be teaching in the next two weeks and work out how you could best use an interactive whiteboard.

- What are the aims and objectives of the lesson?

- **Presentation phase:**
  - Which materials can you use in the presentation phase of the lesson? (To help you with this, try to think of any images, animations, real-life applications or items in the news connected with this topic.) From where could you obtain the most suitable images?
  - How are you going to stimulate the pupils' interest in this topic? How will you get the pupils to think, rather than just presenting information to them? Are there any key questions you can ask? Are there any images which will prove to be particularly thought provoking? Can you tell a story from the past or raise an issue from the news within this topic?
  - Which techniques will you use to create interactivity and promote discussion?

- **Closed practice:**
  - What task will you ask the pupils to undertake?
  - How can you practise this first as a class?
  - How will you identify within a whole class the pupils who have understood what to do and those that may need more support?

- **Open practice:**
  - Will you leave anything displayed on the board? If yes, what?

- **Plenary:**
  - How can you bring the lesson to a close in an interesting way?
  - Is there a way of pointing pupils to further work?
  - Is there a suitable game / task from a CD-ROM or can you invent one?

- How much of this can be prepared before the lesson? Will you save your work at the end of the lesson? If yes, are you saving it for yourself or for your pupils? Is there anyone with whom you can share any work you have created?

SOME QUESTIONS TO CONSIDER

Interactive whiteboard technology is still a relatively new tool for teaching. New methods and ideas are emerging on an almost daily basis as teachers, manufacturers and publishers seek to exploit the potential of this technology. At present, research is only just beginning to look at how the interactive whiteboard may impact on the classroom environment, but there are some key questions that are being asked and which you may want to ask yourself as you begin working with the interactive whiteboard.

Does an interactive whiteboard change classroom dynamics and teaching style?

By now, you will have observed some lessons using an interactive whiteboard and you will have planned a lesson using the technology. What are your feelings about this?

Research to date has shown that the dynamics of the classroom do change in some ways for some teachers. Glover and Miller[3] (2001, p. 272) talk about 'evidence of changing teaching techniques' although they do not go into any detail about what these may be. Research by The Review Project[1] noted that teachers were talking about being more 'provocative', using visual images to encourage pupils to discuss and hypothesise. They also felt that their planning for lessons improved as they structured their work around a single file on their computers. This helped to keep the lesson flowing and there were fewer breaks for the teacher to write on the board, which led to more conversation and discussion in class. In general, teachers who had become confident with their boards were happier with the quality of their lessons than they had been in the past.

Does an interactive whiteboard improve results?

To date, there is no published academic research which proves that having an interactive whiteboard does improve results. However, there is also no evidence that results have got worse in classrooms that have a whiteboard. To the contrary, anecdotal evidence from teachers has been very positive. The Headteacher of Shireland Language College, Mark Grundy, speaking in October 2002 said, 'Teaching has been transformed and GCSE results have shot up … whiteboards are not the only reason, but they played a key role. Used individually they are effective. Used collectively with the right training and the right pedagogy, they are extremely powerful' (Grundy, 2002).[4]

Teachers are certain that the board raises motivation in class and there are many references to this. It is believed that this is due to the range of materials which a teacher can use with a board. The use of bright, colourful resources, video clips, animations and games with instant feedback all contribute to make lessons more interesting. It also appears that this appeal does not diminish over time. Teachers have said that pupils are responding better in tests and exams, but this does seem in part to be in line with how enthusiastic the teacher is about using the board and seeking out good materials to use. If lessons are lively and interesting, pupils are more inclined to engage and learn.

What do I need to learn to use my interactive whiteboard?

Teachers generally adjust very quickly to using an interactive whiteboard. If you are at the start of your teaching career, it may be that you are able to use a board from the very start of your training in school. You may well need some specialist training. The whiteboard comes with software, which you should learn in order to exploit all the resources on the board efficiently. There are basic skills to learn, but then you will have to learn how to exploit these skills for your own teaching. For example, you can learn how to insert pictures, but you will then need to find pictures suitable for your own teaching and decide how those pictures can form part of a task for your pupils. You should consider that learning to use an interactive whiteboard is ongoing. There will always be new ideas from colleagues, new websites, new software and new techniques to learn, practise and incorporate into lessons.

What are the advantages of using an interactive whiteboard?

- **Motivation:** In a study carried out by MirandaNet, it was reported that 78 per cent of staff at one school felt that pupils were motivated by lessons with interactive whiteboards. 'When students were spoken to they all enjoyed the lessons and said they had been motivated. They liked the large image and the visual aspect of their learning' (<http://www.mirandanet.ac.uk/pubs/smartboard.htm>). Further evidence and interviews have since shown that pupils get more involved in the lesson when there is an interactive whiteboard present and there are more verbal interactions and discussion work. It should also be noted that teachers feel motivated as the resources available for an interactive whiteboard provide much greater opportunities for delivering exciting and motivating lessons.

- **Wealth of resources:** We have already looked at the range of resources that can be used, especially if the computer attached to the interactive board has an internet connection. As an example, a word emerges in a lesson which pupils do not understand. The teacher asks how the meaning of the word could be discovered and a pupil suggests looking at the 'Google Images' website. Within seconds, the class have a large picture of the item on the screen in front of them. This saves a lot of explanation from the teacher, helps pupils to develop their own skills in searching for information and gives a clear, visual image to aid the pupils' understanding.

- **Large display area, with the use of colour:** Time and again pupils mention the clarity of images and the use of colour on the interactive whiteboard. Pupils in today's world live in a very visual environment, and they learn to interpret visual messages. Within learning styles, it would appear that the visual learning style is very strong for many pupils. Learning to use colour in teaching and helping students to understand concepts through visual representations can be facilitated with the use of an interactive whiteboard. A Secondary History teacher remarked: 'Everything is just so much bigger, bolder, more colourful … you can be far more explicit about what you're doing.'

- **Pace during the lesson:** Teachers using whiteboards remark upon the rate at which they can deliver new material and swap between different activities. This helps to keep the lesson moving quickly and to keep pupils alert. 'The ready availability of the board in the classroom means that the computer can be used for short periods … Use of the computer no longer has to be the focus of the whole lesson' (Steed, 2002).[5]

- **Being able to save resources:** 'Once saved, new resources can be re-used either with or without adaptation' (Levy, 2002).[6] This has the advantage of being able to readily call on materials with which the pupils are already familiar and to improve and adapt materials already used, leading to higher-quality resources and time-saving.
- **Use of multimedia resources:** In many subject areas, being able to add sound and video clips can literally bring a subject to life. Modern Languages teachers can more easily incorporate the target language; History teachers can show video clips from newsreels and old soundtracks; Geography teachers can show video from remote locations and Science teachers can show examples of experiments and real-life applications of Science, which would be impossible to recreate in the laboratory. If clips are digitised, they can be quickly triggered, reinforcing the messages about the pace of a lesson.

However, before making the assumption that the interactive whiteboard is the panacea of educational technology, let us look at some of the potential disadvantages.

- **Preparation time:** Ironically, whilst it has been said that interactive whiteboards can save time, Glover and Miller (2001, p. 268)[3] note that amongst teachers 'there is a feeling that they have insufficient time to develop the technology and the materials for its successful use.' This is almost certainly true when teachers first begin using the boards, particularly if they have a low level of ICT skills.
- **Confidence:** If teachers lack confidence in their ICT skills, then everything on the board can be a struggle and there are a few teachers who may seem to have a 'mental block' when it comes to using an interactive whiteboard. At present, this is not a problem as they can continue to use their traditional methods. However, as resources for the whiteboard become more readily available, there may be an expectation that teachers will use this technology. If it is then proved that progress is better with an interactive whiteboard, teachers will be expected to use what is available.
- **Technical problems:** As with any use of ICT, there is always a risk that problems may arise. This is potentially quite serious if you cannot start a lesson or have to change your plans half-way through. The technical problems could arise in a variety of ways:
  - Crash on the computer: The computer stops working or fails to respond in the way you expect.
  - Failure of the network: You lose your internet or network connection but other functions on the computer continue to work.
  - Problem with the projector: The most common cause of a projector failure is the bulb blowing. The bulb's life can be prolonged by regular cleaning of the filters and the school technician should take responsibility for this. You may also wish to check that a replacement bulb is kept in school.
  - Problem with the board: Sometimes the board itself can fail. This could be a problem with the 'driver' which enables your computer to recognise input from the board or it could be a technical problem with the board itself, which may lead to replacement of the board.

Despite this long list of potential problems, interactive whiteboards are designed for classroom use and many teachers use them for months or years with no problems. However, you should go to class equipped for the eventuality that the technology could fail.

- **Cost:** Interactive whiteboards have come down in price significantly, but they still stretch the budget of many schools or departments. The government is injecting significant funding into this area, but the chances of having a classroom with your own board are still slim. This may be something you would like to ask about at job interviews.

- **Maintenance requirements:** As mentioned above, an interactive whiteboard system does require some maintenance, unlike traditional boards. You should check that filters are cleaned monthly and avoid writing on your board with an ordinary whiteboard marker – use only the special electronic pens provided.

SUMMARY

Using an interactive whiteboard can be a stimulating experience for both the teacher and the pupils. It can lead to an informative and exciting presentation of materials and ideas which pupils understand better and have more time to practise. However, this is entirely dependent on good choices being made by the teacher. A lesson taught with the aid of an interactive whiteboard is only as good as the resources selected and the way in which the teacher chooses to exploit those resources. Asking appropriate questions, provoking discussion, maintaining the pace of delivery and selecting suitable tasks away from the board are all key elements in achieving the aims and objectives of the lesson. Transferring good traditional classroom management skills is also essential to maintain a suitable atmosphere for whole-class teaching and learning.

In the majority of schools, the purchase of one interactive whiteboard tends to lead to more purchases. As there is support for the use of interactive whiteboards from central government in the UK, it seems certain that for anyone embarking upon a career in teaching today, an interactive whiteboard will be a key tool in their classroom.

NOTES

1   The Review Project – This is a 2-year research project (August 2002–4) which has undertaken observations of 200 lessons taught using interactive whiteboards. The results are, as yet, unpublished but much of the content of this chapter is based upon the initial findings. Online. Available HTTP: <http://www.thereviewproject.org>.

2   Medtropolis.com. Online. Available HTTP: <http://www.medtropolis.com/VBody.asp>. This website contains a useful animation of a beating heart, which works well on an interactive whiteboard. This was located by running a search on 'heart animation' within a search engine.

3   Glover, D. and Miller, D. (2001) 'Running with technology: the pedagogic impact of the large-scale introduction of interactive whiteboards in one secondary school', *Journal of Information Technology for Teacher Education*, Vol. 10, No. 3: 257–78.

4   Grundy, M. (2002) quoted in 'The White Stuff', *TES Teacher*, 11/10/2002.

5   Steed, A. (2002) 'Use of an interactive whiteboard', BPRS paper, 31 December 2002. Online. Available HTTP: <http://www.teachernet.gov.uk/professionaldevelopment/opportunities/bprs/search/index.cfm?report=345>.

6   Levy, P. with Crehan, C. and Hamooya, C. 'Interactive whiteboards in learning and teaching in two Sheffield Schools: a developmental study', DIS, University of Sheffield. Online. Available HTTP: <http://dis.shef.ac.uk/eirg/projects/wboards.htm>.

FURTHER READING

BECTA (2004) *Getting the Most from your Interactive Whiteboard: A Guide for Secondary Schools*, Coventry: BECTA.

BECTA (2003) *What the Research Says about Interactive Whiteboards*. Online. Available HTTP: <http://www.becta.org.uk/page_documents/research/wtrs_whiteboards.pdf>.

The Review Project. Online. Available HTTP: <http://www.thereviewproject.org>.

7 Teaching and Learning with Digital Video

Andrew Burn

INTRODUCTION: WHAT IS DIGITAL VIDEO?

Digital Video (DV) is essentially the digital version of the video we are all familiar with, usually recorded on DV tape cassettes. Its main advantage is that it is much higher quality than its analogue forebear; good enough, in fact, for television broadcast and for use in the film industry, where it is rapidly becoming the medium of choice for low-budget independent film-makers.

However, the general idea of digital video also encompasses the practice of *digital video editing*, and it is here that the real revolution for schools has taken place. Instead of an analogue editing system (basically two or three video-cassette recorders with a mixing desk), digital editing uses a computer with software which displays the raw footage, the edited version, and a timeline on which the assembled edit is represented (Figure 7.1). As an increasing number of schools are realising, it is now both relatively simple and affordable for students to shoot their own film on digital camcorders, and edit it on the school's computers. Though there are some residual practical issues here, the real question then becomes, 'How might students learn what they need to learn in my subject through the medium of the moving image, alongside the more traditional modes of reading, writing and number; or as part of curriculum areas already involved in forms of making in other media, such as Art, or Design Technology?'

The immediate benefit for learning of the digital medium, as all the early studies pointed out, was that the edited video could be constantly reworked. Instead of being made all in one go, with no room for mistakes, as was basically the case with analogue editing, the

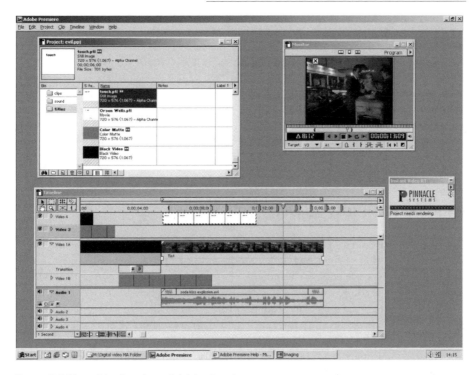

Figure 7.1 The editing interface of Adobe Premiere

new medium allowed for students to draft and redraft their edit, with limitless room for peer or teacher advice on each version.

The first few years of the twenty-first century saw a rapid expansion of uses of DV in schools. Teachers began to use this new medium with pupils to make videos in a wide range of curriculum contexts, and increasingly with younger children; though at the time of writing, this spread is still quite patchy and we are only beginning to understand how video can serve different learning needs in different curriculum contexts.

The question of how digital video production – filming and editing – can be used in schools is a big one, and this chapter will address the main questions and possible solutions. For reasons of space, we will not attempt to consider the wider question of how digital video sources, either in the form of DVD or of downloaded movie files from the internet, might be used in classrooms, though this is a related issue which teachers might like to consider. We will also not consider the use of DV in specialist media education and media studies programmes. Teachers in these fields should look for more specialised accounts of media education in general and media production in particular, perhaps beginning with Buckingham's *Media Education: Literacy, Learning and Contemporary Culture* (2003).

This chapter will ask, and try to answer, four key questions: What do we know about digital video so far? Why would video be useful in learning contexts as far apart as, say, PE and Geography? What do we have to know to use video in teaching? How can we tell what kinds of hardware and software to get, with an increasing array of kit on the market; what principles should guide our choice?

OBJECTIVES

By the end of this chapter you should be able to:

- gain an overview of the existing research about DV in teaching and learning;
- have an opportunity to map this against the curriculum of your specialist subject;
- become acquainted with an example of the use of DV in the broad area of your subject field;
- have an opportunity to consider how DV might assist in wider, whole-school questions about teaching and learning.

WHAT DO WE KNOW SO FAR?

Digital video was taken up first by specialists in media education who already valued students' production of their own video work, and had previously taught them to film and edit using analogue editing equipment, editing videotape across two or three video-recorders. Early accounts of DV in the classroom (Buckingham *et al.*, 1995; Burn and Durran, 1998) described secondary students making short videos such as trailers for films or pop videos. The opportunity to actually edit their own short videos gave students a practical understanding of how the moving image is put together, as well as how it tells a story, or sells a commercial product. These studies also emphasised a question of profound cultural significance: that the moving image, produced as cinema for a century and television for half a century by powerful industries, had for this time positioned the population at large as audiences, able to receive these new media, which changed their cultural landscape forever; but not able to make their own moving image productions. The advent of new digital production technologies has, for the first time, allowed ordinary people (in this case, school students) to become producers as well as audiences of media texts. If we think of the moving image as a literacy, it has been, for a century, a literacy which only consisted of reading. Now, finally, the writing has arrived.

This version of media literacy, though it might seem obvious and logical, is in fact exceptional in international terms. Though the term media literacy is often invoked as a desirable critical skill for future citizens by many governments across the world, from Taiwan to the UK, this almost always means the development of critical reading skills – the ability to interpret media texts. The UK government's new media regulator, OFCOM, has a media literacy unit which also promotes this view of media literacy; but it has developed it further to include the importance of production.

A few years later, studies by the British Film Institute (*bfi*) (Parker, 1999, 2002) looked at how for primary school children making films could help them to imagine the visual aspects of stories better, and improve this and other aspects of their writing. Again, there is an obvious literacy emphasis here, arguing that conceptions of literacy need to be widened to include digital media production; but also that children's development in print literacy is related to and affected by their experience of representation on the moving image.

A series of studies by teachers, working with the *bfi*, Cambridge University, and the London Institute of Education from 2000 to 2004, explored DV both in media education and in different curriculum contexts. The first of these studies (Burn *et al.*, 2001) suggested that digital editing was seen by the teachers in three ways. First, it was a creative process, which involved students making aesthetic choices about how to represent themselves and their world. Second, it was a social process, in which students took different roles, collaborated with each other, and drew on their cultural experience of film and television to make sense of this new medium. These processes can be seen as an example of situated learning (Lave and Wenger, 1991), in which children learn from their peers, especially if the situation is appropriately structured by the teacher, and peer learning is integrated with instructional processes. Third, this study also developed the idea of a moving image 'literacy', which involved using a 'language' of the moving image with its own 'grammar' of shots, transitions, soundtrack, titles and so on.

Most recently, the British Educational Communication Technologies Agency (BECTa) ran a pilot study of DV in a wide range of curriculum contexts, both primary and secondary. The evaluation of this project (Reid *et al.*, 2002) found that much of the best work by students was produced where the teacher had a clear idea of how the moving image worked, both technically and conceptually, and communicated this to students.

This study also clarified the benefits of the digital medium: that it was **iterative** (the edit developed through successive versions); it provided **feedback** (the developing edit could be immediately viewed, informing the next iteration); it **integrated** different digital technologies (digital audio compositions, graphic designs, or text could be imported from other applications); and it could be **distributed** in much more versatile ways – in multimedia formats on the internet; on DVD, as projected video in a cinema, on television at broadcast quality.

In summary, then, we can say some things about successful DV work in schools with some confidence:

- it is a practical way for children to understand the nature of the powerful media of film and television in their lives;
- it has the potential to change the cultural relation of children to the media of the moving image, making them producers as well as audiences;
- it can be a valuable accompaniment to literacy work, showing how ideas and narratives can be transformed from print to film, and vice versa;
- it is a creative activity, requiring aesthetic judgement and many kinds of compositional effort (visual composition, control of time and rhythm, manipulation of sound and music);
- it is a social activity, in two senses: it is often collaborative; and it draws on students' own media cultures;
- it can be seen as (and taught as) a kind of literacy, with its own language;
- it is best taught by teachers who have some understanding of this 'language';
- it is a fluid, flexible medium, ideally suited for learning, providing **iteration**, **feedback**, **integration** and versatile **distribution**.

One more thing can be added, which emerges from the research story so far. This is that teachers overwhelmingly report the motivating power of DV – the ability to control the moving image when children's biggest experience of it by far is as an audience of film and TV, can be a powerful experience for them.

**Task 7.1
Identifying opportunities for DV
production in the curriculum**

The only real value of such research is in its capacity to inform future classroom practice. Readers might like, then, to try the following task:

Look at the curriculum for your subject across one Key Stage. Highlight any curricular requirements (either nationally prescribed or emphasised by your own department) which could benefit from the use of DV production work. Next to any highlighted areas, write in the number(s) of the relevant benefit of DV from the list above (see Chapter 4 for examples).

WHY WOULD WE USE VIDEO IN DIFFERENT SUBJECTS?

In this section, some possible uses of DV are sketched in different curriculum areas. These are all intended only as examples, to raise possibilities and principles. Schools will want to consider for themselves how the moving image, as well as other audiovisual and digital media, are used as part of the rapidly expanding array of communication technologies available to teachers and children. The argument of this chapter is that this consideration should begin by thinking what needs to be taught, and how the moving image can serve that need, rather than beginning from the technology, as we are often tempted to do.

Narrative

Much of children's experience of television and film from an early age is narrative. They know that stories can be told in pictures and words, both in books and in films. They have an extensive, if unconscious, understanding of the conventions of the moving image – how it frames places and people; how it chops up time and reassembles it, speeding it up, slowing it down, splitting it between present, past (flashback, or *analepsis*) and future (flashforward, or *prolepsis*).

Wherever narrative is used in the curriculum, video will always provide an alternative mode to explore it. So, for instance, it could be used to tell stories from history, from myth, from literature, or from the contemporary world. In the classroom, this might appear as children making videos of key scenes from *Oliver Twist*, perhaps, looking carefully at the language of Dickens' book for clues about which character to focus on, what details of the workhouse to show in close-up, how to angle the camera to make the workhouse master look threatening and Oliver look vulnerable.

DV also offers a halfway house between the analysis and production of media texts. One school studies *Romeo and Juliet* with Year 8, for example, by importing a collection of clips from the Baz Luhrmann film into Microsoft Moviemaker, giving students the relevant bit of script from the play, and asking them to edit together a sequence to go with the script. This activity prompts a close critical attention both to Shakespeare's words and to the film-text; but it is also a creative and disciplined piece of production work, requiring an understanding of the editing process, and the importance of juxtaposition, duration, tempo and music.

Or DV might be used to tell stories from the life of the Buddha in RE, with groups within the class each making one episode, and editing the whole piece together at the end. Alternatively, this kind of narrative could be made as a stop-frame animation, using the processes described below.

Narrative appears in curious places – many pieces of music have a narrative quality, either because they tell a story themselves (*Peter and the Wolf*), or because they are often used to accompany filmic narratives (*Ride of the Valkyries*; *Carmina Burana*). Also, because video editing is a time-based medium, it has much in common with music, and can be used to expand students' understanding of, and practical experience of rhythm, tempo, duration. One school developed a Year 9 music project based on the music of horror films, which have often used more avant-garde musical styles than other mainstream genres, because of their usefully disorientating effects! In this project, students had to compose their own music for a short sequence of the film, and then edit it onto the sequence.

Narrative is also, importantly, about dialogue. A simple use of film narrative in Modern Foreign Languages is to take short clips from English movies which use particular repertoires, such as meetings-and-greetings, and ask students to do their own dubbing. This requires them to translate the dialogue, practise speaking it in an appropriate voice and accent (and attempting to lip-sync with the actors in the film), recording the voices, and editing the new soundtrack.

Documentary

Documentary films are widely used in classrooms as accessible and engaging sources of information. What DV offers is the possibility of students making their own documentary film. This allows all the benefits of active, practical learning, and also encourages students to consider profound questions about how truth is constructed and contested. In considering how events and ideas are represented through the selection and combination of elements, and through the use of different forms of address, they should have the chance to learn that the apparently factual basis of documentary and historical fact is actually highly mediated, manipulated, and sometimes distorted.

This could apply, for instance, to a history lesson, in which video is used to interview mediaeval serfs and villeins about their life in a feudal manor, interspersed with footage showing them about their daily work, and contrasted with an interview with the lord of the manor. The class could make quite specific decisions about how to represent the different interests of the lord or the peasants, through the juxtaposition of their points of view, through the scripting of their words, even in quite direct ways, such as through the use of a voiceover commentary.

Similarly, one school turned its annual Geography field-trip into a documentary-making session. GCSE students studying coastal erosion on the North Norfolk coast filmed examples of the eroded coastline, of the coastal defence systems, and interviewed local council officers and local people in Cromer about the issue. This allowed them to put opposing views side by side, about, for instance, who should be liable to pay for coastal defences. In this way they were able to explore the politics of the issue as well as visually representing the physical processes of erosion and defence structures like timber groynes and gabion cages.

Another school used the documentary genre to make a video of a French daytrip, in which the emphasis was on particular language repertoires. The different parts of the day were filmed, such as a visit to a French baker, and his explanation of the baking process, along with a question-and-answer session. These were then edited together with a voiceover commentary in French.

Some documentary sub-genres relate specifically to domains of subject content. In PE, for instance, it might be interesting to explore how matches are conventionally analysed in sports television. The genre of the match report, with its selected footage of the match, its use of slow motion to emphasise and clarify key moments, its discussions between sporting pundits, and its interviews with players and managers, is easily imitated by students in the context of the school match, or even practice session. One school also uses DV to analyse and improve targeted skills in team sports. Students film each other practising the skills, then edit the footage with a critical commentary, using slow-motion, repeated sequences and freeze-frames to emphasise particular movements, errors and successes.

Similarly, all the sciences have their place in television in popular science programmes, from David Attenborough's natural history documentaries to Robert Winston's ponderings on the wonders of human biology. Though the high-quality camerawork or computer-generated imagery of these programmes are difficult to imitate in schools, other aspects are not, in particular what is arguably their greatest asset – the use of a charismatic presenter, who, in the role of expert, presents much of the information to camera, in close-up. Perhaps the most valuable aspect of this kind of approach to science is not so much as a technical exercise, but rather as a way of exploring what science means to people and what makes it interesting. This kind of televisual presentation is a long way from the neutral, objective tone of the conventional written science report. For that very reason, it allows some discussion of the place of such objective reporting in science, and how presentations of popular science serve a different purpose, making room for a more subjective experience, for enthusiasm, imagination, even fantasy.

Animation

Children bring an extensive knowledge of animation to school, and it makes sense to recognise this experience. But animation is a tool often used to represent abstract ideas also, not least in science and maths. Distance learning models of education, such as Open University television broadcasts, have been using this technique for many years, to give the abstract ideas of maths and science concrete form. One group of schools has used computer animation software in Maths to represent ideas of space, and how to calculate the area or volume of different shapes. So they would ask children to show how a kite shape or a parallelogram are made up of simpler triangles and rectangles, by animating the shape so that it broke up and reformed, revealing the simpler shapes and the key to calculating its area. To explain the principles at work, the children also used voiceovers, and on-screen text. They were able to consolidate their learning by inventing ways to make newly acquired ideas visually concrete. This package was the cheap 'edutainment' software, 'The Complete Animator', which produces an AVI movie file as its outcome. This in turn can be edited further in a digital editing package, allowing for voice tracks, music, titling and re-editing. Alternatively, animation of this kind can be carried out in Macromedia's 'Flash' animation software, which many schools are currently acquiring.

Another form of animation is claymation, or stop-frame animation using plasticine models. One department of Design Technology has built a project round this form of animation as part of a Year 9 course in Design (construction). Students had to construct small sets for their animation, build the models from plasticine with a pliable aluminium wire armature, film the animation, record the vocal track, and edit the whole thing. The time-consuming part of this is the filming, which uses a stop-frame setting on the digital camcorder, filming four frames a second (this is slow compared with the standard 24 frames per second of film; but it can be speeded up in the editing process). After each frame, the models are adjusted slightly, so that the illusion of movement is built up frame by frame. Here, the model-making and set-building were obviously central to the curriculum.

Yet another school incorporated animation in a Year 7 Art project. Students researched African folktales, storyboarded them, and drew pictures for each frame, which they then filmed, again using the stop-frame setting. In this case, visual design was the central curriculum concern.

Task 7.2
Planning lessons using DV

Take one class that you teach, or are about to start teaching. Choose one topic or project which could benefit from the use of DV, using or adapting the examples given above. Plan a lesson or sequence of lessons thinking through what kinds of learning DV could promote, and how you would set up these opportunities. (NB: you might like to read the following section also, before trying this activity.)

WHAT DO TEACHERS NEED TO KNOW?

Two things are important – an understanding of how the 'language' of the moving image works, and a grasp of the technology (see the next section).

DV is, in some ways, different from other ICTs. If we teach word-processing, spreadsheets, or presentational devices such as PowerPoint, these have no important references to children's lives or cultural experience. Teaching with video, on the other hand, uses a medium which is saturated with culture, a form of entertainment of which almost all children will have extensive and profound experience. Furthermore, these media have developed through half a century of television and a century of cinema, and have long and complex histories. Students' parents and grandparents will also be familiar with different parts of these histories. Teachers need to help students to make explicit the largely implicit knowledge they have gained as members of these viewing cultures. The following points are basic ones which can easily be taught to classes.

Planning

Students should plan the shape and detail of their video carefully, shot by shot. This can be done by making a shot list, which just describes each shot; or by making a storyboard.

In either case, what needs to be planned is how the shot will be filmed. Students should be encouraged to film what they will need for the final edit, not to film long, rambling, unplanned sequences thinking that they can edit these down later. A good discipline, especially where time is short, is to ask them to 'edit in camera' – to film the shots as close as possible to their vision of the final edit. The editing can then concentrate on reworking, developing soundtracks and rhythm, and other post-production decisions.

It is at this point that students' own media experience can be explored. They will have extensive knowledge of what the genres they are imitating look like. It is worth analysing examples in class, to find out what they know about their structures, visual styles, and detailed conventions. They will have concrete ideas about what kind of voice a newsreader uses, or how a conversation can be filmed, or what the key elements of a music video are.

At the same time, it can be difficult for them to plan shots if they have never really used a camera in this way. Ideally, they should have a chance to try constructing different kinds of shot, before trying a storyboard, so that they can understand clearly what a shot is, and realise that a frame on the storyboard represents a shot. Younger children often use frames of a storyboard to represent much bigger structures, such as a whole scene, which then has to be broken down.

As well as planning the filming and editing, students should plan for other aspects of the film. Recent work in this field has observed that the moving image is a *multimodal* form – it incorporates several modes of communication, such as language, gesture, music, visual design, lighting, costume. It is very easy to neglect some of these. So, if students are using speech, they may need to plan it carefully, script it if appropriate, and practise it. If the video involves drama or role play, this mode deserves as much attention as filming and editing. It can be developed carefully, stopping to refine it, to deepen the quality of the drama, to explore motivation, to model physical aspects of the drama, to explore alternative ways of presenting the dramatic content or narrative. Similarly, music needs to be thought about, and chosen carefully, even maybe made specifically for the project, if the students have those skills.

Filming

- **Framing**: shots need to be framed carefully. This will take into consideration the establishing shot, which shows the whole scene, and lets the viewer know where everything is before the sequence moves into closer shots. It will also include shot distance: whether to show people or objects in long shot (the whole person), medium shot (perhaps waist-up) or close-up (most frequently a face, or head and shoulders).
- **Camera angle**: the angle, conventionally, signifies power. A level angle will signify neutral power – that is, the subject of the shot is neither more nor less powerful than the viewer. A low angle shot will signify power (the subject is more powerful than the viewer). A high angle shot will signify weakness (the subject is weaker than the viewer). In schools, it is particularly important to think about the filming of children. It is all too easy for taller people (older students or adults) to film younger children from a slightly high angle, unintentionally reinforcing a sense of them as relatively powerless.

- **Camera movement**: the most important movements are pan (side to side), tilt (up and down), track (the whole camera moves, traditionally on tracks, to follow the subject). These movements take place with the camera on a tripod, which should generally be encouraged with young film-makers, to produce steady, stable shots. Tracking, however, can be done with a handheld camera, with care; or with a homemade 'dolly', such as a wooden triangle to hold the tripod, with castors at each corner. The other movement is the lens movement of the zoom. This should be used sparingly – in television journalism, for instance, it is almost never used.
- **Sound**: the natural sound that comes with the shot, especially dialogue, needs to be as good as possible, so if an integral microphone on the camera is used, it needs to be fairly close to the speaking subject. It is better to use an external microphone if possible. It is also a good idea to re-record the dialogue just with the speaker talking close to the camera. This second audio track can be very useful for parts where the dialogue is unclear; even for a whole sequence in a piece of drama.
- **Continuity**: this is a conventional method of filming and editing typical of mainstream film and television drama. The idea is to film events in fragmented pieces in such a way that they can be edited together to show the relationships between elements in a situation, allowing the viewer to grasp these relationships. The most familiar example is the shot-reverse-shot structure often used to film a conversation. The film wants to show each speaker in turn, to allow them to fill the frame, to keep changing the point-of-view, and to show each speaker as they are seen by their interlocutor. A little reflection with students will show why a simple two-shot, with both speakers shown in profile simultaneously, is not a satisfactory representation of a conversation. In the shot-reverse-shot, there are usually not two cameras, as is often supposed; nor does the camera change position between each line of the dialogue. Instead, the whole conversation is filmed from one point of view, and then performed again, filmed from the other point of view. The alternating shots are then edited together; and other options appear, such as cutting the soundtrack from one speaker into the reaction shot from the other.
- The other continuity convention typically observed in the shot-reverse-shot is the 180 degree rule. This means that an imaginary line is drawn on one side of the actors, and the camera never crosses this line. Therefore, the shot is on the same side for each speaker, so that each speaker occupies the space we expect them to occupy, their gaze apparently directed at the other speaker, avoiding any disorientation for the viewer. There are many other continuity 'rules', all developed to create the illusion of a complete and coherent space through shots which are actually carefully planned and fragmented, not 'continuous' in reality at all. There is no space here to elaborate – teachers who want to go further with these ideas can find useful guides, most comprehensively in Bordwell and Thompson's *Film Art* (2001), though there are plenty of simple guides on the internet.

Editing

- **Assemble editing**: this refers to the practice of assembling all the shots in the right order on the timeline of the editing software. In fact, it will usually mean two other procedures first – chopping up the footage into relevant chunks, if it has all been imported as one long sequence; and then trimming each shot to get rid of unwanted footage at the beginning and end. All of these procedures can be done by simple, intuitive drag'n'drop movements of the cursor in most editing software. However, this is not just a technical process. Deciding how much information a shot needs to contain can be complex. Students will usually err on the side of too much information, resulting in shots which are too long, and which labour the point. Giving strict constraints about length can often be very productive.

- **Audio**: it can be tempting to leave extra audio tracks until the end. However, it is a better idea to lay down extra audio early. This might be music, in which case the rhythm and duration of sections of the music may determine the length and cutting of the visual track. Or it might be a voiceover commentary, in which case, again, the length of spoken segments may determine how much visual footage is needed.
- **Transitions**: the default transition is the cut, where one shot stops and the next immediately begins. The next most common is probably the dissolve, where one shot dissolves into the next. It is also common for sequences to fade in from black, and fade out again at the end. There are many other transitions, which beginners will want to play with; but they quickly realise that these can look confusing and inappropriate unless they are used for a specific meaning, or are conventional in the genre, such as the use of wipes in sports television. The important principle is to discuss with students why they want a particular transition, such as a dissolve to signify the passing of time.
- **Colour**: the most common colour effect, perhaps, is black-and-white, which can signify a particular artistic style, or can suggest a gritty, bleak, documentary approach. Other effects may be useful for specific reasons, such as producing bizarre effects in a pop video.
- **Speed**: slow motion is often useful for emphasis, or for producing a dreamlike effect. Examples might be a key moment in a football match, a turning point in a drama, or an action of historical importance in a documentary. Speeded up film is less common.

Exhibition

When the students' videos are completed, the other affordance of the digital medium comes into play – that they are very flexible in terms of exhibition, so offer opportunities well beyond showing the video to the class. A popular option is to project them in a bigger venue, such as a school hall. Some schools even build partnerships with local arts cinemas, who can screen work when the cinema is not being used for commercial screenings.

It is becoming increasingly common, however, to export the films in multimedia formats, such as AVI, Quicktime or MPEG. These formats allow for different sizes and quality of image, so that they can be incorporated into web pages, and the download speed can be taken into consideration.

The learning opportunity here is to encourage students to think about audience, a key concept in media education. Real audiences, such as younger children, students in a partner or twinned school, parents and governors, will all require different forms of address, different levels of sophistication, different cultural styles. These are valuable lessons for students to learn.

WHAT KINDS OF HARDWARE AND SOFTWARE TO GET

This involves decisions which are about both learning principles and hard practical considerations. Try discussing the following points with colleagues to establish the principles important to you.

Task 7.3
Choosing cameras and editing software

Discuss the principles below to consider your choices of cameras and editing software.

Cameras

Digital camcorders are becoming increasingly affordable. Here are some important principles to evaluate different products.

- You need to decide the balance between quality and quantity. The same amount of money could buy you one camera or six; the question is whether you need very high quality of lens or functionality, or whether it is more important to have a camera for each of six groups of five students in a group of thirty.
- DV is the most commonly used format at the time of writing. It comes in tape cassettes, most commonly in a small size (mini-DV).
- The footage from the tape is most easily transferred to the computer via a firewire lead, a high speed data transmission cable. You need to ensure that the camera has 'DV out'. You may also want to buy one with 'DV in', so you can record finished films back on to DV tape on the camera.
- Cameras are increasingly available in very compact sizes – so-called palmcorders. These are not necessarily cheaper, and not necessarily better for school purposes. They are more easily lost or stolen, and the smaller controls are sometimes less visible and harder for younger children to use, especially if they have problems with fine motor skills.
- Many cameras have flip-out LCD viewfinder screens. The learning advantage of these is that a group of students can all see the shot which is being composed. The practical disadvantage is that they use up battery power more quickly.
- Finally, invest in tripods, spare batteries, external microphoness and well-padded bags, budget permitting.

Editing software

Again, there are an increasing number of packages on offer. These are key points to consider.

- **What do you want to teach?** If students need only to learn the basics, and they need to do this quickly, then a simple, intuitive package is best. Apple's i-movie, Microsoft's Moviemaker, or Pinnacle's editing system are all ideal. They will enable students to see the basic structure of a timeline, to learn the basic procedures of drag'n'drop editing, and to add at least one extra audio-track. On the other hand, if you want them to learn about more complex editing, how to layer graphic and video tracks, how to edit multiple audio tracks, something more sophisticated is needed, such as Adobe Premiere (now only available for PCs), or Apple's Final Cut Pro. These packages are better suited to older students, and to curriculum contexts which can spare more time for the editing process. They are also more expensive.

- **What experience do the teachers who will use the software have?** If they have little or no experience, and little time for training, then again one of the simpler, cheaper packages should be adopted. Using the more complex tools suggested above will need careful planning for teachers to become comfortable with them. This may involve a series of structured training courses, ideally in the school, leading soon into the first classroom use. Alternatively, it may mean providing a laptop with the software for the teacher to take away and play with.

- **PC or Mac?** Many packages only come for one or the other. For several years, the only package available free was Apple's i-movie, which led to teachers in PC-based schools struggling to buy Macs against their school or LEA preference. Now, in PCs running Windows XP, Microsoft's Windows Moviemaker is included as a free package. This offers simple, intuitive, free editing. The only thing to be aware of with PCs is that they do not include connection points for firewire as standard, unlike Macs. This makes it difficult to import video from DV tapes. Editing with digital video files, perhaps downloaded from the internet, is still possible – or buying a single PC with a firewire port, so files can be imported onto this, then shared across a network or put onto DVD disks or small portable drives to transfer to other machines.

DV IN THE WHOLE-SCHOOL CONTEXT

Finally, it may be worth considering the value of digital video in the context of whole-school work. Three particular areas are especially relevant.

Learning styles

All schools have invested effort in exploring how the traditional learning regimes of print literacy, still dominant in many subjects, can be expanded. They know that many students are more comfortable learning in a visual way, or through physical activity, or through practical problem-solving. Digital video is a valuable addition to the range of styles on offer – it allows students to represent their ideas visually, but also dramatically, orally and musically. Learning Support departments may find DV a useful tool to widen the expressive range of students with identified print literacy problems. Furthermore, as we have seen, DV offers a mode of communication embedded in rich audiovisual traditions which are important elements in the cultural landscapes of young people.

ICT

Digital video editing is, of course, an ICT tool, employing many generic features common to presentational and graphic design software. It has an obvious place in programmes of work (both discrete and cross-curricular) which aim to teach generic skills of multimedia design, and digital video is often an important component of CD-ROMs and web-pages. As well as teaching discrete courses, ICT departments invariably have a whole-school co-ordinating role. If this includes DV, then student progression in digital video-making can be planned coherently across the curriculum and the age range, and resources can be acquired and deployed cost-effectively.

Literacy

A good deal of the research on DV in school has seen it as a form of literacy. Video editing is, arguably, a writing-like form – it is composed of horizontal segments which are sequenced and connected in ways which construct the meaning of each part and the whole. Students can be encouraged to think about how this process happens, how a cut between a close-up and a long shot operates like a preposition of place in language, how the moving image handles narrative time, how it structures dialogue, develops characters, represents thoughts, describes places, conveys emotion, constructs arguments; and how it does these things differently from language. At the level of the whole text, film and television have text-types and genres in much the same way as print texts, and their functions and structures will be both similar to and instructively different from their print-based cousins. Students' conceptual grasp of the nature and purpose of genre could and should embrace the variety of digital television channels, the local multiplex and the shelves of the video store as well as the local or school library.

SUMMARY

This chapter has proposed a number of rationales for the use of DV production technologies across the curriculum. Central among these are the cultural benefits for students of becoming producers as well as consumers of the moving image, the extension of literate practices beyond print and into audiovisual media, the benefits of collaborative learning, and the development of a wider set of creative competencies in the use of ICTs.

The key question for teachers is to think, then, where their own subject requires students to use traditional modes of representation, and how these might be augmented, or even replaced, by the moving image. Forms of print literacy are still overwhelmingly dominant here, disproportionately so when we consider how texts in the world at large are moving rapidly towards complex multimodal electronic formats. Of course, the moving image is not always the best medium for any given purpose; but where narrative and documentary modes are most valuable, moving image media come into their own.

The increasing mismatch between forms of representation used in the school and those used outside the school walls is one important reason why the use of digital video as a powerful, creative and motivating tool in different curriculum areas is of growing interest to teachers. It harnesses a medium with an extensive cultural history, and the making of video is a natural extension of the many uses of video resources which all curriculum areas have routinely used for years. Making video, as well as being a satisfying and creative way to handle ideas, helps students to relate school learning and ICT procedures to the (increasingly digital) media cultures of their home and leisure lives.

REFERENCES

Bordwell, D. and Thompson, K. (2001) *Film Art: An Introduction*, 6th edn, New York: McGraw-Hill.

Buckingham, D. (2003) *Media Education: Literacy, Learning and Contemporary Culture*, Cambridge: Polity Press.

Buckingham, D., Grahame, J. and Sefton-Green, J. (1995) *Making Media: Practical Production in Media Education*, London: English and Media Centre.

Burn, A. and Durran, J. (1998) 'Going non-linear', *Trac*, 2 (Winter).

Burn, A., Brindley, S., Durran, J., Kelsall, C., Sweetlove, J. and Tuohey, C. (2001) 'The rush of images: a research report on a study of digital editing and the moving image', *English in Education*, 35(2) (Summer): 34–48.

Parker, D. (1999) 'You've read the book, now make the film: moving image media, print literacy and narrative', *English in Education*, 33: 24–35.

Parker, D. (2002) 'Show us a story: an overview of recent research and resource development work at the British Film Institute', *English in Education*, 36: 38–45.

Reid, M., Parker, D. and Burn, A. (2002) Evaluation Report of the BECTa Digital Video Pilot Project. BECTa. Online. Available HTTP: <http://www.becta.org.uk/research/reports/digitalvideo/index.html>.

8 Special Educational Needs and ICT

Yota Dimitriadi and Nick Peacey

INTRODUCTION

This chapter explores the role of ICT as a teaching and learning resource for pupils with special educational needs (SEN) and disabilities. It will also discuss how ICT can support the professional development of educators involved in supporting learners with SEN and disabilities and refer to ethical, legal, health and safety issues in using ICT.

OBJECTIVES

By the end of this chapter you should be able to:

- select from the types of resources that can support learners with SEN and disabilities;
- understand the potential of ICT as a tool for consultation and as a tool to support your professional development in SEN;
- consider some of the challenges of ICT in relation to SEN.

BACKGROUND: DEFINITIONS AND STATUTORY REQUIREMENTS

We use the term SEN[1] to include learners whose educational requirements fall into at least one of the four categories identified in the Revised SEN Code of Practice (DfES, 2001):

- communication and interaction (speech and language, autistic spectrum disorders);
- cognition and learning (dyslexia, learning difficulties);
- behavioural, emotional and social development;
- sensory and/or physical.

Under the Disability Discrimination Act (DDA) 1995, revised 2001, institutions are required to make 'reasonable adjustments' to support disabled members of their communities: pupils, student teachers on school experience, and visitors such as parents or therapists. Adjustments include access to the curriculum for pupils on roll at the school as well as working conditions and resources for disabled staff so they are not at a disadvantage in comparison to non-disabled employees.

The DDA also applies to staff with disabilities. Reasonable and necessary adjustments at work include adaptations to premises, access to customised or modified resources and other employment arrangements that can make their practice manageable. Computers and associated technology can transform the workplace and open up opportunities for teachers with disabilities. Seelman (2001) refers to assistive technology in terms of 'medical' devices that support hidden disabilities like diabetes and heart arhythms and 'social' devices which facilitate individuals' communication capabilities. Social devices that can help educators in their practice range from digital hearing aids, specialist voice synthesizers and amplification systems to single-handed keyboards, PC tablets and other portable equipment that can support lesson planning and report writing.[2]

We value ICT as including:

- technological media that can assist, enrich or replace pupils' practices
- interactive settings that can support communication and enhance the lives of all users with special needs and disabilities.

We will not be evaluating specific applications but we will be discussing families of programs and equipment and reflecting upon their educational role in the field of special needs. References to websites that can provide you with information about particular digital resources are included.

This chapter emphasises that consideration of individual needs when choosing appropriate resources is just one aspect of ICT planning for SEN and disability.[3] Teachers should also consider pupils with SEN as active members of a bigger group of learners which can be the class, the school, the local or the global community (Figure 8.1). This chapter focuses on planning at individual and classroom level but includes some suggestions about ICT, SEN and the school and wider community.

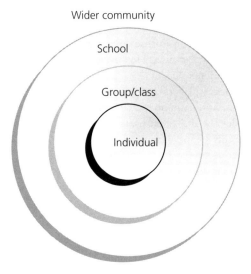

Wider community

School

Group/class

Individual

Figure 8.1 Levels of consideration in ICT provision

Task 8.1
Familiarising yourself with the
DDA

Have a look at the SKILL (National Bureau for Students with Disabilities) website (<http://www.skill.org.uk/dda_quiz/index.asp>). They host a quiz on the DDA that can help you identify key issues in supporting individuals with disabilities at an educational institution.

USING ICT TO SUPPORT PUPILS WITH SEN TO BECOME AUTONOMOUS LEARNERS

Access

Technology can minimise physical or cognitive barriers and support success in learning. Hawkridge and Vincent (1992, p. 91) described the liberation felt by Louis, a 24-year-old disabled pupil who typed 'I am not retarded' as soon as he got access to a computer.

Personal aids in the form of voice-activated software,[4] programs that convert words to symbols and vice versa, joysticks and switches for access provide disabled users with opportunities to learn and exchange information by using more natural and diverse ways of communication. Learners supported in using their voice, their body, pictures and symbols are involved in a multisensory approach to learning, one of the fundamentals of inclusive teaching methodology.

Resources like phonically structured spellcheckers, touch screens and Braille printers respect users' differences and empower them. Accessibility options, such as those in Microsoft Windows, offer the opportunity to customise your browser or personalise your desktop view and support successful use of packages. However, the support of the teacher is often crucial if learners are to gain independence.

Portable technology such as minidisk players and laptop computers are sometimes appropriate for pupils who find organisation and note taking, both as a skill and a physical act, challenging. You need to consider the skills that users need in order to operate such aids effectively. For instance, the ability to touch type or type fast can be important for pupils who intend to use a portable computer as part of usual classroom practice. Franklin and Litchfield (1999) also point out that spare batteries, chargers and print-out points are among the basic requirements for portable technology in class. Work with pupils whose behaviour is a concern will be severely disrupted if such back-up provision is neglected.

Sometimes it is assumed that the same software package will benefit all learners with dyslexia, autistic spectrum disorder or other category of SEN. While some packages have wide application, pupils' individual learning profiles, along with an understanding of the task in hand, must guide decisions as to what is appropriate (Figure 8.2). Technological provision should also be considered as an intervention that needs to be reviewed regularly since pupils' profiles and learning priorities change over time.

Communication and social inclusion

Users with similar interests or anxieties can create new cultures and social identities through digital technologies. The internet is a research and learning tool and one that can support

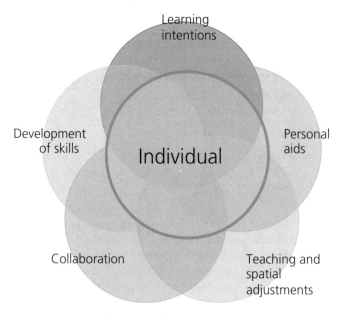

Figure 8.2 Interrelationship of ICT provision

the development of self-esteem. The inspiring website of Barnaby, a teenager with dyslexia, shows how he deals with his disability and invites others to participate with ideas and comments (www.iamdyslexic.com).

Some internet uses require careful consideration. Chris Abbott (2002) alerts us to the unmoderated nature of some online chats which allow the exchange of personal information among users who can choose to remain anonymous. Even if the use of chat rooms has been reduced significantly in the last two years (Livingstone and Boder, 2004), some of the risks identified there can apply to the current popular use of mobile phones.

Livingstone and Boder (2004) note that mobile phones and texting have become pervasive in the lives of many young people as their favourite way to keep in touch with their local social networks. While they neither focus on nor identify children with SEN, they raise many issues that are relevant to this group in terms of exposure to risks and unsuitable materials.

The use of such digital technologies liberates users with SEN from conventions imposed by more formal methods of written communication. They can respond at their own pace and participate in social interactions in a way that is user-friendly and unthreatening. For children who find 'reading' and responding to body language difficult, mobile phones and emailing can be positive ways to contact other people for advice or a friendly chat. Software like Inter_Comm by Widgit Software allows symbol users to email symbol-supported text which the recipients can view as a symbol-processed text, if they have access to such a program or as any other text email (<http://www.widgit.com>).

While we are aware of the positive contribution of digital technologies to support users with SEN in developing autonomy over learning tasks (BECTA, 2003), we also need to be aware of some factors that act against inclusion. First, most assistive technology comes in the form of add-on specialist applications rather than as part of the generic resources; users are segregated rather than included in learning practices. For instance, while the accessibility options on platforms like Windows XP have become more sophisticated, facilities like phonically structured spellcheckers, text readers and mind mapping still need to be purchased separately. Moreover, individuals who use specialist resources can be excluded again when access is limited by weaknesses in design: for example, frames on webpages can make the use of screen readers or head switches difficult; inappropriate colour combinations make even magnified text hard to decipher.[5]

Task 8.2
Mapping resources for a pupil with SEN

Look at the range of assistive technology that is available for children with SEN and disabilities. Try to map appropriate resources for one of your pupils by considering:

- how the pupil learns best;
- the special features of ICT that can support the learning task in hand;
- software and hardware identified (e.g. by the SENCO) as suitable for the pupil's type of SEN. Have a look at the following website for some starting points in identifying suitable resources for your SEN pupils: <http://www.ioe.ac.uk/nof/tfi/subjects_home_page.htm>.

USING ICT TO SUPPORT TEACHING AND LEARNING FOR PUPILS WITH SEN

The technologies described above can break down 'barriers to learning' by providing young people with access to information and practices. For instance, simulations of 'real-life' experiences can support social skill development for young people who find face-to-face communication challenging. Storyboarding programs like Kar2ouche offer pupils opportunities to engage in multimedia authoring by discussing and reflecting on the stages of compositional processes, like writing. Digital video productions can reinforce social interaction and exchange of ideas along with speaking, listening and sequencing skills (Dimitriadi and Hodson, 2005). Children are motivated to observe, evaluate their own performance and discuss their decisions. These discussions can also support subject learning (bfi, 2002). Digital cameras can capture learning instances, encourage dialogue and personalise content to support understanding by pupils with a range of learning styles (Hegarty, 2004).

The importance of ICT as a rich and effective medium for formal and informal communication is highlighted by initiatives like the Communication Aids Project (CAP). The scheme works alongside school and LEA provision to support pupils aged up to 16 years with additional technology which can facilitate oral or written communication (<http://cap.becta.org>).

Interactive whiteboards are becoming increasingly common classroom resources (see Chapter 6). Their popularity lies in the opportunities they provide for multimedia presentations that accommodate a range of learning styles and motivate pupils to participate in learning tasks. The option of operating a whiteboard without always using a keyboard can empower users who find conventional computer systems difficult to use. These pupils, who may use assistive technology like keyguards or alternative keyboards, find it liberating not to stand out in front of the group. Finally, the handwriting recognition options that are included in the operational software are becoming increasingly sensitive to a variety of writing styles. This can motivate pupils who experience handwriting difficulties.

In this way ICT can create 'functional learning environments' providing young people with multimedia tools and resources that can engage them in ways traditional resources fail to do. The 'notschool' project is an example of a password-protected virtual learning environment for teenagers who have been out of school for an extended period of time, usually a year (<http://www.notschool.net>). Initiatives like this demonstrate how the generic features of ICT, considered alongside users' experiences and profiles, can engage disaffected learners and encourage them to share ideas and work within a supportive community. A webquest is another example of moderated use of the internet for educational purposes (<http://www.webquestuk.org.uk>). A collection of internet sites is presented under a theme which the users are asked to research. The inquiry approach that the tasks have and the opportunities for self-evaluation that they provide can make webquests an engaging learning approach for pupils with SEN. The planning stage of such an activity needs to include:

- careful selection of appropriate websites;
- monitoring the availability of sites;
- consideration of technical and presentational issues related to the use of the web.

We need to draw the distinction between computers as 'teaching machines' (Skinner, 1968) and as media for exploration and communication. A range of commercial packages can support the development of basic skills in areas like numeracy and literacy. The packages offer tasks in a drill-and-practice format, give immediate feedback to pupils' responses and keep records of the users' performance. Integrated Learning Systems (ILS) is an example of such software. It provides extensive coursework through individualised practice and a management system that can inform educators about the pupils' attempts at tasks. However, the use and effectiveness of such packages is debatable. Hedley (2004) gives a balanced view on the advantages and limitations of using ILS at school for children with SEN. He supports the view that careful consideration of the children's needs and timetable will need to precede decisions about purchasing such an expensive package.

DISTANCE LEARNING

Video-conferencing is an example of distance learning technology which can provide access to real, exciting and distant settings so the pupils can reinforce or develop further skills and knowledge. The best use of this resource for SEN though involves opportunities for interaction; teachers can organise a consultation with a specialist, who may be geographically distant, for a learner who needs speech and language input or involve pupils from a specialist unit in real-life situations that they find difficult to manage face-to-face (Peacey and Dimitriadi, 2004). Global Leap is a DfES-funded project that supports the implementation of video-conferencing at educational institutions by providing advice and information about UK schools and colleges that already use it (<http://www.global-leap.org>). The project has a particular SEN focus.

Banes and Walter (2002) suggest that use of the internet can promote access to whole language experiences (speaking, listening, reading and writing) and support individual educational aims and cross-curricular work. Careful selection of appropriate sites, support with search skills and critical evaluation of information is needed for all learners; support is a priority for pupils with special educational needs whose reading and comprehension levels present barriers to effective and safe use of the internet. Widgit Software has recently developed software that can take a webpage and arrange the layout in a single column. The user can choose to view the content with symbols or as plain text at any size. Spelling may pose less of a threat as most search engines are equipped with a predictive spellchecker. Pupils with poor organisational and writing skills may also find it difficult to quote digital sources appropriately or remember what information they downloaded. Consistent good practice of skills like bookmarking visited pages and careful recording of sources is essential, especially when this online information is used to support coursework.

Safety in exploring, producing and receiving online content is important. Apart from the physical danger that may emerge as an outcome of providing personal information, legal consequences, exposure to violent or pornographic material and online bullying have been identified as other risks that children may be exposed to (BECTA *et al.*, 2003).[6] Schools are required to have clear policies on internet access to limit such instances and will choose technical solutions to regulate the extent of online access. While these are universal concerns, judgements about the vulnerability of young people with special educational needs will determine the level of enhanced support that needs to be in place in order for them to develop 'safe' internet behaviours. Careful adult supervision while pupils are trained to use the internet responsibly and thoughtfully is one of the most satisfactory responses.

Classroom arrangements

Digital resources may demand changes in classroom arrangements (Figure 8.3). Consider for instance the use of text readers. If their use benefits autonomous learning in a young person with dyslexia or visual impairment, headphones may be needed to avoid hindering the learning of other pupils at the same time. The teacher will also need to ensure that the technology does not obstruct partnerships among pupils and organise activities accordingly.

Task 8.3
Getting to know the school's ICT resources from an SEN perspective

- Look at an up-to-date audit of the school's/classroom's ICT resources. Consider the use of peripherals like printers, scanners and digital cameras that may be particularly helpful in supporting learners with SEN.
- Discuss the access to dedicated resources such as laptop computers, PC tablets, touch screens or safeguards that children with SEN have at your school. Explore the organisation and management implications that are involved in using these resources during a school day, perhaps by trying a lesson plan against the chart in Figure 8.3.
- Consider alternative ways that can encourage children with SEN in your class to record and present their ideas (e.g. use of digital cameras).
- The example in Table 8.1 looks at classroom uses of ICT to support literacy skills. How would you modify this diagram to support effective use of ICT in your subject? What resources and approaches would you emphasise?

ICT AND ASSESSMENT FOR PUPILS WITH SEN

ICT can allow pupils to show their achievement in summative assessments, like GCSE or the National Curriculum tests (SATs). For instance, the use of personal computers is often permitted during exams for pupils with SEN with for whom such technology constitutes part of everyday classroom practice. This can be a positive move towards supporting pupils in tests and examinations but careful consideration of learners' basic IT skills and their confidence in their use is necessary in order to decide whether such an option will allow pupils to show their full potential under a stressful exam setting.[7]

Computer programs are also employed to support other forms of assessment. Diagnostic assessment is used to determine provision and courses of action for children with SEN, especially for those who are on School Action Plus of the Code of Practice (DfES, 2001). There has been a lot of debate about the appropriateness of computerised assessment as a formal measure of identifying and reporting on children's learning differences. The specificity and objectivity of the process that digital technology offers has to be measured against the qualitative aspects of performance that human assessors can detect during their observations (Singleton, 2004). Singleton provides a detailed account of computerised assessment, listing the advantages and limitations of that method. He points out that the

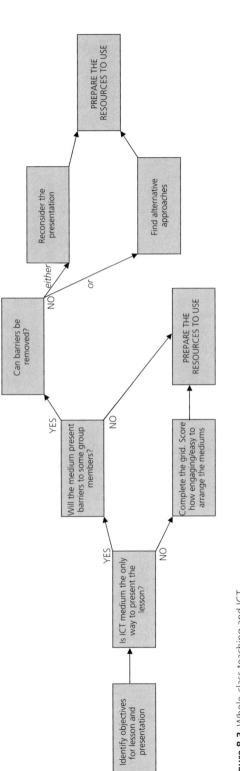

Figure 8.3 Whole-class teaching and ICT

Table 8.1 Classroom use of ICT to support literacy skills

Area	Prepared support	Activities	Software	Hardware
Language and communication	Tasks pre-taped on audio or videotape. Bookmark webpages with activities and information. Check the accessibility and availability of those sites in advance.	Simulations and (online) games for practising situations.	Electronic Wordbanks Pictures, diagrams and symbols. Video-editing software Storyboarding programs.	Good sound system in class (e.g. sound field systems). Touch screens. Concept keyboards. Interactive whiteboards.
Writing	Pre-devised writing 'frames': computer files to scaffold pupil writing. Changes to key press functions / font size / colour settings etc.	Word-processor for drafting and re-drafting. Phonically structured spell checker; grammar checker.	Planning software (mindmapping programs). Talking word-processor with word predictor. Voice-activated software Using annotations in Word.	Good colour printer for quality and valued result. Portable minidisk player for note taking. Portable devices (laptops, PC tablets etc.).
Reading	Changing the look of the screen: typeface, colours, etc. Prepare electronic wordbanks. Listen to narratives. pre-taped on audio or videotape	Symbols, text and pictures together in prepared material.	Talking word-processor with word predictor. Making their own books (using PowerPoint).	Enlarging photocopier. Interactive whiteboard. Larger monitor.

ICT test results must always be integrated with other information about learners, something that may well be considered as the basis of any worthwhile assessment.

Formative assessment (Assessment for Learning) can also be facilitated through the use of ICT. The use of digital video in recording children's performance can document achievement in an accessible form for learners with SEN. This becomes an important resource in cases where social interaction and physical engagement are measured or where recording in written format is a problematic issue for the respondents. This approach can support detailed evaluation of the learning task by peers and others, and also serve as a medium to demonstrate to parents and carers their children's attainment over time.

Databases also provide ways of systematically recording and monitoring the progress of children with special needs. They can hold information about individual learners and produce reports regarding their documented progress. This can support processes like transition from primary to secondary school, when formal communication and exchange of information is needed. More sophisticated management systems can also provide templates and information to support other processes related to SEN practices, like the development of individual education plans (IEPs).

The important role of support staff and the impact of their presence in the classroom is widely recognised nowadays (DfES, 2004). It is useful to consider their competence and confidence in using a range of ICT resources. The British Computer Society has produced an online guide 'Using Adult Helpers in the Classroom' that makes suggestions of how Teaching Assistants can support effective implementation of ICT in the classroom (<http://www.bcs.org.uk>).

Task 8.4
Assessing copyright, health and safety policy and practice for pupils with SEN

Ask for the school's policy on copyright, health and safety issues around computer use. Reflect on how these policies take into consideration the range of differences children with SEN may have.

Ensure you are clear about the school's policy on images of students. Are such images identifiable on the school's website?

Task 8.5
Listening to the experts: what works in the classroom?

Interview a teaching assistant about effective uses of ICT for SEN they have seen in the classroom.

Ask the SENCO to facilitate your interviewing a pupil with SEN who uses assistive technology.

USING ICT TO SUPPORT LINKS WITH THE WIDER COMMUNITY

ICT can play a positive role in strengthening links between school and other local and international communities. A number of online resources produced by BECTA, the DfES and other national agencies provide suggestions and guidance for setting up and maintaining effective partnerships, for instance, school–home links which can be so vital for SEN work (see also Chapter 10). Family engagement has been highlighted as an important factor for successful school intervention (Somekh *et al.*, 2003). Some of these reports are accompanied by case studies which show how commitment between parents, pupils and school is fostered and encouraged through ICT.[8]

The web can be a central resource in building these links, especially with governors, parents and carers. A number of schools showcase the work of their pupils and celebrate their achievements. Parental permission to publish images of students electronically should be requested (Abbott, 2002). Special schools like Meldreth Manor (<http://atschool. eduweb.co.uk/meldreth/index.html>) use symbol processing software like Writing With Symbols 2000 (WWS00) to make their online content widely accessible. Other educational establishments make public their schemes of work, homework titles and sometimes put advice on the website for parents and carers who want to support their children at home. This is invaluable; one of the major issues for pupils who are slow at writing is the alternative view's clear understanding of the requirements of homework or other independent study tasks.

The web can also create school and individual links with local colleges and support transition of pupils. Young people who need more time to adjust to new settings will find it comforting to familiarise themselves with the next educational phase slowly. The distant access can develop to a visit and interviews with teaching staff at the college.

Some schools encourage computer-mediated communication, like email, between home and school. They may offer free ICT courses to parents and carers to help them develop basic IT skills that are required for such partnerships. Such initiatives show that schools are committed to engage all participants in a dialogue about the learning activities that they organise and support. These activities require planning and careful management to balance the school's vision with realistic targets for teachers' workload.

**Task 8.6
Reflecting on effective links between school, home and the community**

Look at the school's website. How is it used to support links with the community?

How does the school use ICT to support communication with parents (e.g. email, computer classes etc.)?

Does the school organise any computer clubs? What support can be given to children with SEN during these sessions?

YOUR PROFESSIONAL DEVELOPMENT, SEN AND THE WEB

The web provides educationalists with the opportunity to extend their supportive social networks to global communities of practitioners, something that can facilitate, among other practices, better understanding and engagement of the multilingual children with special needs that they may have in the classroom. Email communication, specialist databases, access to examples and developments from all the over the world can support dialogue and knowledge among disparate communities.

There are a lot of established digital networks that encourage practitioners in the special needs field to share and exchange ideas and expertise. Online discussion forums hosted by organisations like BECTA include the 'senit' group explicitly set up to discuss issues around ICT and SEN, while specialist databases like 'Inclusion' offer information, advice and ideas on resources for learners with special needs and those who support them (<http://inclusion.ngfl.gov.uk>).

SUMMARY

This chapter has discussed how ICT can support independent learning and communication skills for pupils with SEN. It has emphasised the importance of considering educational aims and pupils' individual profiles before deciding on resources. We have examined a number of issues and concerns that we, as educators, need to address in order to make effective and safe use of the technology. Good ICT teaching is the foundation of success in the curriculum for all learners, including those with SEN. The way to effective teaching for young pupils with SEN or disabilities is to listen to them, their parents, carers or specialists on the 'accommodations' that can be made and find ways of using these suggestions to enhance preparation.

NOTES

1   A fuller discussion on issues around inclusion and special educational needs in the secondary school can be found in Peacey (2005).

2   Access to Work is a government scheme set up to provide information, advice and financial assistance regarding the equipment, support and training that can be made available to employees with disabilities.

3   The structure we have followed is not exclusive. The literature refers to a number of different ways that the educational use of ICT has been organised. Florian (2004) comments on how overwhelming the plethora of information available in the field of special needs can be and identifies six uses of ICT to support SEN practice. If you want to find out more about Access to Work and how you can apply for support, you will need to contact your nearest Access to Work Business Centre. Contact details can be found on the Employer's Forum on Disability (<http://www.employers-forum.co.uk/www/guests/info/factsheets/sheet1.htm>).

4   Comparison of various voice-activated software and other access technology equipment can be found at many websites including the RNIB site (<http://www.rnib.org.uk>) and the iANSYST site (<http://www.dyslexic.com>).

5   If you want to get an idea of the extent of accessibility standards, you can visit 'Bobby' (<http://www.cast.org/bobby>). It is a free online service that can check webpages and report on presentational points that may make them less accessible. The service does not cover the reading level of the page. Bear in mind that no single electronic device can give an effective check on every point.

6   This pack focuses on Key Stage 2 pupils. However, it provides useful starting points and activities about internet use that are relevant to older pupils.

7   Spellcheckers and similar resources cannot be used in those assessments that specifically test written language skills (for example English).

8   The Impact2 study provides in-depth information about the influence of networked technologies on educational attainment. Home–school links are also explored in the project (<http://www.becta.org.uk/research>). See Chapters 10 and 11.

REFERENCES

Abbott, C. (2002) 'Making the Internet special', in C. Abbott (ed.) *Special Educational Needs and the Internet*, London: RoutledgeFalmer.

Banes, D. and Walter, R. (2002) *Internet for All*, London: David Fulton.

BECTA (2003) *ICT Research: What the Research Says about Supporting Special Educational Needs (SEN) and Inclusion*, Coventry: BECTA.

BECTA ICT Advice, DfES, GridClub, QCA (2003) *Internet Proficiency Scheme for Key Stage 2 Pupils. Teacher's Pack*, Nottinghamshire: DfES.

bfi (2002) *bfi Evaluation Report of the BECTA DV Pilot Project*, Coventry: BECTA (full report available at <http://www.becta.org.uk/research>).

DfES (2001) *Special Educational Needs Code of Practice*, London: DfES.

DfES (2004) *Trainer Manuals for TA Induction (Secondary)*, London: DfES.

Dimitriadi, Y. and Hodson, P. (2005) 'Children as digital video producers: using digital video to support speaking and listening', in P. Hodson and D. Jones (eds) *Unlocking Speaking and Listening*, London: David Fulton.

Florian, L. (2004) 'Uses of technology that support pupils with special educational needs', in L. Florian and J. Hegarty (eds) *ICT and Special Educational Needs*, Maidenhead: Open University Press.

Franklin, G. and Litchfield, D. (1999) 'Special educational needs and ICT', in M. Leask and N. Pachler (eds) *Learning to Teach Using ICT in the Secondary School*, London: RoutledgeFalmer.

Hawkridge, D. and Vincent, T. (1992) *Learning Difficulties and Computers. Access to the Curriculum*, London: Jessica Kingsley.

Hedley, I. (2004) 'Integrated learning systems', in L. Florian and J. Hegarty (eds) *ICT and Special Educational Needs*, Maidenhead: Open University Press.

Hegarty, J. (2004) 'Managing innovations in ICT', in L. Florian and J. Hegarty (eds) (2004) *ICT and Special Educational Needs*, Maidenhead: Open University Press.

Livingstone, S. and Boder, M. (2004) *UK Children Go Online: Surveying the Experiences of Young People and their Parents*, London: Department of Media and Communications, London School of Economics and Political Science.

Peacey, N. (2005) 'An introduction to inclusion and special educational needs', in S. Capel, M. Leask and T. Turner (eds) *Learning to Teach in the Secondary School. A Companion to School Experience*, London: RoutledgeFalmer.

Peacey, N. and Dimitriadi, Y. (2004) 'Communication across boundaries: video conferencing architecture and education', paper given at The Future of Educational Inclusion – The Royal Institute of British Architects Client Forums 12 July 2004, Brunei Gallery, School of Oriental and African Studies.

Seelman, K.D. (2001) 'Is disability a missing factor?', in G.L. Albrecht, K.D. Seelman and M. Bury (eds) *Handbook of Disability Studies*, London: Sage.

Singleton, C. (2004) 'Computer-based assessment', in L. Florian and J. Hegarty (eds) *ICT and Special Educational Needs*, Maidenhead: Open University Press.

Skinner, B.F. (1968) *The Technology of Teaching*, New Jersey: Prentice Hall.

Somekh, B., Mavers, D. and Lewin, C. (2003) *Using ICT to Enhance Home–School Links: An Evaluation of Current Practice in England*, London: DfES.

9 ICT and Assessment

Norbert Pachler

INTRODUCTION

It seems important to stress at the outset of this chapter that, in view of the interdisciplinary and cross-curricular approach taken in this book, I focus here on generic issues of ICT and assessment as opposed to assessment of ICT skills. In other words, I am concerned in the main with the question of what impact the introduction of ICT has on assessment.

> It goes without saying that the general principles of assessment apply; assessment should:
> - be an integral part of teaching and learning and follow from curricular objectives;
> - inform future teaching and learning;
> - provide useful information about the progress, achievement and attainment of (learners) to relevant parties;
> - involve the learner in the process;
> - come at regular intervals to provide a critical mass of data to validate judgements and to motivate the learner;
> - consist of a variety of methods to make data more reliable; and
> - be manageable.
>
> (Pachler and Field, 2001, p. 204)

But the introduction of ICT into secondary education requires us to ask ourselves some fundamental questions about key aspects of school-based learning, including what to teach and how to assess it. Arguably, it brings with it fundamental transformations of traditional epistemologies, i.e. what we teach and what pupils learn, as well as of the learning process, i.e. how we learn.

Angela McFarlane (2001b, p. 237) enumerates three perspectives on ICT in schools, namely ICT as

- a set of skills or competences;
- a vehicle for teaching and learning; and
- an agent of change which impacts in a 'revolutionary way'.

Depending on which view(s) of ICT prevail(s) different implications for assessment of ICT follow.

OBJECTIVES

By the end of this chapter you should have an awareness of important issues concerning:

- the impact of ICT on the curriculum and pedagogy;
- the use of ICT for assessment purposes;
- computer-based and online assessment;
- the implications of ICT for cheating and how to prevent it.

THE IMPACT OF ICT ON THE CURRICULUM

As I noted earlier, a particular interest for our current purposes is the use of ICT for teaching and learning and as an agent of change. In this context, the question arises what effects, if any, high levels of ICT use have on learning and attainment. McFarlane (2001a) rightly notes that, whilst ICT can impact favourably on a range of important attributes of effective learners, such as problem-solving, critical thinking or information-handling, research largely identifies factors with indirect rather than direct effects on the sorts of things established standardised tests, such as Key Stage tests and the GCSE, traditionally test.

In a recent publication of research it commissioned into its impact, the Department for Education and Skills (DfES), was only able to make the most tentative of claims:

> Though it is evident that ICT has potential to contribute to transforming educational achievement, potential benefits cannot be taken for granted … Generally something positive happens to the attainment of pupils who make (relatively) high use of ICT in subject learning.
>
> (Pittard *et al.*, 2003, p. 3)

Findings such as these point towards the need for tests which have task and content validity, i.e. tests which measure the specific contributions made by ICT to the subject content and curriculum. If, for example, the use of particular (educational) programs, such as computer-mediated communication (CMC) software, is particularly prevalent in the teaching and learning of a subject, this needs to be reflected in the nature and content of the tests, for example by incorporating the use of video-conferencing or access to CMC software etc.

David Buckingham notes the challenges posed by digital media and how schools can take account of the new styles of knowledge creation and learning these media develop and require, in particular in relation to what he calls 'digital literacies'. He argues the importance of integrating digital – elsewhere called 'electronic' – literacy with print and audio-visual literacies and for it to become part of the core curriculum. Buckingham (2001, p. 7) also posits that an engagement with the implications of new technologies is essential if schooling is to remain relevant. According to him, literacy education of the future will need to 'seek to empower children both to understand and to participate in the digital culture that surrounds them' and 'aim to create informed, critical, active users of digital media' (Buckingham, 2001, p. 12). Of particular importance for current purposes is the focus on participation in the sense that new technologies enable young people to become active participants in knowledge and culture creation processes, for example through the creation of webpages or, more recently, weblogs or 'blogs'. Increasingly weblogs are a means of self-publishing, often in the form of a digital diary. According to Kirsten Kennedy (2003) a blog is produced with 'an active writer in mind, one who creates in an online writing space designed to communicate an identity, a personality, and most importantly, a point of view'. Buckingham (2001, p. 12) deems three broad conceptual aspects of digital media literacy to be essential:

- representation: the way in which digital media present the world;
- language: the ability to use language and understand how it works including the 'grammar' of particular forms of communication; and
- production: an understanding of who communicates to whom and why.

Arguably, therefore, without looking in any detail at individual subject areas here, new technologies have fundamental implications for what we teach.

THE IMPACT OF ICT ON PEDAGOGY

Similarly, new technologies have serious implications for how we teach.

Loveless *et al.* (2001, pp. 80–1), for example, offer a two-page typology of differing perspectives of 'old' and 'new' pedagogies in relation to knowledge. Due to lack of space I can only enumerate some of their descriptors here and refrain from listing the juxtaposed descriptors of 'old' pedagogy. Under new pedagogy, among other things, they list the following:

- use strategies to decide what is worth knowing in the head;
- teacher helps students access, select, evaluate, organise, and store information coming from a wide range of sources;
- students write to disks or publish on the web for a wider audience to see;
- texts are editable;
- students' personal choices are expected;
- intellectual products are revisable living documents subject to addition, subtraction and change.

Hand in hand with these descriptors goes the emphasis in effective ICT use on inter-disciplinary collaboration and on web-based projects. Not only do these modes of working raise the question of how to discriminate between individual contributions but also the question of what grading criteria might be most appropriate, in particular in view of the danger of foregrounding the product, e.g. the finished website, video or digital artefact, over the process, e.g. what students learned from collaborating and working in teams:

> What is assessed in schools and how the assessment is performed exercises a very powerful influence on the curriculum. The potential of ICT will not be realised as long as assessment is primarily in terms of student achievement in single subjects, by means of conventional written tests.
>
> (CERI, 2001, p. 31)

Whilst multimedia authoring software can give students the tools to produce a genuine representation of their understanding of the material produced, there is a need for the development of a shared set of criteria for assessment that take into account technical manipulation and content exposition (see e.g. McFarlane *et al.*, 2000).

THE IMPACT OF ICT ON ASSESSMENT

From the above it follows that, if specific pedagogical approaches are prevalent in subject teaching, such as collaborative project work in intra-institutional teams or web-quests (see also Chapters 1, 4–7 and 12), the assessment arrangements for that subject need to reflect these approaches to teaching and learning.

Task 9.1
Familiarising yourself with the statutory requirements

An important aspect of your role and responsibility as an effective subject teacher is familiarity with the requisite statutory requirements. Analyse how ICT can be used, for example, to cover the curriculum requirements of your subject specialism in the context you are in. For example, the National Curriculum (NC) Orders for England for all curriculum subjects can be found at <http://www.nc.uk.net>. The ICT in subject teaching part of the *NC in Action* website at: <http://www.ncaction.org.uk/subjects/ict/inother.htm> is also worth looking at.

Independence from the teacher is an important feature of ICT use. In assessment terms this means on the one hand that the teacher is less likely to be able to make valid and reliable judgements about the learning process; on the other hand, due to the features of ICT applications, such as spell checkers, on-line dictionaries, access to huge data banks of information through the internet and cut-and-paste functionality etc., it is becoming increasingly difficult to ascertain how much of the product is the student's own work and how much of it she has actually understood. In other words, the nature of assessment through ICT sits ill-at-ease with traditional educational paradigms of testing the retention, recall and understanding of knowledge by individual learners as opposed to the more skill- and application-based, collaborative modes supported by and intrinsic to working with ICT. It seems, therefore, that assessment paradigms will need to evolve in the light of emerging technologies and the learning objectives they are predicated on.

This issue was identified, amongst others, by John Brown as early as 1994:

> One of the continuing educational limitations is the value that is placed on timed examinations as a way of measuring an individual student's ability and achievement. Virtually no other situation that students will meet as members of society, as workers or as individuals will require the formality and isolation of the examination room. And yet, no matter how reliant on information technology they might have become, we continue to measure their ability to answer questions in two paperback-pages-worth of writing, in isolation and with only a ball-point pen to assist them. So although IT enables students to do different things, current examination and assessment systems continue to measure their ability on an increasingly inappropriate scale.
>
> (Brown, 1994, p. 38)

Task 9.2
Sarah's project

'Sarah is investigating how rivers change from source to sea. The class has collected data on the local river. Sarah enters all this data into a spreadsheet to generate graphs and check for correlations. She chooses suitable axes, prints her graphs and wonders whether the relationships she has identified are true for other rivers. She searches on the Internet for references to major rivers and locates a number of relevant sites. She prints out an academic paper on the river Nile. The language used is beyond her so she copies the text in electronic form and runs it through a précis program. This gives some useful information for her report, most of which contradicts her findings. She wonders whether the difference in sizes between the two rivers is an issue. She goes to a pupils' bulletin board and posts a message offering to trade her findings with other pupils' data on rivers in their localities. Of the six responses, two contain data and charts which she can cut and paste into her project, and two others give her raw data in need of processing.

She assembles the project, runs it through a grammar and spell-checker, and removes all uses of the passive voice. The grammar checker tells her that the work has a Flesch reading ease score of 75 per cent. She prints it out' (McLean, 1998, p. 33).

On the basis of the information in the above case study, what subject-based and what learning outcomes are likely to be in evidence through Sarah's final product? Which learning outcomes can be implied judging by the description of the process? How do these learning outcomes relate to the curriculum and its assessment frameworks, i.e. would Sarah be getting good marks in an exam situation based on what she has learnt carrying out this project? Is Sarah's approach in any way problematic?

In his preface to *ICT, Pedagogy and the Curriculum – Subject to Change*, Stephen Heppell makes the point that education traditionally, 'rightly conservative with children's lives, is downright paranoid about technology, seeking to confiscate, assimilate or smother it before any damage can be done' (Heppell, 2001, p. xv). He, rightly in my view, notes that new technologies can no longer be confiscated at the school gate but that, instead, they are embedded in the social and economic fabric of our lives and have to be seen as change agents of institutions of learning.

Yet, despite considerable achievements in the use of ICT in teaching and learning, the relationship between ICT and assessment remains at best strained. At a time when ICT has become 'a pervasive influence and working medium throughout the curriculum' (CERI, 2001, p. 29), its presence in the assessment process is negligible. At the time of writing, the general teaching requirements of the National Curriculum for England (see <http://www.nc.uk.net/nc_resources/html/ict.shtml>), for example stipulate the following concerning the use of ICT across the curriculum. Pupils should:

- be given opportunities to apply and develop their ICT capability through the use of ICT tools to support their learning in all subjects;
- be given opportunities to support their work by being taught to:
  find things out from a variety of sources, selecting and synthesising the information

  - to meet their needs and developing an ability to question its accuracy, bias and plausibility;
  - develop their ideas using ICT tools to amend and refine their work and enhance its quality and accuracy;
  - exchange and share information, both directly and through electronic media;
  - review, modify and evaluate their work, reflecting critically on its quality, as it progresses.

The crucial questions that follow are how examination specifications for various subjects match up to these expectations. To what extent are students allowed to make use of a variety of sources when answering their exam questions? How much use of electronic media and ICT tools is permissible? How much does computer-enabled assessment count overall?

A recent OECD study (CERI, 2001, p. 30) rightly stresses that unless assessment procedures reflect the levels to which ICT influences teaching and learning they lack validity. Or, as Heppell puts it:

> Our examination and assessment system is a creaking edifice built on failed and antiquated technology; for example, the inability of past technology to moderate spoken contributions pushed oracy out of an examination process where performance was distilled down to be simply mastery of notional representation, but when computers appeared they were seized immediately by the examination system, not to repair the damage from a fatal over-reliance on pen technology, but to produce a further distillation of learning into the execrable OCR sheets of multiple-choice tests. Other than that, by and large, the possession of a computer in the examination room is still regarded as cheating. Twenty years after we introduced the skills of authoring by word processor into schools our children are still frisked at the door of the examination room to ensure that they do not enter with a computer and, heaven forbid, actually evidence those skills.
>
> (Heppell, 2001, pp. xvi–xvii)

One might add the difficulties policy makers and consequently awarding bodies appear to be having with more traditional technologies such as graphical calculators in maths or dictionaries in modern foreign languages.

Yet, the affordances of ICT in relation to assessment can be profound.

COMPUTER-BASED AND ONLINE ASSESSMENT

McFarlane (2001a, p. 232) rightly points out that there is a need to distinguish between computer-based tests which replicate traditional tests and those which test in new ways or which test what couldn't be tested before. Within computer-based tests traditional computer-based tests and online- or web-based tests can be distinguished. The former are tests which are hosted on an individual computer or a closed network whereas the latter are 'delivered' via the web. Roever (2001) enumerates some potential positive characteristics of computer- and web-based assessment such as immediacy of feedback, self-scoring, flexibility, automatisation of feedback and marking, tracing the behaviours of test takers or authenticity. Web-based or online assessment, according to him, has the additional advantage of being available anytime and anyplace, is comparatively easy to author, only requires basic software such as a web-browser for display and apparently is very inexpensive. On the downside he mentions the increased risk of cheating, item exposure and confidentiality due to lack of security as well as the problem of server failure. Another important potential difficulty concerns the computerised assessment of free-text responses. In other words, limits in the advance of artificial intelligence appear to impose considerable constraints on the ability of algorithm-based, automated feedback on free text as opposed to, for example, multiple-choice formats. This can have a considerable impact on task and test types used and, consequently, on test validity and authenticity. Roever also advances the view that the appropriacy of web-based testing depends largely on the stakes associated with the test and that the lower the stakes involved, the higher the levels of appropriacy.

The Australian National Training Authority (2002, p. 6) list the following online assessment options:

- written assignments;
- essays;
- quizzes and questions;
- collaborative assignment work;
- exams (open-book; structured; timed);
- practicals;
- participation in online discussions;
- publication of student work/presentations;
- experiental activities, such as role-play;
- debates;
- reviews/journals and reflections.

In terms of modes of assessment they note: teacher, self, peer and external.

As can be seen, assessment opportunities making use of the web are still rather similar to non-computerised methods and often only use computer communication to submit or comment on students' work in traditional ways. Where computer-testing per se is used it often comprises short answers and multiple-choice questions. In short, computer-based and online assessment are still only in their infancy.

The Australian National Training Authority (2002, p. 6) also list a number of challenges concerning the use of computer-based assessment including whether and how to measure student participation in online discussion and activities, how to measure individual performance within group assignments, authentication of student work and detecting plagiarism – an issue I discuss in more detail below.

The US-based National Centre for Fair & Open Testing (no date) inter alia points out that students tend to score higher in traditional paper-and-pencil exams, that computerised tests can constrain test-takers compared with paper-and-pencil tests and that computers may worsen test bias and disadvantage weaker typers.

The University of Cambridge Local Examinations Syndicate (UCLES) presented some interesting findings about the impact of assessment mode on student performance, strategies, perceptions and behaviours at the 2004 annual British Education Research Association Conference. Papers presented by Johnson and Green (2004a, 2004b) draw attention to previous research which suggests that the use of computers has a beneficial effect on students' intrinsic motivation and that it can lead to greater cognitive gains. In addition they note the potential of computer-based assessment for saving time and money, in particular through individualised formative assessment. Quite rightly, in my view, they refer to Ashton, Schofield and Woodger (2003) who argue that the challenge for online assessment is not technical but pedagogical in nature. For example, is the task/test difficulty dependent on the mode of presentation? And, does the mode affect performance, assessment strategies used by students and their perceptions of difficulty? Their literature review posits that studies examining the relationship between assessment mode and student perception suggests that – contrary to student perception – computer-based was generally harder than paper-based assessment and that differences between children's overall performances on paper and the computer were not statistically significant. This phenomenon is explained in the literature by students' generally positive attitude towards computers (high face validity) which affects their stance towards answering questions. It is also noted that presentational differences such as the use of colour illustrations or neatness of typing, might be contributory factors. In other words, the medium 'computer' offers certain technical affordances (see e.g. Bearne and Kress, 2001 or Laurillard et al., 2000) which appear to have a noticeable washback effect, i.e. influence the way in which students perceive assessment and go about completing tasks. A particularly strong concept according to Johnson and Green's work appears to be 'task ease' in relation to doing less writing (2004b, p. 13). Their findings (2004a) also suggest that children showed a greater commitment to the task and less off-task behaviour as well as less responsiveness to extraneous influences and distractions. Also, they rightly wonder whether question types and the way questions are asked interact with the modality, i.e. computer or paper test. Children, particularly boys, are said to be more likely to 'take a chance' about submitting an answer on the computer even if they were not sure about their answer.

Overall, the research surveyed here clearly shows that the issue of online assessment is far from straightforward and that numerous variables interact, including the content being tested, the age of the students, the nature of tasks, the wording of questions, interface design etc.

From the teachers' point of view, online assessment on the one hand holds the promise of innovation in assessment, for example through the use of e-portfolios, digital video or other artefact creation, but it also brings with it considerable concerns in relation to workloads. Despite the assertions by government that increased ICT use would lead to a freeing up of teacher time (e.g. DfES, 2003a, p. 8), in relation to assessment the possibility of electronic submission of work 24 hours per day, 7 days a week, potentially exposes the teacher to unrealistic expectations by students and their parents and can lead to expectations in relation to speed and automaticity that put pressure on teachers to provide feedback to unrealistic timescales.

E-portfolios hold a particular promise in relation to online assessment as they potentially offer a so-called learner-centric (as opposed to assessor-centric) repository 'supporting reflection, growth, accomplishment and collaboration over time and the demonstration and projection of self (skills, competence, [knowledge,] personality and mastery) to others for multiple, unpredictable purposes' (quoted in Grant, Jones and Ward, 2004). In order for e-portfolios to become a reality in the secondary school context at least one of Heppell's (2001) demands in relation to a children's e-charter would need to be fulfilled, namely for them to be offered progression and continuity for the ICT activities they collect on their way through schooling.

Managed learning systems, which revolve around computerised assessment, appear to feature prominently in the government's thinking about ICT use in compulsory schooling (DfES, 2002, p. 16). They tend to be predicated on a model of centrally prescribed content which is delivered and assessed through ICT; learners are tracked by ICT; and, in addition, teachers are communicated with via ICT. In this model, ICT is seen predominantly as a cost-saving device enabling flexible 'delivery of learning' 'in order to reflect the personalisation of pupils' programmes of sudy' (DfES, 2002, p. 15). Such a model accords little with Buckingham's notion of active student participation and culture and knowledge construction. For practical examples see Chapter 5.

From work by the Qualifications and Curriculum Authority (QCA) as well as the DfES consultation paper on an e-learning strategy (DfES, 2003b) it is clear that electronic assessment, or e-assessment, is very high on the government's list of priorities.

The DfES e-learning strategy consultation paper notes (2003b, p. 32) that assessment is one of the most powerful drivers of innovation and change in education and points out that e-learning systems could greatly enhance the value of assessment through data analysis for the teacher and interactive feedback for the learner. In other words, they can offer assessment for learning and personalised support. The paper claims that e-assessment has the potential to reduce time spent on marking and to increase the time spent on directing and supporting learning. It also suggests that e-assessment has the potential to widen participation by overcoming barriers of time, location and cost through what it calls 'on demand' testing (p. 33). According to the consultation document, simulations, information gathering, data presentation or modelling offer challenging and interesting ways of e-assessment (p. 34).

The Qualifications and Curriculum Authority (QCA), which oversees the examination system in schools in England, according to its website (<http://www.qca.org.uk/adultlearning/workforce/6877.html>), has a strategic objective whereby by 2009:

- all new qualifications must include an option for on-screen assessment;
- all awarding bodies should be set up to accept and assess e-portfolios;
- all existing GCSEs, AS and A2 examinations should be available on-screen;
- the first on-demand assessments are starting to be introduced; and
- at least ten new qualifications, specifically designed for electronic delivery and assessment, should be developed and live.

Through the eVIVA project the QCA has been experimenting with the compilation of online portfolios of ICT Key Stage 3 work for pupils, i.e. formative assessment, to show what they know and can do as well as the processes they have used and the decisions they have made (see <http://www.eviva.tv>). In addition, work is being carried out on summative Key Stage 3 ICT onscreen tests including performance tracking. The test will cover processes such as finding things out, developing ideas and exchanging and sharing information. Also, the QCA have done work on multiple-choice onscreen testing of basic and key skills at levels 1 and 2 and plans to develop tests in other formats such as short answers, multiple completion and extended responses.

PLAGIARISM

One increasingly central issue in the context of ICT-based assessment is plagiarism. The functionality of new technologies, in particular of the web and word-processors, have made it very easy for students to pass off the work of others as their own. This unacknowledged presentation of another person's intellectual property is commonly known as plagiarism or electronic cheating.

A number of strategies can be and have been suggested for tackling e-cheating. I find Robert Harris' anti-plagiarism strategies (2002) particularly appealing. They include the following:

- Strategies of awareness:
    - understand why students cheat;
    - educate yourself about plagiarism;
    - educate your students about plagiarism;
    - discuss the benefits of citing sources;
    - make the penalties clear.

- Strategies of prevention:
    - make the assignment clear;
    - provide a list of topics;
    - require specific components;
    - require process steps;
    - have students include an annotated bibliography;
    - require most references to be up to date;
    - require a meta-learning essay;

- Strategies for detection:
    - look for clues;
    - know where the sources are;
    - search for the sources;
    - use a plagiarism detector.

Task 9.3
Anti-plagiarism strategies

What are the implications of the practical advice above on tackling plagiarism for your own teaching context? Which other strategies might be appropriate and effective?
For plagiarism advice also see <http://www.jiscpas.ac.uk/>.

SUMMARY

In this chapter I have argued the case of the interrelationship of ICT, teaching, learning and assessment. I have tried to show that ICT not only has implications on what we teach and how but also on assessment. ICT was shown to have considerable potential for assessment, but I have pointed to some of the systemic barriers for it reaching its full potential. In short, ICT will pose a sizeable challenge for all of us in education for some time to come.

REFERENCES AND FURTHER READING

Ashton, H., Schofield, D. and Woodger, S. (2003) 'Piloting summative web assessment in secondary education', paper presented to the 7th International Computer Assisted Assessment Conference, Loughborough, July.

Australian National Training Authority (2002) *Assessment and Online Teaching*. Online. Available HTTP: <http://flexiblelearning.net.au>.

Bearne, E. and Kress, G. (2001) 'Editorial', *Reading, Literacy and Language*, 35(3): 89–93.

Brown, J. (1994) 'Tomorrow's curriculum: the necessary or the possible', in SCET (ed.) *All our Learning Futures: The Role of Technology in Education*, Glasgow: SCET.

Buckingham, D. (2001) *New Media Literacies: Informal Learning, Digital Technologies and Education*, London: Institute for Public Policy Research.

Centre for Educational Research and Innovation (2001) *Schooling Tomorrow. Learning to Change: ICT in Schools*, Paris: OECD.

DfES (2002) *Transforming the Way we Learn: A Vision for the Future of ICT in Schools*, London: DfES.

DfES (2003a) *Fulfilling the Potential: Transforming Teaching and Learning through ICT in Schools*. London: DfES. Online. Available HTTP: <http://www.dfes.gov.uk/ictinschools/uploads/docarchive/fulfilling_potential.pdf>.

DfES (2003b) *Towards a Unified e-Learning Strategy*, Consultation document. London: DfES.

Grant, S., Jones, P. and Ward, R. (2004) *E-portfolio and its Relationship to Personal Development Planning: A View from the UK for Europe and Beyond*. Online. Available HTTP: <http://www.inst.co.uk/clients/jisc/e-portfoliodef.html>.

Harris, R. (2002) *Anti-plagiarism Strategies for Research Papers*. Online. Available HTTP: <http://www.virtualsalt.com/antiplag.htm>.

Heppell, S. (2001) 'Preface', in A. Loveless and V. Ellis (eds) *ICT, Pedagogy and the Curriculum: Subject to Change*, London: RoutledgeFalmer.

Johnson, M. and Green, S. (2004a) 'On-line assessment: the impact of mode on students' performance', paper presented at the BERA Annual Conference, Manchester,

September. Online. Available HTTP: <http://www.ucles.org.uk/assessmentdirectorate/articles/confproceedingsetc/BERA2004MJSG.

Johnson, M. and Green, S. (2004b) 'On-line assessment: the impact of mode on students' strategies, perceptions and behaviours', paper presented at the BERA Annual Conference, Manchester, September. Online. Available HTTP: <http://www.ucles.org.uk/assessmentdirectorate/articles/confproceedingsetc/BERA2004MJSG2>.

Kennedy, K. (2003) *Writing with Web Logs*. Online. Available HTTP: <http://www.techlearning.com/db_area/archives/TL/2003/02/blogs.html>.

Laurillard, D., Stratford, M., Luckin, R., Plowman, L. and Taylor, J. (2000) 'Affordances for learning in a non-linear narrative medium', *Journal of Interactive Media in Education* (2000/2). Online. Available HTTP: <http://www-jime.open.ac.uk/00/2>.

Loveless, A., DeVoogd, G. and Bahlin, R. (2001) 'Something old, something new … . Is pedagogy affected by ICT?', in A. Loveless and V. Ellis (eds) *ICT, Pedagogy and the Curriculum: Subject to Change*, London: RoutledgeFalmer.

McFarlane, A. (2001a) 'Perspectives on the relationships between ICT and assessment', *Journal of Computer Assisted Learning*, 17(3): 227–34.

McFarlane, A. (2001b) *ICT and Attainment – Planting Apple Trees to Harvest Oranges?* London: Institute for Public Policy Research. Online. Available HTTP: <http://www.ippr.org.uk/research/files/team25/project75/digital_curriculum.pdf>.

McFarlane, A., Williams, J. and Bonnet, M. (2000) 'Assessment and multimedia authoring: a tool for externalising understanding', *Journal of Computer Assisted Learning*, 16(3): 201–12.

McLean, N. (1998) 'No more marking time', *TES Online Education*, May 15, p. 33.

National Centre for Fair & Open Testing (no date) *Computerised Testing: More Questions than Answers*. Online. Available HTTP: <http://www.fairtest.org/facts/computer.htm>.

NCET (1994) *ICT Work*. Coventry: NCET.

Pachler, N. and Field, K. (2001) *Learning to Teach Modern Foreign Languages in the Secondary School*, London: RoutledgeFalmer.

Pittard, V., Bannister, P. and Dunn, J. (2003) *The Big pICTure: The Impact of ICT on Attainment, Motivation and Learning*, London: DfES. Online. Available HTTP: <http://www.dfes.gov.uk/ictinschools/uploads/docarchive/The%20Big%20Picture%20B.pdf>.

Roever, C. (2001) 'Web-based language testing', *Language Learning Journal*, 5(2): 84–94. Online. Available HTTP: <http://llt.msu.edu/vol5num2/roever/>.

10 Linking School with Home Use

Norbert Pachler and Ana Redondo

INTRODUCTION

Recent advances in Information and Communications Technology (ICT) make new things possible; this is as true for the so-called 'real world' as it is for education. As access to new technologies grows outside schools, particularly in homes, and as more and more learning resources become available in digital form, the role and function of school as the best place of learning are being called into question.

OBJECTIVES

By the end of this chapter you should have an awareness of:

- issues concerning the increase of computer use in the home / outside school;
- how new technologies might be used to support home-based learning;
- what schools can do to maximise the potential of ICT for home-based learning.

THE PROLIFERATION OF ICT AND ITS IMPLICATIONS

Work by Lewin *et al.* (2003, p. 45) commissioned by the DfES (see also Comber *et al.*, 2002; Somekh *et al.*, 2002a; Somekh *et al.*, 2002b) stresses the breadth of computer-based activities that are happening in many homes allowing young people, and their parents, to access specialist information and knowledge relevant to their own interests to an extent and in a way that has not previously been possible. These developments considerably challenge teachers and schools among other things in their role as gatekeepers. Lewin *et al.* posit that schools generally fail to draw upon these experiences of knowledge creation outside school.

> Rather than technologies having any impact on transforming knowledge in the majority of schools, the traditional structures of curriculum and pedagogy were colonizing technologies and directing students' energies in schools to doing 'more of the same more efficiently'.
>
> (Lewin *et al.*, 2003, p. 45)

Whilst subject to transformation, the role of the teacher does not become redundant with the proliferation of 'edutainment' nor, indeed, more overtly instructional applications. Suggestions that the coherence teachers provide to the learning process will, in the foreseeable future, become less important, can be seen to be misguided. Nevertheless, there exists a clear move in the world outside school towards self-directed, autonomous learning and knowledge creation which requires learners to identify their own goals and plan and structure their learning that sits ill-at-ease with current practices and curricula in schools.

> Pedagogy is no longer merely a process of teacher–student interaction, but a complex process of interaction between teacher, student, peers, family and technology.
>
> (Lewin *et al.*, 2003, p. 28)

Currently prevailing notions of schools as institutions and places of learning need to be seen as having social and historical functions, amongst others 'as repositories and transmitters of knowledge' (Hutchinson, 1996, p. iv). In view of the increasing ease of access to information through new technologies as well as the expansion of our knowledge bases, the so-called information explosion, the idea of 'virtual schooling' is no longer inconceivable.

David Hargreaves, for instance, argues that if we want to make conceptions such as 'the learning society' or 'lifelong education' a reality,

> (the) traditional 'education system' must be replaced by *polymorphic* provision – an infinite variety of multiple forms of teaching and learning. Future generations will look back on our current sharp disjunction between life and education and our confusion of education with schooling as a barrier blocking a – perhaps the – road to the learning society.
>
> (Hargreaves, 1997, p. 11)

From a teacher's, rather than a policy maker's perspective, proclamations about an 'infinite variety of … forms of teaching and learning' are, often quite rightly, bound up with concerns about the impact on personal professional practice. Not only in terms of pedagogical challenges and implications – and of course these do exist – but also in relation to workload. Anybody with experience in technology-enhanced teaching and learning will know about the complexities involved and the increased amount of teacher time required. From a teacher's, as well as schools' perspective there will be concerns about the professional development implications of familiarisation and appropriation of ever-changing technologies and the psychological challenge in working in environments in which young people often show less inhibition and a greater knowledge and skills base than their teachers.

In the context of ICT use for increased home–school links the issue of (a lack of) familiarity on the part of parents with new technologies also comes into play. A number of schools have launched special initiatives to overcome such barriers such as laptop loan schemes or parent clubs.

A survey conducted in Autumn 2002 (Hayward *et al.*, 2003) suggests critical mass in home computer use:

- 81 per cent of households had access to a computer in the home, up from 78 per cent in the 2001 survey;
- 68 per cent of households had access to the internet at home, up from 64 per cent in 2001;
- 98 per cent of 5–18-year-olds used computers at home, school or elsewhere, with 92 per cent using them at school and 75 per cent using them at home;
- 84 per cent of 5–18-year-olds used the internet at home, school or elsewhere, with 71 per cent using it at school and 56 per cent using it at home;
- Young people of all ages used computers at home for a wider range of activities than in 2001.

Somekh *et al.* (2002b, p. 10), referring to Harrison *et al.* (2001), point out that there has been a dramatic increase of home ownership in ICT of late:

- 88 per cent of Key Stage 4 pupils have computers at home;
- 64 per cent of secondary pupils can access the internet at home;
- 67 per cent of secondary pupils reported to have their own email address;
- 49 per cent of KS3 and 60 per cent of KS4 pupils reported having their own mobile phone.

In view of these statistics and the transformational potential of ICT discussed earlier, schools should examine the potential of new technologies for the purposes of communicating with parents and the wider community and how to involve them in the learning process.

New technologies have the potential for fundamentally changing home–school relationships not only by enabling better access to information but also by providing tools for knowledge creation and participation in new cultural practices. Nevertheless, there is a real danger of new technologies increasing disadvantage for young people without ready access to computers and other technology at home, for example, for reasons of social deprivation. According to Lewin *et al.* (2003, p. 47), social class can be seen to be a particularly significant factor.

In addition to differences in amount of computer use in the home, there are differences in the type of use:

> While a significant *minority* of students do not have access to the internet at home, a significant *majority* do not choose to use technology to help them with their school work on a daily or frequent basis.

Research by Furlong *et al.* (2000) suggests that whilst boys tend to prefer to use computers for entertainment, especially skill and strategy games, girls tend to favour their use for homework, writing and information retrieval. This can be seen to have potential implications for the achievement differential between girls and boys. Millard (1997) found that boys tend to have more and easier access to computers at home than girls, particularly in lower socio-economic groups.

There is, in other words, a 'digital divide' between 'haves' and 'have nots' and a full range of educational concerns need to be understood by schools in relation to the implications of widespread use of ICT in the home. Schools need a comprehensive awareness of equal opportunities in terms of the differential of computer access by learners not only across the social divide but by gender and ethnic background. In schools with a high population of refugee children, for example, these issues will be particularly pronounced.

This is, of course, not to ignore some of the seemingly more encouraging evidence. According to a survey commissioned by BT, the use of computers at home seems to increase fathers' involvement with their children's school-related work:

> 16 per cent of dads with home computers were involved with their children's home learning, compared with just 9 per cent of fathers relying on traditional homework resources. Computers and the Internet provide men with the opportunity and incentive to interact more with their children, BT suggests.
>
> (*The Guardian*, 13 January 1998)[1]

When considering such evidence it is important to remember that home-based use of ICT to support learning is a growing market with considerable commercial importance. Publicity material is inherently characterised by vested interests and it is often not possible to make informed judgements about the validity and reliability of the research carried out by service providers.

Significantly, there are many pupils who have a strong preference for using ICT at home (see e.g. Furlong *et al.*, 2000, Sutherland *et al.*, 2000) due to enhanced hardware and software availability as well as increased access, choice and agency. Schools and teachers ignore the resulting ICT capability of pupils at their peril.

TYPES OF HOME AND SCHOOL USE OF ICT

The DfES-funded research carried out by Lewin *et al.* (2003, p. 34) identifies a number of what the researchers call 'special initiatives' to develop links between home and school including:

- virtual classrooms;
- homework guidance on the web;
- emailing parents;
- emailing homework to teachers;
- home access to school servers;
- online tutoring;
- parental access to school attendance registers via the internet; and
- online conferencing for parents and school governors.

The web and email, therefore, play a crucial role in the interface between home and schools.

The Becta website[2] offers the following examples of ICT linking home and school:

- email;
- a basic school website;

- a resource-rich or interactive school website;
- online learning/'virtual school';
- student, parent and community use of school-based ICT facilities;
- loan and subsidy schemes, including portable ICT schemes;
- local TV – locally produced educational content on TV networks;
- community intranets; and
- additional online resources of use to parents and pupils.

However, the 'Home and school use of ICT' section of a report by Comber *et al.* (2002, pp. 30–1) notes the following key findings:

- the use of email to bridge the gap between and school is still under-exploited;
- teachers have concerns about the nature and quality of some of the resources researched by pupils themselves; and
- there is frequently a lack of clear guidance from schools for parents in relation to effective ICT support.

This suggests that there is still a problem with suitable content and school strategies being under-developed.

Task 10.1
Establishing patterns of home computer use

Carry out a survey amongst your classes to establish prevailing patterns of computer use at home amongst your pupils. What are the implications of your findings for the work you ask your pupils to do to in the class and at home?

THE ROLE OF HOMEWORK

One obvious opportunity of linking home and school use of ICT is through ICT-enhanced homework. Pupils often find homework a chore. Encouraging the use of ICT for homework purposes is one way of capitalising on the motivational potential of new technologies. Equity of access is an important issue here and schools must ensure that strategies are in place to enable those pupils who have not got access to ICT at home to enhance their classroom-based learning as well as their more fortunate peers who do. This can be done, for instance, through lunchtime or after-school ICT/homework clubs.

Findings by Comber *et al.* (2002, p. 31) suggest that teachers tend to encourage, rather than require, internet use for homework because of concerns over equity of access. Yet, there are real advantages to be had by students being able to access their schoolwork from home for continuation, extension and refinement (see Lewin *et al.*, 2003, p. 39). Homework can supplement and/or differentiate what happens in the classroom and it can reinforce or consolidate work carried out in school.

Homework, in a sense, can be seen as the space between school-based and out-of-school learning, where teacher- and curriculum-specified tasks meet a learner-defined curriculum and culture. A report of emerging findings from the evaluation of the impact of ICT on pupil attainment (Harrison *et al.*, 2001, p. 5) uses the concept of a 'socially contextualised integrated model of learning' to explain this interrelationship.

Pupils can benefit from the attention given to them by 'significant others', e.g. their parents/guardians at home or ICT/homework club supervisors in school, as well as make use of reference material which might not be available during lessons.

Competition for access to computers is likely to be less fierce at home as well as in ICT/homework clubs, i.e. the user–hardware ratio is bound to better than during normal classwork. In 2003, according to OFSTED (2004), the average number of pupils per computer in secondary schools was 5.4.

Computer-supported work outside the classroom still causes anxieties in certain quarters, traditionally in relation to spelling and handwriting but more recently in relation to plagiarism. In order to ameliorate some of these anxieties it is important that explicit assessment criteria are used which recognise the work done using ICT but at the same time do not disadvantage those pupils unable to use ICT. See Chapter 9 on assessment on how to tackle the issue of plagiarism.

Task 10.2
Integrating ICT use into homework tasks

1. Examine your current scheme-of-work for one class you are teaching with a view to how ICT resources could be used to supplement homework tasks.
2. Also, what ICT-based revision material do you know of for your subject area? Talk to colleagues in your department, get in touch with your subject association and look out for subject-specific software catalogues as well as reviews in the educational press for ideas. See, for example:
   – BBC Learning at <http://www.bbc.co.uk/learning>;
   – BBC Bitesize Revision at <http://www.bbc.co.uk/schools/gcsebitesize/>;
   – Channel 4's Homework High at <http://www.channel4.com/homework/>;
   – Kevin's playroom at <http://www.kevinsplayroom.co.uk/>; and/or
   – S-cool at <http://www.s-cool.co.uk/>.

OFFERING ADVICE TO PARENTS ABOUT EFFECTIVE ICT USE

A key consideration for schools in relation to home-based ICT use for learning is the provision of guidance on when, where and how to use computers. Ever since the internet emerged, there has been a lot of hype about its potential dangers:

> Child porn, adult porn, instructions on how to make bombs, how to engage in autoeroticism …, the finer points of glue-sniffing, rants against the black and Jewish world conspiracy and why we should all have the freedom to carry guns are just some of the Net's offerings that have been whipping up a frenzy of paranoia, moral outrage, medium-level concern in the media and, consequently, among parents and teachers.
>
> The simple, rather banal fact is that the Internet is only as bad and as good as society itself.
>
> (Klein, 1995, p. 20)

If these potential dangers and the anxieties parents might have are not taken seriously and tackled head-on, it is difficult to see how significant progress can be made in terms of ICT use within and outside school. As far as ICT-enabled work within school is concerned, the adoption of an acceptable use policy such as the one suggested by the National Association for Co-ordinators and Teachers of IT, ACITT, seems imperative.[3] Guidelines for ICT use outside school are also available online. Stephen Heppell offers some useful advice on the *Schools OnLine* webpages,[4] see Figure 10.1 for a summary.

Advice is also available from a number of other websites, including government-sponsored ones.[5] Schools might wish to develop these guidelines, tailor them to their local needs and disseminate them to parents.

A different type of support can come in the form of open days or open evenings during which pupils can demonstrate what they have learnt, what equipment there is available at school and what software is used by subject departments. But also, events like these can be used to offer parents and the wider community training in (basic) ICT skills in the

---

The internet reaches out across the whole world and has come of age as a communication medium. This is exciting but also means that the full spectrum of individuals that make our world interesting and occasionally dangerous are also 'out there' on the Internet too. Common-sense rules that work in the rest of our lives also work on the Internet. Common sense is valuable in any context, including this one.

- Never give out identifying information – your home address, phone number, school – in a public messaging area like chat or user groups.
- People at the other end of an email are not always what they seem. Someone claiming to be 'she' and 14 could be 'he' and 40. This may not matter but think carefully before giving personal information out, or developing a relationship.
- If you come across messages that are deliberately provocative, obscene, racist, illegal, pornographic, threatening or that simply make you feel uncomfortable, do not respond to them. In doing so you would be opening a dialogue with the person who posted the message.
- If you receive messages that are harassing or otherwise disturbing, talk about it with people you trust and forward the message(s) to your service provider with a note about your concerns.
- Just because it comes out of a computer doesn't mean it is true! Be sceptical of information off the net until you have identified its source. Seemingly credible stories can be invented and circulated for many reasons (for example, political advantage).
- Any offer that is 'too good to be true' is probably neither 'too good' nor 'true'!
- Put computers in social areas. Our own (and our friends') social rules and habits are a good check of our behaviours. In schools don't place monitors facing the wall, in homes get computers out of the bedroom. It will be worth the move for the discussion around the screen that will result.
- Never, ever, ever arrange to meet as a result of an electronic contact unless parents and/or teachers are aware of what is happening. If you do meet, make sure the first meetings are in a public place in the presence of friends, parents or adults that they know.
- Don't panic! There is simply so much that is good and useful and exciting on the net; working together on projects and tasks will always be less likely to cause problems than just browsing around endlessly.
- Talking about what we all discover and exploring each other's discoveries will all help to build constructive use of time.

Figure 10.1 Safety guidelines for students, teachers and parents

hope that this will bridge the fear barrier for some parents and facilitate them working with their children on ICT-based work. The fact that there are lots of benefits to be had from pupils learning with their parents or even from teaching their parents is well known. Once parents see how proficient their children are and what motivational effect ICT might have on them, it is likely that they are going to be positively disposed towards ICT use in school.

Schools might consider providing parents with suggestions about what software would be beneficial in supplementing school-based work in various subject areas. Experience suggests that it is preferable to discourage parents from purchasing software which forms an integral part of a department's scheme-of-work as use outside school of such core applications might take some of the excitement out of their use in school. Also, the fun element of learning through computers at home might be diminished in that way. Teachers could concentrate on recommending supplementary as well as revision material. Parents, could, for instance be directed to vetted web-based revision and supplementary material (see Task 10.1 above).

Apart from technical considerations, schools might consider discussing with parents some of the most pertinent pedagogical implications of ICT use such as the tensions between presentation versus content, i.e. 'not all that glitters is gold', the dangers of plagiarism or the importance of fostering in pupils research skills etc.

One area parents, as well as pupils, tend to be particularly interested in is advice and guidance concerning examination periods, particularly during the study leave period in preparation for GCSEs and A/AS level examinations. Again, ICT-based materials are available such as guidance on exam stress[6] or study skills.[7]

Also, parents could be in touch with relevant organisations such as the Parent Information Network (PIN),[8] an independent national support membership organisation with the aim of helping parents support children using computers. Of interest is, of course, also Becta's *Information Sheet: Parents, ICT and Education*[9] which gives an introduction to how ICT can be used to support children's learning. Figure 10.2 summarises Becta's advice.

- Keep the computer in a communal area of your home, such as the living room.
- Take an interest in what children are doing with the computer.
- Ask children to show you how it works and explain how they use computers in school.
- If a modem is being used, control the activity by monitoring times used and numbers dialled.
- Advise children to take care whenever they are online, reminding them never to give out any personal information about themselves – particularly full names, addresses, phone numbers, or financial information.
- Ask children to avoid responding to anyone who leaves obnoxious, sexual or menacing email and report all electronic harassment and/or abuse to their parents.
- Make sure that computing and video games are only two activities amongst many that children enjoy.

Figure 10.2 Becta's advice to parents

THE ROLE OF A SCHOOL WEBSITE

As we have noted above, together with email, school websites[10] are particularly potent in linking home to school use and in engaging parents in school matters. Lewin *et al.* (2003, p. 35) point out that in order to realise their full potential or to play a significant role in empowering parents and families, school websites need to contain detailed information about educational issues and choices about the curriculum and assessment. According to their research this is, however, generally not the case. Often school websites are conceived of mainly as marketing tools and they tend to focus on static information such as a school prospectus, curriculum information, school rules, information about the school mission and ethos, key dates and contact details.

It seems very important that there is one single individual with overall responsibility for the website who draws on the work of a group of teachers from different subject areas in order to ensure consistency of approach and regular updates. In addition, it seems advisable to involve views from across the school including pupils, non-teaching staff, parents and governors. A working party which meets regularly might be a useful vehicle to ensure all the work gets done and that as many people as possible are able to contribute. Importantly, pupils themselves can make a very valuable contribution to the development of a school website through specific curriculum activities.

Stephanie Davies (1998) suggests the publication of a regularly updated school 'newspaper' produced by pupils. She also notes that school field trips lend themselves to web-presentation including actual pictures and links to websites providing background information. Davies points out that classes could be given web-space to publish information about the topics they are working on and include actual pieces of work. This way school-based learning can become more transparent to parents at home. In order to entice pupils to engage with the school website outside school the inclusion of homework guidance, activities and links seems important.

Becta offers useful guidelines on planning and designing effective school websites entitled 'Making web sites work'.[11]

Task 10.3
School websites

Find out whether your school has a web-presence.

1. View the site and consider what its aims and purposes are. What type of material can be found on it: curriculum-related links, publicity material, information about the local area? Who is the target audience: pupils, parents, teachers, the wider public?
2. Find out about its management and production. Who is responsible for creating it? Who is updating it? What curriculum areas are contributing?
3. Find out how you could contribute and make your own contribution, preferably in conjunction with one of the classes you teach.

Should your school not have a web-presence yet, look at the websites of Netherhall or Ashcombe schools (for URLs see note 10).

SUMMARY

In this chapter we have attempted to demonstrate how ICT can meaningfully be used for bridging the gap between school and home learning. Communicating with pupils and parents through email, for instance informing them about school events or even allowing pupils to submit homework etc., nevertheless remains problematic as it can easily represent extra workload for already very busy professionals.

In concluding, we want to refer to Thomas *et al.* (1998, pp. 149–50) who voice a note of caution when they point out, on the basis of their experience of working for a big distance-learning provider, that certain pre-requisites for successful, large-scale internet-based teaching are necessary:

- a culture of *supported* learning;
- recognition of cost;
- integration of technology with the administrative infrastructure, as well as with teaching practice;
- transformation of practices (both teaching and administrative) to take advantage of technology in order to provide needed functions, rather than superficial translation of existing practices.

NOTES

1   See <http://home.campus.bt.com/HomeCampus/pub/sampler/endorse.html> (accessed 1999).
2   See <http://www.becta.org.uk/research/research.cfm?id=2606>.
3   The policy document can be downloaded from ACITT's website at <http://acitt.digitalbrain.com/acitt/web/guest/freebies/aup97.doc>.
4   Available at <http://sol.ultralab.anglia.ac.uk/pages/schools_online/userSupport/Safety_advice/>.
5   See e.g. <http://safety.ngfl.gov.uk/schools/>; <http://www.gridclub.com/>; <http://www.thinkuknow.co.uk/parents/>; <http://www.parentcentre.gov.uk/>; <http://www.parentsonline.gov.uk/parents/>; or <http://www.parentsonline.gov.uk/safety/>.
6   See e.g. <http://www.childline.org.uk/Examstress.asp>; <http://www.adelaide.edu.au/counselling_centre/brochures/exams.html>; <http://stress.about.com/cs/schoolstress/a/aa020501.htm>; <http://www.isma.org.uk/exams.htm>; or <http://www.city.ac.uk/healthservice/exam.htm>.
7   See e.g. <http://www.bbc.co.uk/learning/returning/betterlearner/studyskills/index.shtml>; <http://www.how-to-study.com/>; <http://www.studygs.net/>; <http://www.ucc.vt.edu/stdysk/stdyhlp.html>; <http://www.d.umn.edu/student/loon/acad/strat/>; or <http://www.howtostudy.org/>.
8   See <http://www.pin.org.uk/>.
9   Available at <http://www.becta.org.uk/leas/leas.cfm?section=13_1&id=2189>.
10   For good examples, see e.g. the Netherhall School at <http://www.netherhall.cambs.sch.uk>; or Ashcombe School at <http://www.ashcombe.surrey.sch.uk/>.
11   Available at <http://www.becta.org.uk/subsections/awards/website_awards/documents/making_websites_work.pdf>.

REFERENCES AND FURTHER READING

Comber, C., Watling, R., Lawson, T., Cavendish, S., McEune, R. and Paterson, F. (2002) *Learning at home and school: case studies*. ImpaCT2. ICT in Schools Research and Evaluation Series – No. 8. DfES/Becta. Online. Available HTTP: <http://www.becta.org.uk/research/research.cfm?section=1&id=563>.

Davies, S. (1998) 'More than just a prospectus', *TES Friday*, 10 July: 15.

Furlong, J., Furlong, R., Facer, K. and Sutherland, R. (2000) 'The national grid for learning: a curriculum without walls?', *Cambridge Journal of Education*, 30: 91–110.

Hargreaves, D. (1997) 'A road to the learning society', *School Leadership and Management*, 17(1): 9–21.

Harrison, C. *et al.* (2001) *ImpaCT2. Emerging Findings from the Evaluation of the Impact of ICT on Pupil Attainment*. Research and Evaluation Series – No. 1 DfES/Becta. Online. Available HTTP: <http://www.becta.org.uk/page_documents/research/ngflseries_impact2.pdf>.

Hayward, B., Alty, C., Pearson, S. and Martin, C. (2003) *Young People and ICT 2002*. ICT in Schools Research and Evaluation Series – No. 12, London: DfES/Becta. Online. Available HTTP: <http://www.becta.org.uk/page_documents/research/full_report.pdf>.

Hutchinson, C. (1996) 'Snares in the charmed circle', *Times Higher Educational Supplement*, 12 April: iv–v.

Klein, R. (1995) 'Naughty toys and dirty pictures', *TES Computers Update*, 20 October: 20–1.

Lewin, C., Mavers, D. and Somekh, B. (2003) 'Broadening access to the curriculum through using technology to link home and school: a critical analysis of reforms intended to improve students' educational attainment', *The Curriculum Journal*, 14(1): 23–53.

Millard, E. (1997) 'New technologies, old inequalities – variations found in the use of computers by pupils at home with implications for the school curriculum'. Online. Available HTTP: <http://www.leeds.ac.uk/educol/documents/000000362.htm>.

OFSTED (2004) *ICT in Schools. The Impact of Government Initiatives Five Years on*, London: OFSTED. Online. Available HTTP: <http://www.ofsted.gov.uk/publications/index.cfm?fuseaction= pubs.displayfile&id=3652&type=pdf>.

Somekh, B., Mavers, D. and Lewin, C. (2002a) *Using ICT to Enhance Home–School Links: An Evaluation of Current Practice in England*, ICT in Schools Research and Evaluation Series – No. 4, London: DfES/Becta. Online. Available HTTP: <http://www.dfes.gov.uk/ictinschools/evidence/subject.cfm?articleid=255>.

Somekh, B., Lewin, C., Mavers, D., Fisher, T., Harrison, C., Haw, K., Lunzer, E., McFarlane, A. and Scrimshaw, P. (2002b) *Pupils' and Teachers' Perceptions of ICT in the Home, School and Community. ImpaCT2*, ICT in Schools Research and Evaluation Series – No. 9, London: DfES/Becta. Online. Available HTTP: <http://www.becta.org.uk/research/research.cfm?section=1&id=562>.

Sutherland, R., Facer, K., Furlong, R. and Furlong, J. (2000) 'A new environment for education? The computer in the home', *Computers and Education*, 34: 195–212.

Thomas, P., Carswell, L., Price, B. and Petre, M. (1998) 'A holistic approach to supporting distance learning using the internet: transformation, not translation', *British Journal of Educational Technology*, 29(2): 149–61.

11 ICT and Classroom Pedagogies

Colin Harrison

INTRODUCTION

This chapter draws on the detailed evidence gathered over a number of years by the ImpaCT2 project (Becta, 2002), a government-funded project that investigated the relationship between ICT and school achievement at Key Stages 2, 3 and 4 (pupils aged 11, 14 and 16). The design of the ImpaCT2 study was innovative, in that the research team not only conducted a large-scale statistical analysis of data on ICT usage and attainment, it also set up research teams in 60 schools to gather case-study data on how computers were used in classrooms and out of lessons, sometimes using pupils as well as teachers as researchers. Bringing together information from a range of studies, therefore, the ImpaCT2 team was able to obtain detailed evidence on how computers were being used in schools, and on how a variety of pedagogies connected pupils to information and communication technologies in a wide range of subjects.

OBJECTIVES

By the end of this chapter you should have considered:

- the relationship between technology, pedagogy and learning, in a range of curriculum areas;
- the importance of computers in children's learning in a variety of locations, both in school, and at home;
- the nature of software in a range of subjects, and the very different ways in which computers are used in different curriculum areas, particularly English, Maths and Science.

ICT AND ATTAINMENT

What is the linkage between ICT and school achievement, and how does the teacher's pedagogy – the instructional methods and strategies that the teacher uses – help to shape that achievement? In order to answer this question, the ImpaCT2 project team (Becta, 2002) homed in on five key areas:

1.   What is the involvement of pupils with computers and the Internet at home and in school?
2.   Does curriculum-related usage have a measurable effect on performance and attitude?
3.   Are any effects confined to usage in school?
4.   Are all kinds of computer usage equally productive of learning?
5.   If ICT-based learning involves interactions between home and school, what are the related problems and how can these be met?

In order to consider the nature of the impact of ICT on learners, and subsequently on school achievement, the ImpaCT2 evaluation team attempted to model these relationships, and in particular to consider the ways in which the impact of computers on school students has changed in more recent times. One possible representation of these relationships is shown in Figure 11.1.

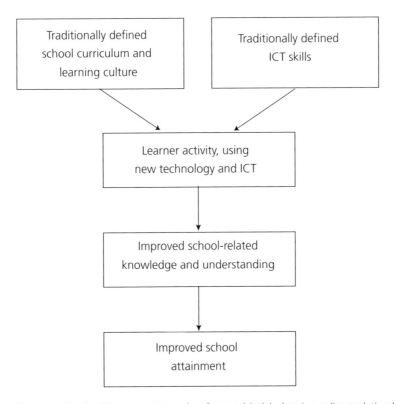

Figure 11.1 The Direct Impact Learning Context Model, showing a direct relationship between use of ICT and learning outcomes

The Direct Impact Learning Context Model assumes a direct relationship between the levels of ICT integration into learning tasks and subsequent performance on attainment measures, and, we would suggest, it is this model that underpins most of the research into ICT and learning reported in our preliminary study (McFarlane *et al.*, 2000), which reviewed research in the field. The research methods that adopt this perspective usually classify the nature of ICT use in terms of tool type and some offer particular emphasis on tasks using these tools. However, these models rarely if ever offer a detailed cognitive model of likely cause and effect, for example by asking why using spreadsheets and databases in science might improve performance in science reasoning tasks. The Newcastle study is an exception in that it offers the most detailed link between features of IT use and impact on understanding (Moseley *et al.*, 1999).

Clearly some research evidence is weak in that it deals with scenarios where there is a very limited pedagogical model, for example with no attempt at integration of computer-based tasks with other learning. However, the Direct Impact Learning Context Model could be representing sophisticated, thoughtful teaching, with the use of excellent software. However, the evidence from the research literature is that:

- it is extraordinarily difficult to demonstrate a *direct* relationship between implementation of new technology and improved attainment as measured by national, standardised assessment measures;
- by contrast, other outcome measures, which are more *indirectly* related to improved learning, have been regularly demonstrated, e.g. enhancements in specific skills, higher-level conceptualisation, better problem-solving, more complex small-group talk, improved motivation.

The apparent mismatch between these two sets of outcomes needs some explanation. The examination boards would say that national tests such as SATs and GCSE should pick up such improvements in what are effectively learning strategies. But there is also some evidence that use of IT can impact negatively on content knowledge, e.g. data-logging might expand the problem-solving/experimental design phase of practical work, but lower content knowledge of pupils using traditional practical methods.

The ImpaCT2 study used end-of-Key-Stage standardised outcome measures as one area of focus, but the team also wanted to attempt to represent the relationship between ICT and learning in a more complex and subtle manner, and this is represented schematically in Figure 11.2, the Socially Contextualised Perspective on Learning. There are a number of reasons for doing this:

- networked technologies introduce knowledge structures and knowledge authority relationships into learning which are fundamentally different to those which have previously obtained in schools;
- these different structures in turn imply the need for learners to acquire a new or modified set of skills in dealing with these structures and authority relationships;
- the ImpaCT2 project was asked to examine particularly closely learners' use of ICT in their homes; this in turn implied the need for a broader conceptualisation of computer use than one focused solely on school learning;
- increasingly, simple causal models of the impact of ICT are being replaced by models which acknowledge a complex set of interactions between the learner, the task and new technology, a set of interactions which do not posit an inevitable

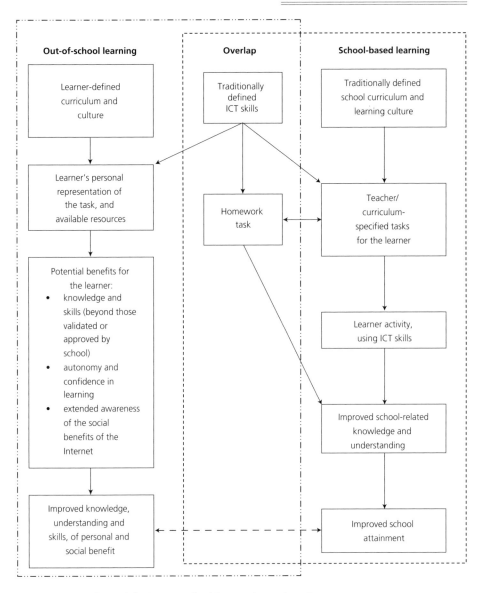

Figure 11.2   The Socially Contextualised Perspective on Learning

causal linkage between ICT and attainment, but rather propose that useful learning occurs only when certain conditions are met (and that these are met comparatively rarely in most learners' school experience);

- using the Internet almost inevitably raises issues of social responsibility and personal autonomy; whether schools foreground these or not, those who advise governments have a moral responsibility to attend to these issues and to include them in any account of a learning/benefit analysis.

The ImpaCT2 evaluation argued that networked technologies have changed the nature of knowledge. What is certain is that they have facilitated new ways of representing knowledge. As a result, a pupil's interaction with these texts, as reader, author or more frequently co-author, requires a skill set which varies from that required to interact with other text forms.

The process of gathering information from sources and creating a personal representation is affected by the increased access to both primary and secondary sources in electronic format. The concept of network literacy includes the ability to select from a range of digital sources, and careful thought needs to be given to this ability. To cut and paste a coherent collage of information is a valuable skill – but can be dismissed as mere plagiarism. There is a need, therefore, to distinguish between the following skill sets:

- *manipulation*, e.g. the ability to capture an image;
- *editorial*, e.g. the ability to select an appropriate image;
- *design*, e.g. the ability to place the image effectively;
- *authorial input*, e.g. the ability to use an image to contribute to and enhance the meaning-making process.

Networked technologies offer access to an unprecedented range of information, and where home access is available this gives individual learners potential for a high degree of autonomy in their learning. Users can choose when and what they learn. The authenticity of the resulting experience will contrast sharply with at least some of the learning that pupils experience in school, and what they are required by school to do at home. Where school learning complements the powerful autonomous learning culture facilitated by new technologies, there is likely to be a synergy, e.g. in a GCSE or 'A' level research topic. However, where it conflicts there may well be a rejection of the task and a subsequent drop in attainment, e.g. in a memorisation task.

From the outset, therefore, the research team was convinced that it would be essential to look beyond the classroom walls in order to explore the influence of ICT on the construction of knowledge, on learning and on subsequent achievement, and the team therefore gathered data from a wide range of sources:

- A daily diary of computer usage over a period of a week (based on 400 pupils).
- A specially constructed questionnaire bearing specifically on Internet usage both for school purposes and personal interest (answered by 210 pupils).
- Reports on a single ICT project chosen by the pupil as one where the computer had been especially helpful in the execution of a school assignment (invariably carried out outside of lesson time, usually outside school, and generally occupying several sessions) (165 pupils).
- Reports based on some 50 interviews conducted by pairs of pupils interviewing each other using a common semi-structured format.
- Further insights were obtained from two sets of concept-maps representing the pupil's idea of 'a computer'. These were elicited from every pupil in the sample on two occasions separated by a year and were designed to offer an insight into his or her own ideas about ICT and how it impinges on a person's life (approximately 4,000 concept maps).
- Interviews and video diaries kept by pupils and teachers in 15 schools that were conducted towards the end of the project in order to elicit additional information about ways in which ICT was being used outside of school, as well as in school.

Task 11.1
Reviewing practice in your school

Keep your own diary of computer usage for a week, then use the information you gather to compare with the picture of school learning presented in this chapter. Keep careful records not only of the time, minute by minute, that you spend on different tasks, but also consider some of the following:

- What software have you used? How much of it was bundled, bought, pirated, downloaded?
- How might you classify your computer usage (professional, personal, fun, learning, administration, etc.)?
- How much time were you online? Did this change what you did?
- What were the tangible outcomes/products of your computer activity?
- What were the intangible outcomes?
- Of what audiences were you a member? For what audiences did you create material?
- How has your use of sound/video/multimedia files changed over the past year?
- If you can, persuade a colleague or friend to do this exercise as well, and compare notes.

WHAT WERE THE CENTRAL FINDINGS OF THE IMPACT2 PROJECT?

At the time of data collection, from 1999 to 2002, the use of computers in schools was increasing, and about to increase still further, but the baseline data on computer usage in schools was disappointing to those who had hoped to see massive impact; across all age ranges the modal amount of ICT in school lessons was 'hardly ever', and the modal amount of networked ICT (wireless or hard wired) was 'never'. Having said this, however, most of the teachers whom we interviewed saw this picture as one that was changing rapidly.

Differences in attainment associated with the degree of ICT involvement were explored in relation to the end-of-Key-Stage tests in English, Maths and Science for KS2, KS3 and KS4, and also in other GCSE subjects. Differences were never large, but were nonetheless clearly present in more than a third of all comparisons. In none of the 13 comparisons was there a statistically significant advantage to groups with lower ICT involvement (as had been found in some earlier studies); in other words, ICT was never strongly associated with poorer performance in exams.

The differences that were found were not consistent across Key Stages:

- At Key Stage 2, there was a highly significant positive association between ICT and SAT test results in English.
- Also at Key Stage 2, there were similar trends for Maths and Science, but these were less clear-cut.
- At Key Stage 3, there were no clear-cut associations between ICT and SATs results, but there were indications of a positive association in Science.
- At Key Stage 4, there was a highly significant positive association between ICT and attainment in two GCSE subjects: Science, and Design Technology.
- Also at Key Stage 4, there were strong indications of a positive association between ICT and attainment in Modern Foreign Languages and Geography.

However, it should be stressed again that the proportion of lessons involving ICT was generally low over the period concerned (although the team's view was that this was likely to rise as teachers gain in experience, as equipment is made available in more classrooms and with improvements in the availability of quality software, both on the Internet and on CD). Second, there was no consistent relationship across all three Key Stages between the average amount of ICT reported for any subject and its apparent effectiveness in raising standards. It therefore seems likely that it is the type of involvement that is all-important.

Another very important point to make is that the ImpaCT2 team looked not only at ICT usage in lesson time, it also took account of ICT used at home for school purposes. The statistical results make it clear that, where there were statistically significant differences, home use for school work was a contributing factor where there was an association between ICT and achievement.

ICT AND PEDAGOGY

ICT in lessons and in learning

The statistical findings of the ImpaCT2 project were not clear-cut, but there was a much more even set of findings in relation to attitudes towards ICT in schools. Over the two years in which the team collected data, and with very few exceptions, almost all those who participated in the ImpaCT2 project – teachers, managers, parents and pupils alike – spoke positively about ICT in education (and most were not volunteers – their head teachers had signed their schools up). There were very few 'ICT resistors'. The main benefits that were cited often came under the heading of motivation. ICT was perceived as raising confidence and self-esteem, and improving the motivation of pupils by giving them a sense of autonomy. These effects were sometimes most notable among pupils who had seemed to be disengaged from learning. The one outstanding benefit of ICT (singled out from among many by teachers) was its ability to enhance both the products of the pupil's learning and the quality of the learning process. Using ICT, the team was told, pupils learned how to interrogate information sources in a variety of ways and to produce rapid and accurate representations of what they found. Teachers could then focus attention on meanings and implications.

Conversely, lessons were less successful where pupils were allowed to get bogged down in problems of managing the equipment and resources. ICT, by its nature, requires that the teacher allow a greater measure of independence to pupils. It was clear that this was appreciated by pupils, parents and teachers, but was not always easy to manage and exploit in the classroom. Some teachers had adapted with enthusiasm, others were still struggling. Some of the best examples of ICT usage were observed in lessons that moved through different modes of teacher/pupil interaction and involved both parties in a variety of roles, and where intended use and actual use came together.

School intranets were common in effective ICT-using schools and were used to provide resources, for data storage, and for the exchange of work. The Internet was appreciated by teachers and by pupils, both for its dedicated learning sites and for the wider sources to which it gave access. Email was used to great advantage in at least some primary and some secondary schools, especially in creating links with pupils in a different country. At the time of data collection, few schools were using email for transfer of work between school and home, though of course this picture was rapidly changing.

Authentic paired work at the computer was rare; pupils were rarely seen to collaborate, even when working side by side (though they might consult). On the other hand, there were many examples of projects that involved sharing aspects of the work before pooling their outcomes and, among the activities that were observed, these were some of the most successful and popular.

The constrained use of ICT in lessons entailed that more learning activity had to be undertaken outside of lesson time. Though this was clearly beneficial, it could and did sometimes give rise to problems associated with access and assistance both at home and in school.

Principal constraints

There were problems and, as you would expect, many of these related to the shortage of time or money – or both:

- The ever-growing demand for maintaining adequate and up-to-date ICT resources presented problems to all schools because staff and pupils tended to get de-motivated when hardware and software became unreliable.
- The demands of ICT instruction often required an undue concentration of resources in computer suites, thereby reducing the opportunities for integrating ICT into the teaching of other subjects, and making it difficult for teachers and pupils to access the computer when they needed to.
- There were universal problems of underfunding in schools and many where pupils preferred using their own machines at home for schoolwork as they were faster, more efficient, more reliable, and had better Internet connectivity than school machines.
- Many teachers felt that their experience of in-service training (funded by the New Opportunities Fund, NOF) had increased their technical skills but that they still needed support to develop their ability to exploit the full potential of ICT in relation to the curriculum.

The ImpaCT2 team found that there were many more uses being made of different ICT resources in mathematics, science, ICT and English than in other subjects. This meant that there were a greater number of ICT resources available to these subject teachers, and there was a greater body of knowledge about educational practices for ICT in these subjects, and a greater body of evidence of the effects of ICT on these subjects. The positive impact on attainment was greatest for those ICT resources which had been embedded in some teachers' practices for a long time. There is an emerging body of knowledge about the effects of specific types of ICT, such as email or the World Wide Web, but the evidence of the effects of these on pupils' attainment is not yet consistent and extensive.

There was substantial evidence from smaller focused studies of the contribution of specific uses of ICT to pupils' learning. These include the use of simulations and modelling in science, ICT and mathematics, and the use of word processing in English. Many small studies have shown consistently positive results over the last 20 years, but this does not yet extend to all types of ICT use, nor does it exclude the input of the teacher.

This sense of ICT developing and extending the ability of learners to manipulate and process information was a theme to which many teachers returned when asked to consider the impact of ICT on achievement. In essence their claim was that ICT could enable learners to interrogate information in a variety of ways, and to produce rapid and accurate representations of data. This allowed the teacher to focus on developing their understanding of the outcome of their investigations instead of spending most of the lesson supervising them while they made laborious (and often imprecise) charts by hand. As one teacher put it:

> Networked technologies give students a breadth of resources and access to information potentially so much greater than a project box or a book. It puts students more in control of what they are accessing and they can speed ahead if they are more able, and as long as information is accessible for all abilities, it can be a very positive experience.
>
> (Classroom teacher, Arkwright Secondary School)

Task 11.2
Reviewing practice in classrooms

Try to negotiate access to a classroom in which one or more computers are in use every day, and log carefully how the computer is used. Then use the information you gather to compare with the picture of school learning around the computer presented in this chapter.

Keep careful records not only of the time, minute by minute, that children spend on the computer, but also consider some of the following:

- What software is used?
- What decisions were made by the teacher concerning how the software was used, and what decisions were made by the pupils?
- How might you classify the computer usage (curriculum-based, personal, fun, learning, administration, etc.)?
- How much time was the computer online, connected to the Internet? Did this change what the user did?
- What were the tangible outcomes/products of the computer activity?
- What were the intangible outcomes?
- Of what audiences were the users a member? For what audiences did they create material?
- What use was made of sound/video/multimedia files?
- If you can, persuade a colleague or friend to do this exercise as well, and compare what you found.

ICT AND ATTAINMENT: SPECIFIC SUBJECT AREAS

In this section of the chapter, as well as reporting what the ImpaCT2 project researchers found, I also draw upon a useful recent review of the literature on ICT and attainment, the report for Becta by Margaret Cox and Chris Abbott (2003).

Mathematics attainment

The ImpaCT2 team found positive effects of ICT on pupils' learning of different concepts and skills in mathematics at both primary and secondary levels. These effects were more evident where there was a clear linkage between curriculum content and the software in use. The comments of an ImpaCT2 project school's numeracy co-ordinator, discussing the use of a spreadsheet package, show that this potential was not confined to the secondary phase:

> Some of my children came up with some fascinating graphs … they could spend the time thinking about the questions they were asking and the information they were collecting, rather than 'have I coloured this square in properly?'
> (Year 2 teacher/Numeracy co-ordinator, Broadway Primary School)

English attainment

Different uses of ICT contributed to some improvements in achievement in English, but the results were very inconsistent and restricted by the amount of ICT use and access to ICT in schools. The most predominant reported use of ICT has been for word processing, although other English-specific software is widely used by some English teachers. The most positive evidence arises from primary pupils' use when they are at the early stages of language development and when they have a chance to compose, and reflect on their compositions.

Perhaps not surprisingly, although the greatest amount of computer usage time for English in schools was spent on word processing at Key Stages 3 and 4, this was not strongly associated with improved attainment (although ImpaCT2 found a linear trend associating ICT with attainment in English at KS4). There is perhaps one main reason for this; the assessment mechanisms at Key Stages 3 and 4 for English give no credit for improved presentation, or for skills in layout and desk-top publishing, so it is not surprising that the linkage is poor. Our data did not permit close analysis of the relationship between different types of software in English, but our guess is that as pupils spend more time using the Internet for research, rather than simply working on presentation, there will be a correspondingly greater association between ICT and attainment in English.

Science attainment

ICT and science attainment were significantly related in the ImpaCT2 study. The types of ICT use in Science, and the enhancement of pupils' learning, are much more closely related to specific concepts and skills, and tend to be more specific than, for example, the use of word processing in English. The team reported positive evidence related to pupils' improving understanding of science concepts, developing problem-solving skills, hypothesising scientific relationships and processes, and improving scientific reasoning and scientific explanations. As one teacher put it:

> I think like a lot of teachers, I used to be a 'control freak'. I liked to stand at the front and make sure I'd explained very carefully to all the students exactly what

they needed to know by the end of the lesson, then they commenced to write it down. Quite a didactic approach. ICT has certainly encouraged me to produce learning activities where the students have to go and find out things rather than listen to what I am going to tell you sort of lesson. I think I am now getting a balance between the two sorts of lesson.

(Chemistry teacher, Arkwright Secondary School)

ICT attainment

The ImpaCT2 study reported that innovative and challenging uses of ICT could improve pupils' data-handling skills, their ability to construct complex models and their understanding of the value of different ICT systems. The research showed that if teachers were to provide opportunities for pupils to carry out in-depth investigations with, for example, appropriate modelling environments, then they could reach higher levels of abstraction and competency in the field of ICT.

Humanities attainment

Although there was less research reported about the use of ICT in the humanities, there was evidence to show that using simulations could enhance students' reasoning and decision-making in geography, history and economics. There was very little evidence of ICT being used or evaluated in primary schools for the teaching of geography or history, and clearly this is an area of the curriculum where more ICT use and research is needed.

Nevertheless, there were a number of teachers who tried to develop much more structured ways of searching the Internet by introducing their pupils to a variety of procedures which they might use, such as the following: find good keywords, identify likely information sources, evaluate a resource when located, adapt and synthesise information from various sources (including text, graphics, charts and so on), cut and paste from the WWW or a CD-ROM into a word-processing or desk-top publishing document, and so on. Where such approaches were effectively introduced, they had the potential to develop navigation skills as well as evaluation and reporting skills, and all of these could be transferred across the curriculum.

My best practice is with Year 9 history. We have put various exercises on the Internet using proprietary software, and they have to put together their own First World War diary. We use networked technologies because there are a vast range of sources out there; we are not just limited to books. This gives us the ability to use the sources for maximum information, first to answer straightforward questions, then to develop thinking skills about applying the knowledge, think about what they have learned and then they do the empathy piece. By the end, they have got simple answers, then more detailed answers, then they write the diary. It worked very well, particularly with boys, who might not have responded so well to just looking through books. They were able to cope well and responded enthusiastically.

(Classroom teacher, Arkwright Secondary School)

Modern foreign languages attainment

There was evidence of a positive effect of specific software, such as software providing foreign language simulations, on attainment in modern foreign languages. As with the teaching of English, much of the success reported in the literature is linked to particular sub-skills of language learning such as word recognition and vocabulary building. The most consistent evidence of a positive effect of ICT use has arisen when the specific skills developed by the software currently in use have been measured. Clearly the Internet also offers enormous potential for supporting the teaching of modern languages, and presenting pupils with authentic texts and tasks.

Art, music, business studies and physical education attainment

Little research has been published about the impact on attainment of ICT in art, music, business studies and physical education, according to Cox and Abbott (2003). Some papers provide evidence of the enhancement of pupils' learning through specific ICT applications such as sound synthesisers in music, digital imagery in art, and ICT skills in business studies. More research in these subjects would be useful to show other teachers where ICT might enhance their teaching.

ICT and Design and Technology attainment

A particularly good illustration of the use of ICT in Design and Technology came from a teacher's description of the contribution of ICT to the various stages of a GCSE design technology project in which the students were required to plan and build a three-dimensional model. The use of the Internet was said to 'bring a new dimension' to the research phase of the process, extending the relatively limited and dated reference materials available in the school. By using software which allowed them to test out various aspects of their design, the students managed to reduce the time typically given to this aspect of the process. At the same time, they could test out their ideas in a flexible way, all of which would otherwise have been beyond them because of limitations in skills or shortage of materials, or would have been impractical in a crowded GCSE timetable:

> they are not limited by their own manipulative skills … they can play around with different things, like finish, texture, that they couldn't do (in a real situation). So not only does this reduce workload, but it enhances their ability to come up with an answer to that particular problem.
>
> (Design technology teacher, Dalton Secondary School)

Another very effective lesson, this time in a primary school computer suite, was a session with a Year 3 group using a computer-aided design (CAD) package to design a bedroom. This was part of a series of lessons based on a QCA work unit, one that incorporated elements of design and technology, numeracy and literacy. The session that was observed was the second of the series, where the pupils were introduced to the main features and functions of the package.

Using a CAD package (ICT: Year 3)

This lesson began with a brief whole-class introductory demonstration of the computer-assisted design task using a fixed interactive whiteboard. The pupils were reminded, through demonstration, of the work of the previous lesson in this series in which they had begun to explore the capabilities of the software, and the broad objectives of the current session were explained. Pupils were given opportunities to ask questions and seek clarification before commencing the task.

Following this introduction the pupils worked individually. Although there were sufficient PCs for pupils to work on their own design, a considerable amount of spontaneous collaboration took place. Where this was deemed to be moving pupils forward, the teacher encouraged it. The teacher moved around from pupil to pupil, in some cases solving technical problems, but for the most part using open-ended questions and prompting to encourage pupils to solve their own problems.

At several points during the session when it became evident that several pupils were encountering a similar problem, the teacher returned to the whiteboard to explore the problem with the class. This was done using the same 'open question' approach, encouraging the children to offer possible solutions, and then 'trying them out' on the whiteboard, instead of just supplying the 'right answer'. On several occasions pupils were called to the front to demonstrate their solution on the whiteboard.

At the conclusion of the lesson, the teacher explained to the class that he wanted them to learn a new way of saving their files (saving to the server rather than to disk). This was demonstrated, step by step, again via the whiteboard.

(Year 3 teacher, SENCO/St Bedes Primary)

Again, this lesson, though a relatively straightforward one, involved a flexible approach on the part of the teacher and of the pupils. Again, moving smoothly, purposefully and appropriately between the various roles that have been discussed earlier seems to have been a crucial factor in the teacher's success.

While this pattern might be thought good pedagogy with or without ICT, it is also a good example of the appropriate and effective exploitation of ICT resources in the development of key skills. From brief interviews with the children during the session, it was clear that most had a good understanding of the task, they had demonstrated progress from the previous lesson, and they were able have a go at finding solutions either independently or with the help of a partner.

The effects of ICT on motivation and attitudes

The Cox and Abbott (2003) review declared that research indicates a general improvement of pupils' motivation and attitudes to learning attributable to working with ICT, shown through improved commitment to the learning task, greater interest in the subject, and pupils taking more responsibility for their learning and making sustained efforts in difficult tasks. Much of this evidence had been gathered through observations and questionnaires.

More research is needed that measures pupils' attitudes and motivation through established attitude tests.

The ImpaCT2 team found that the prospect of students working on computers away from the direct supervision of the teacher is not without its problems. A number of teachers alluded to the fact that even in relatively 'structured' situations it was not always possible to determine the extent to which the pupils were actually learning, or indeed whether they were engaged in the task in hand at all. Thus, when reflecting in a video diary on a lesson in which a pre-selected Internet site had been used to complete a worksheet, one teacher remarked that it 'wasn't difficult to keep them on task, it was just very difficult to make sure they were on the *right* task'. Observations of ICT-focused sessions confirmed that even with the best-appointed ICT rooms and the most carefully planned lessons, monitoring the activities of 20 or more simultaneous users could be problematic for many teachers. Back in the classroom, where the number of machines was more limited, there could be a different problem; while there were fewer computer users to 'keep an eye on', the teacher had to organise activities for the remainder of the class who were not using ICT.

> I value ICT and I think it's very important, but it's almost like a fringe activity sometimes … when you've got the other 20 or so others doing something else. It's not always easy to home in. As soon as the others are up and running, I can go back to the ICT, but it's hit and miss, and there's no telling whether I get to see all the children that are working.
>
> (Year 6 teacher/Numeracy co-ordinator, Yew Tree Primary)

SUMMARY

Computers and the Internet have already brought about fundamental changes to the nature and authority of knowledge in our society. But this does not mean that computers have changed schooling. As Larry Cuban, has powerfully argued (Cuban, 2001), computers have changed teachers' lives, but they haven't changed classrooms much, and they have hardly changed pedagogy at all.

The vignettes of pedagogy that have been presented in this chapter broadly speaking support the view that computers can, and should, inform good teaching, but Cuban's criticisms that very little is changing in schools are misguided, at least in part. For what is happening is not so much a computer revolution in schools as a diffusion of technologies in society that will increasingly blur the boundaries between school and not-school, and the issue for new teachers will not be so much how to integrate technology into their teaching, but rather to understand how technology is impacting their students' learning – and to understand that this will happen to a large extent in ways that are beyond the teacher's direct control.

ACKNOWLEDGEMENT

The author is very grateful to the following members of the ImpaCT2 project team, whose work on the evaluation, on data analysis and on the Final Report is drawn upon very substantially in this chapter: Bridget Somekh, Peter Scrimshaw, Angela McFarlane, Cathy Lewin, Di Mavers, Kaye Haw, Tony Fisher, and the statistical team, Eric Lunzer and Jane Restorick.

REFERENCES

Becta (2002) *ImpaCT2: The Impact of Information and Communication Technologies on Pupil Learning and Attainment*, Coventry: Becta.

Cox, M. and Abbott, C. (eds) (2003) *ICT and Attainment: A Review of the Research Literature*, Full Report. Coventry/London: Becta/DfES.

Cuban, L. (2001) *Oversold and Underused: Computers in the Classroom*, Boston, MA: Harvard University Press.

McFarlane, A., Harrison, C., Somekh, B., Scrimshaw, P., Harrison, A. and Lewin, C. (2000) *Establishing the Relationship between Networked Technology and Attainment: Preliminary Study 1*, Coventry: Becta. Online. Available HTTP: <http://www.becta.org.uk/research/reports/docs/impact2_prelim1.pdf> (accessed 3 June 2004).

Moseley, D., Higgins, S., Bramald, R., Hardman, F., Miller, J., Mroz, M., Tse, H., Newton, D., Thompson, I., Halligan, J., Bramald, S., Newton, L., Tymms, P., Henderson, B. and Stout, J. (1999) *Ways Forward with ICT: Effective Pedagogy Using Information and Communications Technology for Literacy and Numeracy in Primary Schools*, Newcastle: University of Newcastle.

FURTHER READING

Becta (2002) *ImpaCT2: The Impact of Information and Communication Technologies on Pupil Learning and Attainment*, Coventry: Becta. This was the main ImpaCT2 report, and it gives not only a full account of what was found, but a useful guide to the project's methodology and plenty of links to further reading. Online. Available HTTP: <http://www.becta.org.uk/research/research.cfm?section=1&id=561> (accessed 6 October 2004).

Cox, M. and Abbott, C. (editors) (2003) *ICT and Attainment: A Review of the Research Literature*, Full Report. Coventry/London, Becta/DfES. This comprehensive and balanced review gives valuable subject-by-subject reviews and links to further reading. Online. Available HTTP: <http://www.becta.org.uk/page_documents/research/ict_pedagogy_summary.pdf> (accessed 6 October 2004).

Cuban, L. (2001) *Oversold and Underused: Computers in the Classroom*, Boston, MA: Harvard University Press. Cuban's views on what he considers to be the misspent money that has put computers in every classroom, once considered scandalous, are now listened to much more attentively; in short, this distinguished researcher invites us to think much more carefully about how we want to use computers in the classroom. Among the many web links to articles by him is this, from the intriguingly titled edtechnot.com. Online. Available HTTP: <http://www.edtechnot.com/notarticle1201.html> (accessed 6 October 2004).

12 Teaching in ICT-rich Environments

Using e-Learning to Create a Knowledge Base for Twenty-first Century Teachers

Christina Preston and John Cuthell

INTRODUCTION

The use of advanced technologies in learning has had more influence on workplace practice in the last thirty years, than on the education industry. The term 'e-learning' used to refer to formal courses of instructional learning and self-instruction via computer-mediated materials. However, there is recognition now that the Internet can be used for informal learning too. The best e-learning, in this context, is: just-in-time – available for the users when they need it to complete the task; on-demand – available when they need it, not in a couple of days time, or a week or a month; bite-sized – available in small chunks that take only fifteen to twenty minutes to complete. E-learning opportunities of both types are available to you for both your professional development as well as to support your classroom practice.

In your work on this chapter we ask you to look carefully at the examples we give from teachers' practice-based research case studies that have been published on the web for other teachers. We offer these case studies with all the immediacy and uncertainty that innovative practice presents. Whilst it is recognised that there are limitations in practitioner-led action research projects, the active engagement in evidence-based action enquiry enables teaching professionals and their schools to develop a systematic and rigorous approach to teaching and learning. In this spirit, several of these e-communities of practice will welcome case studies from you as a practitioner.

OBJECTIVES

By the end of this chapter you should be able to:

- articulate the opportunities offered by teachers' e-communities;
- understand the institutional context you are working in and develop teaching strategies to maximise effective use of the school's ICT facilities;
- identify the ICT skills you have, and those you will need to develop, in order to create e-learning materials and deliver them for a range of pupil learning styles.

BACKGROUND AND DEFINITIONS

The term 'e-learning' is used in Further and Higher Education to describe the use of the web and other internet technologies to enhance the teaching and learning experience. Also used are the terms Information and Communication Technologies and more recently Information and Learning Technologies. 'Distance learning' which was once a paper exercise now usually includes a computer-mediated communication element. Many colleges and universities are dependent on web-based learning environments (WLEs) for the overall management of classes as well as the delivery of some learning materials. The WLEs have been widely used for over a decade and, unlike textbooks, are constantly being altered and upgraded. There are two main kinds of WLEs, the Managed Learning Environment (MLE) and the Virtual Learning Environment (VLE) (see Chapter 5 for more details). The MLE, which is widely used in Higher and Further Education concentrates on automating the administration of learners in educational institutions, as well as the delivery of learning resources. Tracking and online assessment modules are sometimes integrated or can be bolted on. The second type of web-based software, the VLE, encourages interactions between learners and learners, and learners and teachers. In VLEs, learners can become creative authors and artists in real time creating web-based publications which are multimodal, multimedia, and potentially multivocal. The VLE is the tool which gives you the greatest opportunity to increase individual pupil's engagement with learning beyond the conventional classroom boundaries. Pupils who are intimidated in face-to-face learning may also find this mode of expression liberating.

E-learning which promotes this kind of informal pupils' learning has not yet been established in schools although innovative schools are now experimenting with new media. The DfES use the e-learning term in a wider sense in reference to schools, that is to embrace all the elements involved in the effective use of an ICT-rich classroom for multi-literate communication rather than just using the web. Advanced technologies are being constantly invented or upgraded, but in general terms an ICT-rich environment will include a variety of multimedia hardware, software and peripherals linked by broadband connections. The electronic media include the internet, CD-ROMs, standalone software, integrated learning systems, web-based learning environments, video-conferencing or the use of such peripherals as interactive whiteboards (IWBs), digital cameras, personal digital

Table 12.1 DfES statistics on ICT provision in schools, 29 July 2004

Sector	Average number of computers	Ratio
Primary	31.6	7.5
Secondary	217.6	4.9
Special	33.4	3.1
	% with IWB	Average per school
Primary	63	1.9
Secondary	92	7.5
Special	71	2.6

assistants (PDAs) and mobile phones (DfES, 2003). DfES statistics show the overall picture for the provision of ICT resources in schools with particular reference to the investment in IWBs, see Table 12.1.

You may want to compare the picture in your school with these national averages.

Teachers who have access to environments which are as ICT-rich as these can focus on the global phenomenon in which the screen is replacing the book, and the image is displacing traditional text as the dominant medium of communication (Kress, 2003). One benefit of introducing rich ICT environments in schools is that all learner styles can be empowered, because learning resources are now presented in a range of media. In our experience, coming to terms with the influence of ICT on the way in which society now communicates also has a vital part to play in reclaiming the professionalism of teachers. Sachs (2003) defines four pedagogical modes for teachers across the world that have developed in the last millennium: the *transformational*, the *managerial*, the *democratic* and *old teacher professionalism*. She goes on to promote a new mode: the *activist professional* who makes changes in the classroom, shares the evidence and helps to build a knowledge base using practice-based research as a Continuing Professional Development (CPD) methodology.

Education commentators like Sachs, Hargreaves, Goodson and Whitty, see the building of an authoritative and democratic community as an important step in reinstating the professional teacher's authentic voice (Hargreaves and Goodson, 1996; Wenger, 1998; Sachs, 2001; Whitty, 2002). ICT provides the opportunities for building new types of communities of practice in which 'activitist professionals' collaborate to build new practice. Examples of 'communities of practice' for teachers include the subject associations like the National Association for the Teaching of English (<http://www.nate.org.uk>); ICT cross-curricula organisations like the Association for ICT in Education (<http://www.acitt.org.uk>), and the MirandaNet Fellowship (<http://www.mirandanet.ac.uk>); and professional organisations like the General Teaching Council (<http://www. gtce.org.uk>). Evidence from the MirandaNet community of practice indicates that 'activist teachers' are now emerging who value the opportunity provided by face-to-face and online forums to consult with policy makers and influence policy (<http://www.mirandanet.ac.uk/ejournal>).

E-LEARNING ISSUES IN CONTINUING PROFESSIONAL DEVELOPMENT

Cautionary tales are now emerging about the early adopters' enthusiasm for e-learning as the antidote for any educational malaise. *Thwarted Innovation* is the title of a USA report which raises concerns about the influence of the commercial market on Managed Learning Environments (MLEs) for education (Zemsky and Massey, 2004). The authors warn that underlying these programs is a formal instruction model. These coding restrictions can prevent institutions from making progress in innovatory modes of learning. Purchasing decisions should not, therefore, be left to the IT department. But the affordances of VLEs are not as yet well understood by teachers.

This lack of knowledge and experience in the impact that e-learning can have means that it is difficult for teachers to enter the debate as equal partners. Zemsky and Massey question four assumptions that policy makers and software design companies make about e-learning in the absence of input from the profession. These assumptions are described with irony:

- if we build one they will come
- the kids will take to this medium like a duck to water
- e-learning will change the way we teach
- international communities will spring up promoting collaborative learning across cultural boundaries.

(Zemsky and Massey, 2004)

In the UK, a training programme for all teachers, the NOF ICT programme, raised the profile of e-learning in schools. The spin-offs have probably been more effective than the core programme itself (Leask, 2001). The report (Preston, 2004a) on emergent trends is drawn from the replies of advisers and practitioners and on the fifteen school case studies which represented a national range of phases, types and catchment areas. The selection was made from the respondees who felt that the national ICT training programme had had a positive impact on the use of ICT in the curriculum. The innovative uses of ICT that were identified were strategies for transformational learning, new leadership approaches, whole-school ICT development, practice-based research, creativity, ownership of learning, communities of practice and long-term CPD. The next steps in ICT CPD strategy which are recommended by these community leaders are a move from an instrumental view of ICT 'training' for teachers, into a transformational mode of learning which seems to be the way that teachers really want to go, both for themselves and for their pupils (Preston, 2004a).

It is inevitable, however, that not all teachers find ICT relevant to their work.

CREATIVE APPROACHES TO E-LEARNING

The DfES (2003) has used evidence of existing good practice to identify five different elements of e-learning that teachers need to understand.

- *Concurrent learning* takes place across a number of venues, for example, home, library, school.
- *Cinematic learning* occurs when visual media influences what, where and how children learn.

- *Collaborative learning* happens in a range of contexts, but is a particular feature of online communities.
- *Communicative learning* with online support and mentoring means the availability of teachers for all pupils.
- *Consensual learning* places the child as a partner in the learning process.

Case studies from practising teachers offer examples of ways in which we can apply the DfES elements of e-learning to different teaching and learning contexts.

Concurrent learning is learning that takes place across a number of venues, for example, home, library, school. A number of schools and teachers have schemes that empower their pupils by providing laptop computers for use at home and at school, while other schools use Think.com, Grid Club and BBC Bytesize to support concurrent learning. These VLEs acts as a powerful motivator for pupils to complete coursework, particularly at GCSE level (<http://www.think.com>; <http://www.gridclub.com>; <http://www.bbc.co.uk/schools/gcsebitesize/pe/>).

Cinematic learning occurs when visual media influences what, where and how children learn. Visualisation is an extremely powerful component of the learning matrix, and anything that promotes this faculty enhances the whole process. For example, teachers in a village on the Berkshire/Hampshire borders developed a citizenship project using multimedia communications to enhance reading and writing between children in other countries. As part of initiating a relationship with a Chinese school they put together a CD of pictures, sound and animation to present a range of 'typical' scenes from the village and the countryside (Scott-Baker, 2003).

Collaborative learning happens in a range of contexts, but is a particular feature of online communities supported by VLEs. Think.com is a closed VLE from Oracle, that facilitates collaborative learning between pupils (<http://www.think.com/>). Drew Buddy explains how he found a colleague to work with in India: 'Setting up conventional exchanges can be time consuming. It's hard to find keen teachers and to sustain programmes after a visit. The use of VLEs makes a big difference. Projects get going more quickly and maintain the collaboration momentum for longer' (Preston, 2004b). World Ecitizens provides a different kind of VLE which offers extensive free citizenship resources designed by teachers. Each pupil has a private web space where they collaborate with other pupils as well as the public gallery and places for debate. One teacher-user remarked that the children were so engaged in the activities that their behaviour improved. 'They have also been more thoughtful towards each other and more aware of social concerns' (<http://www.worldecitizens.net>).

Communicative learning, characterised by online support and mentoring, means that teachers are available for all pupils. Fanning (2004) found that the use of Think.com in the classroom changed teaching practices. Teachers used the system to distribute teaching materials via class web pages; they collected and returned homework by email; they set up online assessment tasks for pupils. This resulted in a move towards a constructivist method of teaching, where teaching becomes more learner-centred and the teacher assumes the role of facilitator.

Consensual learning positions the child as a partner in the learning process (DfES, 2003). For example, 10- and 11-year-old pupils in a citizenship class in an East London school expressed their concerns about the many homeless people they saw on the streets. The artist and the writer in residence who worked on this theme with the pupils were impressed with their mature sensitivity to the complexities of this social problem which they researched locally. Their local searches with adult partners produced a digital video drama, recorded interviews, video reconstructions and documentaries, compelling digital images and *Living*, a graphic novel on homelessness which can be downloaded from the Word Ecitizens gallery. Observations on this website from the artists, film-makers and writer who worked in partnership with the children will help you to replicate a similar e-learning project (<http://www.worldecitizens.net>).

These projects have been undertaken by teachers who are experimenting with the affordances of ICT as well as the skills that they and their classes need to make e-learning a reality. Task 12.1 suggests ways in which you might begin to explore these transformational learning opportunities.

Task 12.1
Identifying your understanding of learning opportunities

Work with a group of colleagues.

Draw a mind map of the way in which computers impact on your professional life and compare this with other teachers. Ask your students to answer the same question with a mind map and share all the results. How much do the students' maps differ and compare with the teachers' maps? Are there areas where students can help teachers?

Analyse a range of e-learning materials from websites and list the ICT skills that were required to produce them.

Which skills do you already have? Which skills will you need to learn?

Develop an action plan which maps ways in which you can both acquire and apply the skills. Look for ways in which you can share this learning with colleagues.

ELEMENTS OF E-LEARNING

In this section we will concentrate on Laurillard's (2002) framework for defining the elements of e-learning that a professional teacher would hope to understand in order to gain the greatest learning advantage for pupils. She defines five categories of learning media: *narrative, interactive, communicative, adaptive* and *productive.*

Narrative media support learning experiences which are attending and apprehending; interactive media encourage investigation and exploration; communicative media prompt learners to experiment and practice, whereas productive media provide the means for the expression of and articulation of learning. Narrative media include the most traditional technologies and learning methods in the form of print, TV, video, CD-ROM and DVD.

Interactive media include research and investigation possibilities in libraries, CD-ROM, DVD, and web resources.

Communicative media embrace seminars, conferences, web forums and WLEs. VLEs have the most innovative potential in the classroom because learners can become creative authors and artists in real time, creating web-based publications which are multi-modal (combining sound, video, text and graphics for ease of information access), multimedia, and potentially multi-vocal. Learners can interact with characters in both virtual and actual situations. Chat Rooms provide a real-time space for discussion, whereas in Multi-User Domains (MUDs) people interact globally as fictional characters of their choice. Some accomplished players take on the role of several different characters simultaneously (Turkle, 1996). Other participative features of VLEs include brainstorms, interviews, forums and blogs.[1] There may be an emerging influence on learners' autonomy when they work unsupervised at home, in homework clubs and in leisure contexts (Scrimshaw, 2004).

Adaptive media include applications like adventures, simulations, and educational games as well as laboratory experiments and field trips.

Productive media include microworlds and modelling environments. Sites such as WebMonkey and Weblogs Compendium provide all the tools and support to create websites and weblogs. Productivity software also includes integrated communications packages like the Office tools. Advanced word-processing skills such as the creation and use of a range of templates, and the insertion in a document of features such as checkboxes, listboxes and option buttons, can all be used to create interactive online documents and materials. These can be used with interactive whiteboards. Presentation software such as PowerPoint can be used in a number of ways. Integrating audio and video clips reinforces the learning experience; animated sequences within a presentation can sequence and highlight key points. Your school may now have an interactive whiteboard which is important in terms of communication to the class and by the class to each other. But to maximise its effect you will need the presentation software that the major manufacturers supply. Your school should have a copy that you can install on your own computer to create teaching and learning resources. The manufacturers' websites also provide resources and ideas for you to adapt. Some teachers' case studies on the use of IWBs in transformational learning can be found on <http://www.mirandanet.ac.uk/interactive.htm>.

The keenness of teachers and learners to represent themselves and create a web identity has been underrated by the designers of software and amongst the current best ten sellers list are packages which indicate the popularity of the web as a means of self-publication: Adobe Photoshop to adjust photographic images, Adobe Acrobat to standardise documents for a wide audience beyond the working or learning environment. The other two are sophisticated tools for creating animated websites: Macromedia Studio MX and Dreamweaver (Zemsky and Massey, 2004).

DEVELOPING YOUR SKILLS?

Think about the age range of the pupils you will be teaching, and the curriculum areas you will be covering. Review the ideas presented here and in the other chapters in this book. You will know the syllabus areas you will have to teach. How will your pupils learn most effectively? How can ICT be used to support this? Some educational software will support specific parts of the curriculum. Talk to your colleagues about what they have found to be most effective. Look at the range of resources that are available online. Curriculum Online (<http://www.curriculumonline.gov.uk>), TeacherNet (<http://www.teachernet.gov.uk>), Channel 4 (<http://www.channel4.com/learning/>) and the BBC (<http://www.bbc.co.uk>) are good starting points. Companies that produce commercial software will usually provide you with access to evaluate the materials. Then think about how you can use your skills to produce teaching materials and learning materials for your pupils to use in a range of different contexts.

Varying contexts

Consider the different patterns of pupils' learning. How will you pace the materials for pupils to use? What other activities will your use of ICT integrate? You will need to think about what you expect the output of the pupils to be – what they will have to do – and what outcomes you expect at the end of the work. Different learning styles and intelligences can be supported by ICT (see Chapter 13). Consider the ways in which your ICT skills can be deployed.

INFORMATION ACQUISITION

An important element of learning is information acquisition, and this needs to be integrated with the ICT materials that are used. Some of this information can be presented for pupils to use. Other information will need to be accessed as part of the learning process. This should lead to the concept formation that will support further learning.

The assessment tools that are used as part of this process should provide pupils with the feedback they need to consolidate their learning. If you can create interactive materials using HTML features such as checkboxes, listboxes or option buttons you can integrate the assessment with the learning.

UNDERSTANDING YOUR PUPILS

Researching your pupils' perspectives can help you to take a fresh view about this controversial subject. Bennison (2002), for example, worked with Year 8 pupils at a school in Essex to identify their views on e-learning, and how these might impact on motivation, learning, roles of teachers, achievement and attainment. He found that Year 8 pupils at Chafford Hundred Campus approached their innovative new, highly connected school with a mixture of both excitement and trepidation. They valued the hard work and input of their teachers and wished to see their roles change, rather than be eroded, by the implementation of newer technologies. They saw value in a goal of working alongside teachers and learning support tutors as both their mentors and as fellow learners. Bennison's pupils indicated that they were very aware of a whole range of applications of technology in schools and that some of these applications, they felt, served their learning needs better than others. There are issues here in respect of staff training. Those who have been thinking exclusively about technology leading to a screen-facing independent learning agenda might begin to consider more imaginative group work with computers (see also Chapter 13). In particular, pupils at Chafford Hundred seemed to value their teachers' willingness to learn. One pupil observed, 'With the power of this technology, teachers here are kind of learning with us and that is exciting'.

Task 12.2
Building your skills and
knowledge

List all the software that you can use that relates to the five categories of learning media: narrative, interactive, communicative, adaptive and productive. How much more do you need to learn to cover them all?

Can you use digital images and video, and can you import audio into your teaching materials? You may not have the equipment yourself, but if you have the skills and concepts you should be able to apply them to any context.

Find out what your students use inside and outside school and elicit their opinions on the best packages to learn and the best websites to explore.

OVERCOMING INSTITUTIONAL BARRIERS TO E-LEARNING

It can take a school up to five years to embed all the elements that are required to ensure that e-learning thrives. Even then, enthusiastic teachers will find it difficult to establish good e-learning procedures and principles in the classroom unless the school development plan is supportive and the school learning policy encourages innovation and change. Most heads and senior mangers have had no training in this area, but if they are approached in a sensitive way they may find the help of newly trained teachers valuable in creating the right circumstances for growth in this area. Parents and governors are usually keen to help as well and can often share professional talents in this field.

Figure 12.1 shows the kind of elements that need to be in place in order to spread ICT capacity within the school and encourage reflection about teaching and learning methods.

Figure 12.2 indicates the way in which e-learning affords new audiences for pupils and teachers across national and cultural boundaries (Preston, 2004a).

Task 12.3
Becoming familiar with the
approach to ICT in your school

Working with colleagues from your school:

- Analyse the elements in Figure 12.1 to see what is already in place. Draw a new diagram which reflects the achievements of your school in this area and discuss the local needs.
- Discuss the learning projects which are taking place in school to analyse how many new audiences are being addressed. If local and international communities are being addressed, think about how this is raising standards.
- Look at the school website to see whether teacher and pupil achievements are receiving enough coverage and consider the accreditation opportunities that are available.
- Consider how e-learning can assist the school's approach to new subjects such as citizenship. How does the school deal with international citizenship? Funding ideas can be found on the DfES Global Gateway site (www.globalgateway.org.uk).

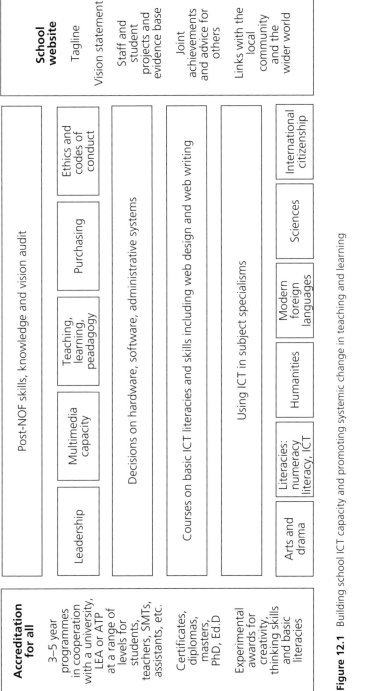

Figure 12.1 Building school ICT capacity and promoting systemic change in teaching and learning

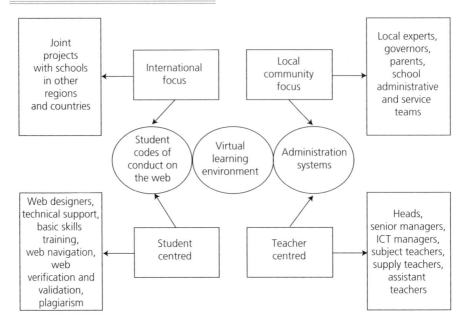

Figure 12.2 The school learning community

EMBEDDING ICT AND E-LEARNING INTO THE SCHOOL DEVELOPMENT PLAN

How does a young teacher surmount the problems that would otherwise limit opportunities for embedding ICT and e-learning into the curriculum? It is worth looking in some detail at one project which focused on Modern Foreign Languages. Hanrahan (2004) explored ways in which ICT could be used to set meaningful and motivating homework in Modern Foreign Languages. She investigated pupils' response to an online language forum. It involved two groups of Year 7 pupils within a large 11–18 comprehensive school in East Sussex: a French class of 29 pupils and a German class of 28.

The idea for this project germinated from two distinct and fairly common difficulties encountered by Hanrahan: limited access to the IT suites in school, and the setting of meaningful, yet interesting, homework. Her aims were to investigate the viability of pupils' use of ICT for Modern Foreign Languages at home including their response to their own private forum, and whether this response had any impact on their attitude to language learning.

The conclusions that Hanrahan drew from the online homework forum that she initiated were positive. The use of the web forum was not only possible in modern foreign languages, but highly desirable. The enthusiastic change in pupils' attitude towards language learning was palpable in the classroom and is corroborated by the data collected. Promoting pupil autonomy and offering them a choice resulted in a higher level of pupil engagement and sense of ownership. Several pupils joined on other language sites of their own accord and also in their own time when no specific homework was set. This surprising spin-off is a clear indicator of how motivating this type of e-learning can be.

Hanrahan believed the forum to have a beneficial effect on pupil confidence and found that work online was good for differentiation by task, by outcome and by expectation. This effect was controlled by the pupils themselves who tended to select online homework activities which were appropriate for their level and which would bring them success. Another interesting factor was the volume of posts and the ease with which the vast majority of pupils engaged with the technology, although only 8 out of the 50 respondents had previously been on a forum before. This form of e-learning was instrumental in facilitating interaction both within and between the two language classes and in raising the profile of languages.

Another study which challenged conventional practice examined the affordances emerging from the use of online communities within a primary school context. In his conclusions, Turvey (2004) found significant evidence of pupils taking responsibility for their own learning and that of their peers. He quotes a pupil exchange as an example of complex learning.

'Ok. To get more than 10 pages you have to delete one page so you have nine pages! Then you go and make the last page. Then when you click "save", keep clicking the "save" button about 5 times to get about 5 more pages! Ok? Hope it works. Tell me if it does!'

This exchange illustrates that whilst children used the online community for socialisation both within and without school, they also took responsibility for their own skills development. Similarly, other colleagues made reference to the relative ease with which children shared information and learnt from each other within the online environment.

Another significant theme that seemed to be evident was the way in which pupil to teacher relationships and dynamics seemed to shift in some cases. Those children who were normally quite reticent in the face-to-face context of the classroom would respond to an online environment. Turvey's evidence suggests that within the context of the online environment children who would not normally initiate conversation with the teacher found it easier to approach the teacher.

There were strong signs that the children perceived the use of the online environment as something other than school work. They were sometimes resentful of using their webspace for school-based, teacher-initiated projects. Pupils remained motivated when using Think.com in school, but some made a clear distinction between home and school use. Where children were able to work on their sites at home there was a strong sense of ownership over their material. This raises the issues of control and censorship which engaged the teachers in a different approach to pedagogy; one that recognised the child's ability to take responsibility for their own learning. Is the next step self-assessment of learning? (See also Chapter 9 on assessment and ICT.)

HOW DO WE ASSESS E-LEARNING?

The attitudes that a school has to assessment can profoundly affect learning strategies. This case study looks at the opportunities for change in a primary school. Riley (2004), a citizenship teacher, examined issues related to the assessment of e-learning in his classroom. He decided that he should focus first on traditional methods, building on existing learning models such as the learning cycle and the Vee Heuristic (Novak and Gowin, 1984; Ahlberg, 1997). He concentrated on the practice-based methodologies which would provide the most convincing results. These methods involved assessing prior understanding as well as understanding after intervention. He then adjusted learning tasks to reflect a pupil's learning progress, resource needs and pace. Traditional literacy-based tasks were developed and the summaries of collaborative discussions were used to develop group-learning evaluations which illustrated understanding. This kind of evaluation was dependent on group interactivity and Riley was aware that the results might not reflect specific individual understanding. However, they did provide some feedback as to the range and depth of discussion that interactivity stimulated.

Riley (2004) was particularly interested in phenomenography which focuses on the ways in which qualitatively different ways of understanding experience can be divided into different categories of description (Marton, 1988). These categories capture the meanings or conceptions of experience (Marton and Booth, 1997). The logical relations between categories of description are identified and described further in the form of an 'outcome space'. One such outcome space is the 'concept map' (Novak and Gowin, 1984; Ahlberg, 1997). This graphic representation incorporates visual and linguistic representations. Concept mapping allows both qualitative and quantitative evidence of learning to be evaluated in the formation of concepts and their relational linkages. Keywords or pictorial representations indicate the range of conceptual understanding; their connectivity assesses differences in complexity of understanding (Somekh *et al.*, 2000). Concept maps drawn before and after the intervention by the participants provide instances by which prior understanding and post-intervention learning can be compared for evaluation. Another outcome space is the saved discussion and the use of the dialogical framework for social modes of thinking to assess the quality of social learning interactions taking place within the discussion forum (Wegerif and Mercer, 1997). These differing contributions to Riley's understanding of pupil thinking and stages of learning enhanced his evaluation of e-learning through triangulation of evidence.

These new methodologies still need further evaluation, but the practice-based study has proved their effectiveness in small-scale class-based research (see <http://www.mirandanet.ac.uk/ejournal).

DEEP LEARNING AND COMMUNUAL WISDOM

If we think of multi-modal resources as ones that incorporate sound, video, image and text, to support information exchange and a range of learning styles, then it follows that the use of these modes in teaching will have a profound effect on the learner who may well also be a teacher. This shift towards a multi-modal pedagogy, which blends more traditional styles of teaching with new innovative styles, emphasises collaborative learning and creativity. A strong theme of the White Paper, 'Towards a unified e-learning strategy', also promotes online communities of practice as a means of bringing learners, teachers, specialist communities, experts, practitioners and interest groups together to share ideas and good practice, contributing to new knowledge and learning (DfES, 2003).

The question at the end of this chapter is whether these communities of practice will encourage 'deep learning' – learning that is complex and connected holistically or 'braided' in that it has evolved out of practice and has been mediated within a community of learners (Preston, 2002). From this communal constructivism perspective, e-learning is not just about transmitting information, although e-learning can be very rich in this sense (Holmes *et al.*, 2001; Leask and Younie, 2002). For example, in an attempt to visualise the process of e-learning, Smith (2004) developed a diagram based on the classroom evidence of peers which had been presented in class and published in the MirandaNet ejournal (<http://www.mirandanet.ac.uk/ejournal>), see Figure 12.3. Some of these studies have been illustrated in this chapter. Smith's diagram, which is of great complexity, was the focus of vigorous discussion about the new learning paradigm that teachers were trying to grasp through practice-based continuing professional development.

Braided Learning refers to the action research learning cycle in which concepts are revisited and develop over a period of time by groups of practitioners. These concepts can be refined by remote community intervention over months or years so that a knowledge base grows from individual submissions (Scardamalia and Bereiter, 1996). Some contributions pursue an obscure thread whilst others are designed to fill out gaps in the knowledge base and signpost new routes for research. But, although we may be able to facilitate this learning process more easily through e-learning, it is not possible to exert control over it for it is a more democratic pedagogical model than traditional instructional modes of teaching. Is this kind of e-learning an idealistic cul-de-sac or a route to democratic wisdom? Some experimentation with e-learning in your classroom may provide some surprising answers.

Task 12.4
What ICT skills and knowledge do your pupils have?

Ask your class to list all the programs they use – at school, and at home.

Then ask them what they do with the programs.

Analyse their responses.

What skills do they say they have that are not being used in school?

How can you use this knowledge to extend their ICT capability and integrate it in the ways that you teach and they learn?

What can the class tell you about theories of e-learning? Ask them to draw a concept map of how they think they learn using computers.

Discuss with the class whether the introduction of e-learning in classrooms will promote new habits of democratic participation and citizenship awareness, or not.

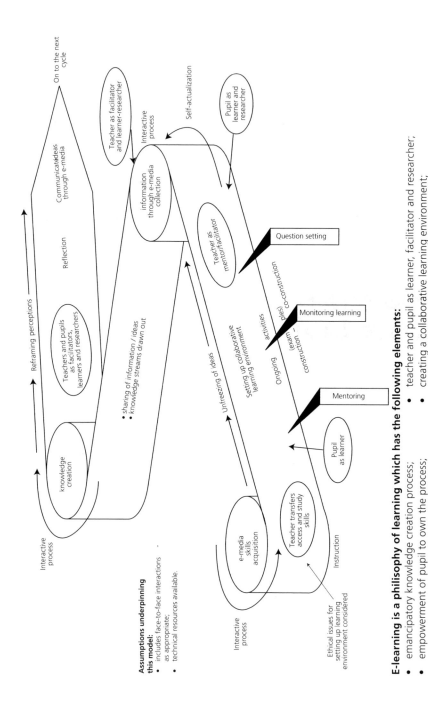

Assumptions underpinning this model:
- includes face-to-face interactions as appropriate;
- technical resources available.

E-learning is a philisophy of learning which has the following elements:
- emancipatory knowledge creation process;
- empowerment of pupil to own the process;
- unfreezing/reframing perceptions;
- use of e-media to facilitate the learning process;

- teacher and pupil as learner, facilitator and researcher;
- creating a collaborative learning environment;
- self-actualisation;
- use of e-media to communicate knowledge.

Figure 12.3 An e-learning model for schools (Source: Smith, 2004)

SUMMARY

In this chapter we have seen how developments in ICT have changed the ways in which teaching and learning are undertaken. An ICT-rich environment creates possibilities for the five elements of e-learning identified by the DfES – concurrent learning, cinematic learning, collaborative learning, communicative learning and consensual learning. The case studies have shown how some teachers and schools have been able to implement these elements.

You will have been able to identify those skills you already have and those you will need to enable you to create resources and teach in the ways that reflect your professional vision of education. At the same time you should be able to work within the environment of your school and create learning opportunities for pupils and colleagues that reflect your ideas and experience.

Above all, the chapter should challenge your understanding about the processes of learning. Is learning communally constructed in professional communities? Is it important that ICT gives you potential access to communities that cross classrooms, continents and cultures? Should you be involved as a professional in creating professional opportunities for democratic participation and global citizenship?

NOTE

1   Shared weblogs have become a popular way to share experiences as they unfold.

REFERENCES

Ahlberg, M. (1997) *Continual Quality Imporvement as High Quality Learning*, Research Report 68, University of Joensu, Faculty of Education.

Bennison, M. (2004) 'Elearning: pupils perspectives' *GTC Efacilitators Ejournal* (C. Preston and J. Cuthell, eds), Southampton: Mirandet International Research Centre, University of Southampton. Online. Available HTTP: <http://www.mirandanet.ac.uk/ejournals/indexgtc.htm>.

Hargreaves, A. and Goodson, I. (1996) *Teachers' Professional Lives: Aspirations and Activities*, London: Falmer Press.

Holmes, B. *et al*. (2001) 'Communal constructivism: pupils' constructing learning for as well as with others', 12th International Conference of the Society for Information Technology & Teacher Education (SITE 2001), Charlottesville, VA, USA, Association for the Advancement of Computing in Education.

Kress, G. (2003) *Literacy in the New Media Age*, London: Routledge.

Laurillard, D. (2002) *Rethinking University Teaching: A Framework for the Effective use of Learning Technologies*, London: RoutledgeFalmer.

Leask, M. (2001) *The New Opportunities Fund ICT Training for Teachers and School Librarians: Progress Review and Lessons Learned through the Central Quality Assurance Process in England*, London: Teacher Training Agency. Online. Available HTTP: <http://www.teach-ttaa.gov.uk>.

Leask, M. and Younie, S. (2002) 'Communal constructivist theory: ICT pedagogy and internationalisation of the curriculum', *Journal for IT for Teacher Education*, 10(1/2): 117–34.

Marton, F. (1994) 'Phenomenography', in T. Husen and T.N. Postlethwaite (eds) *The International Encyclopedia of Education*, Oxford: Pergamon.

Marton, F. and Booth, S. (1997) *Learning and Awareness*, Mahwah, NJ: Lawrence Erlbaum Associates.

Novak, J.D. and Gowin, D.R. (1984) *Learning How to Learn*, Cambridge: Cambridge University Press.

Preston, C. (2002) *Braided Learning: Teachers Learning with and for Each Other*, National Interactive Media Association: Learning Together, Tokyo: NIME.

Preston, C. (2004a) 'Learning to use ICT in classrooms: teachers' and trainers' perspectives'. Online. Available HTTP: <http://www.mirandanet.ac.uk/tta>. London: MirandaNet/TTA.

Preston, C. (2004b) 'Training and transformation', *Times Education Online Supplement*, London: 22.

Sachs, J. (2001) 'Teacher professional identity: competing discourses, competing outcomes', *Journal of Education Policy*, 16(2): 149–61.

Sachs, J. (2003) *The Activist Teaching Profession*, Buckingham: Open University Press.

Scardamalia, M. and Bereiter, C. (1996) 'Schools as knowledge building organisations', in D. Keating and C. Hertzman (eds) *Today's Children, Tomorrow's Society: The Developmental Health and Wealth of Nations*, New York: Guildford Press.

Scrimshaw, P. (2004) *Autonomous Learning in the Educational Borderlands: Will ICT help or hinder? Learning for the 21st Century: What Really Matters*, Budapest: Eotvos Lorand University, IFIT.

Somekh, B., Mavers, D. and Restorick, J. (2002) 'Interpreting the externalized images of pupils' conceptions of ICT: methods for the analysis of concept maps', *Computers and Education*, 38: 187–207.

Turkle, S. (1996) *Life on the Screen: Identity in the Age of the Internet*, New York: Weidenfeld and Nicolson.

Wenger, R. (1998) *Communities of Practice: Learning, Meaning and Identity*, Cambridge: Cambridge University Press.

Whitty, G. (2002) *Re-forming Teacher Professionalism for New Times. Making Sense of Education Policy*, London: Paul Chapman.

Wegerif, R. and Mercer, N. (1997) 'Using computer-based text analysis to integrate quantitative and qualitative methods in the investigation of collaborative learning', *Language and Education*, 11(4): 271–87.

Zemsky, R. and Massey, W.F. (2004) *Thwarted Innovation: What Happened to e-Learning and Why*, West Chester, PA: The Learning Alliance, University of Pennsylvania. Online. Available HTTP <http://www.thelearningalliance.info/WeatherStation.html>.

PRACTITIONERS' PAPERS FROM THE MIRANDANET ONLINE TEACHERS' JOURNAL

Online. Available HTTP: <http://www.mirandanet.ac.uk/ejournal>:

Fanning, J. (2004) 'Can the use of Think.com transform classroom teaching? Computer Mediated Communication in the Classroom'.

Garrett, F. (2002) 'Changing attitudes: underachievers and Think.com'.

Hanrahan, K. (2004) 'Modern Foreign Languages E-learning Project: How can ICT be used to set meaningful and motivating homework in MFL? Investigating pupils' response to an online language forum'.

Riley, N. (2004) 'An investigation using online environments and collaborative e-learning with primary pupils. Using online environments to learn effectively'.

Scott-Baker, G. (2003) 'Using multimedia in international exchanges'.

Smith, M. (2004) 'To observe and describe the process of using an online pupils' community'.

Turvey, K. (2004) 'Online communities within the primary school context. What affordances emerge from the use of online communities within the primary school context?'

FURTHER READING

Brown, A. and Davis, N. (eds) (2004) *The Global Perspective: World Yearbook of Education 2004 Digital Technology, Communities and Education*, London and New York: Routledge. This digest of the impact that the digital revolution is having on education systems and on social habits around the world will have great appeal for teachers who are keen to set up world citizenship exchange projects or those who just want to know what is happening outside the UK.

Cuthell, J.P. (2002) *Virtual Learning: The Impact of ICT on the Way Young People Work and Learn*. Aldershot: Ashgate. This book is based on a five-year study of the ways in which young people in a comprehensive school in West Yorkshire integrated ICT in their work and their lives, and the impact this had on the ways in which they worked and learned. The evidence from the investigation is relevant to the ways in which young people's expectations for learning are shaped by an exposure to technologies that are rarely acknowledged or used by schools.

Thurlow, C., Lengel, L. and Tomic, A. (2004) *Computer Mediated Communications: Social Interaction and the Internet*, London: Sage Publications. This is an accessible book for pupils which covers the theoretical foundations of e-learning, the major social issues and provides information about essential technical skills. Readers who are already interested in the impact of the Internet on identities, relationships and communities in an international context will find a wealth of new facts as well as a consideration of the more complex and deep potential for learning and being.

Wegerif, R. and Dawes, L. (2004) *Thinking and Learning with ICT: Raising Achievement in Primary Classrooms*, London: RoutledgeFalmer. If teachers are going to incorporate the use of computers in their daily lesson plans in any phase it is important that their skills of dialogue, collaborative thinking and group discussion are well developed. The authors outline a strategy for enhancing the effectiveness of computers for teaching and learning with an emphasis on:

- raising pupil achievement in the core subject areas
- developing collaborative learning in small groups
- using group discussions as a way of improving general communication, as well as thinking and reasoning skills.

13 Theories of Learning and ICT

Norbert Pachler

INTRODUCTION

This chapter starts from the premise that any teaching, be it enhanced by Information and Communications Technology (ICT) or not, in order to be effective, i.e. maximise student learning, needs to be based on a good understanding of learning and on insights from educational psychology. Its aim, therefore, is to explore the potential of ICT in relation to some of what is known about how we learn as a basis for sound pedagogical decisions about when and how best to use ICT.

In view of the quick pace of change in the world of new technologies, the use of ICT in educational settings is often predicated on faith in the potential of a particular piece of hard- and/or software by so-called 'early adopters' or on government initiatives, at times with little or no empirical evidence being available. The introduction of interactive whiteboards in recent years is a case in point. Only after enough schools had purchased and installed them in the hope and with the expectation that they would increase standards in teaching and learning and improve, develop and enhance effective pedagogy,[1] is and can research aiming to identify and disseminate leading practice in their use be carried out. Indeed, the government's own ICT agency acknowledges that: 'As interactive whiteboards are a relatively recent technology, there is not a great deal of literature relating to them in refereed academic journals' (Becta, 2003, p. 3). Glover *et al.* (2004), for example, note that the considerable increase in the number of interactive whiteboards installed in schools in the UK is, at least in part, because of government funding and arguably without a very strong evidence base.[2] As it is becoming available, research, whilst acknowledging their potential, inter alia highlights the inherent dangers in terms of didactic teaching and the need for pedagogic change.

Therefore, it is often necessary to rely on what is known about how pupils learn when introducing new variables into teaching in order to maximise positive impact from the start. In his writing, Larry Cuban (2001) bemoans the fact that computers are often oversold and underused. He, rightly in my view, makes the point that frequently new technologies are introduced into schools without giving enough thought to how best to use them. Such an approach is not likely to bring about innovation in and the improvement of teaching and learning. Technology does not in itself empower learners; schools and teachers have a crucial role to play. In my view, the use of ICT as productivity tool as opposed to a creativity tool, for example the use of interactive whiteboards simply as a presentation tool, is missing the point. Instead of doing new things it promotes doing old things in new ways (see Noss and Pachler, 1999).

OBJECTIVES

By the end of this chapter you should have an awareness of:

- some of the claims made about the potential of ICT for learning;
- dominant theories of learning and their implications for the use of ICT;
- criteria for the selection and effective use of ICT applications in teaching and learning.

WHAT IS THE POTENTIAL OF ICT FOR PUPILS' LEARNING?

For some time now, considerable claims have been made about the potential contribution of ICT to pupils' learning by policy makers, researchers and some teachers. Angela McFarlane (2001, p. 230), reflecting on research on the impact of ICT carried out prior to the most recent ImpaCT2 studies, identifies some generic traits and specific educational benefits of ICT such as:

- learner enthusiasm;
- learner confidence;
- cognitive processing speed;
- concentration;
- range of writing forms used;
- quality of revisions to writing;
- spelling, and presentation in writing;
- speed of learning;
- information handling skill;
- critical thinking;
- ability to organise and classify information;
- improved reading and comprehension;
- learner autonomy, leading to improved motivation and improved learning;
- transformed power relationships in learning, leading to benefits for the learner.

ICT can clearly be seen to possess a potential, for example, to liberate users from routine tasks and empower them to focus on creative and cognitive, rather than procedural aspects of writing or to make accessible vast amounts of information. These possibilities are, however, not unproblematic as they can be seen, potentially at least, to deprive pupils of real, first-hand (multi-sensory) experiences at the cost of simulations and models. Also, the quality of the final product can easily become more important than the processes involved in creating it or the quantity of information can easily be misconstrued for quality of experience (see Bonnett, 1997).

A tendency to perceive the value of new technologies in terms of a transmission and delivery model still widely prevails. In this view, learners are seen as empty vessels to be filled by education with the help of ICT.

Increasingly, though, there have been attempts to explore the potential contribution of computers to the social qualities of our lives (see e.g. Crook, 1994, p. 2) and there has been a realisation of new technologies as agents in interaction and collaboration rather than more narrowly as work-related tools. Linked to it are the implications of ICT use not only for how we communicate with each other but also for how we use language.

Mitchel Resnik (2002, pp. 32–3), in my view rightly, points out that in order to take full advantage of new technologies 'we need to fundamentally rethink our approaches to learning and education – and our ideas of how technology can support them'. In particular, he advances the view that there prevails the fallacy that learning is about information which, according to him, is limiting and distorting. Resnik posits that learning is not about information transmission but an active process of construction of new understandings through active exploration, experimentation, discussion and reflection. 'In short: people don't *get* ideas, they *make* them.' He promotes the view that the best learning experiences involve designing and creating things – with the help of new technologies. From this, it follows for Resnik that we need to fundamentally reorganise classrooms and replace what he calls a 'centralised-control model' with a more 'entrepreneurial' approach to learning (p. 36). Key features of this approach are learner agency and autonomy/independence and interdisciplinary topic- and project-based approaches. In addition, he argues for an updating of curricula for the digital age from a focus on 'things to know' to a focus on 'strategies for learning things you don't know' (p. 36).

However, there are also cautionary voices in relation to ICT use. Emma Haughton (1999), in a book review of Jane Healy's *Failure to connect* (1999), discusses Healy's view that '(just) because children … are performing tasks that look technologically sophisticated does not mean they are learning anything important'. Haughton goes on to report Healy's opinion that much of 'educational' software is 'crowded with extraneous and time-consuming effects that accomplish little beyond distracting children and distancing them from real learning'. Among other things, Healy mentions dangers such as impulsive clicking, trial-and-error use or guessing. In Healy's view computer time can subtract from talking, socialising, playing, imagining or learning to focus the mind internally, leading to a loss of ground.

Whilst Resnik's and Healy's views are not directly referenced to empirical work in the field here, they nevertheless seem relevant and valid and merit consideration. Regrettably, in my view, here has been a strong tendency to pay too little attention to writing in the field that aims to theorise and conceptualise the key issues. Predominantly work that is based on statistical measures or that is (pseudo)empirical in nature is valorised. This is the case despite the fact that, for example, the large-scale empirically-oriented impact research funded by the UK government is far from straightforward and, by its own admission, raised more questions than it answered. In part this is due to the complex range of interrelated factors and processes that impact on learning.

> While a study may be able to demonstrate an improvement in a pupil over time, it is very difficult (and sometimes impossible) to determine whether the use of ICT was critical, or played a role in improved attainment because so many other factors will have played a part. ... Additionally, ICT provision and use is likely to be very closely related to factors like quality of teaching and learning more generally, pupil characteristics, and quality of school leadership. For these reasons, isolating 'ICT' as a separate factor is often not meaningful or desirable, and understanding its links with other factors is a key facet of studying its impact.
>
> (Pittard *et al.*, 2003, p. 4)

In summary, whilst there are strong claims to be made for ICT, it cannot be viewed as a panacea, as *the* solution to the educational challenges we face by virtue of its sheer existence.

THE CENTRALITY OF THE ROLE OF THE TEACHER

Whilst acknowledging the fundamental impact on traditional pedagogical modes, it is important to emphasise how the effectiveness of new technologies in the learning process depends on the 'centrality' of the role of the teacher in rendering pupils' experiences and work at and with the computer coherent by embedding them in a context of interpersonal support (see Crook, 1994, p. 101). The role of the teacher remains pivotal, such as, for example, in identifying appropriate learning outcomes, choosing appropriate software and activities and structuring and sequencing the learning process or in facilitating moderating online discussions. Nevertheless, fundamental changes to the role of the teacher are taking place, in John Higgins' terms, from 'magister' (instructor) to 'pedagogue' (facilitator of pupil learning) (see Higgins, 1988). Mauri Collins and Zane Berge (1996) characterise the changes not just in the role of the teacher but also that of the learner as summarised in Table 13.1.

A paper about a research project funded by the Economic and Social Research Council (ESRC) entitled 'Interactive education: teaching and learning in the information age'[3] (John and Sutherland, 2004) notes that a number of tensions emerge when subject teachers engage with ICT. In particular they enumerate tensions between:

- teaching about and teaching through ICT;
- information accretion and information discernment; and
- subject and technological culture.

According to the authors,

> ICT alone does not enhance learning; rather it is the ways in which ICT is incorporated into the various learning activities that is of fundamental importance. Here the role of the teacher is crucial and a focus on design within the project foregrounds the teacher's responsibility to craft a learning situation.
>
> (John and Sutherland, 2004, p. 102)

John and Sutherland (2004, p. 102) go on to stress that what they call 'subject subculture', its traditions and antecedents often influence how innovative ICT practices are developed: 'teachers only tend to adopt new practices if the assumptions inherent in the innovation are consistent with their epistemological beliefs and personal theories'. Subsequently they

Table 13.1 Changes in the roles of teacher and learner

Changing instructor roles	Changing student roles
From oracle and lecturer to consultant, guide, and resource provider	From passive receptacles for hand-me-down knowledge to constructors of their own knowledge
Teachers become expert questioners, rather than providers of answers	Students become complex problem-solvers rather than just memorisers of facts
Teachers become designers of student learning experiences rather than just providers of content	Students see topics from multiple perspectives
Teachers provide only the initial structure to student work, encouraging increasing self-direction	Students refine their own questions and search for their own answers
Teacher presents multiple perspectives on topics, emphasising the salient points	Students work as group members on more collaborative/cooperative assignments; group interaction significantly increased
From a solitary teacher to a member of a learning team (reduces isolation sometimes experienced by teachers)	Increased multi-cultural awareness
From teacher having total autonomy to activities that can be broadly assessed	Students work toward fluency with the same tools as professionals in their field
From total control of the teaching environment to sharing with the student as a fellow learner	More emphasis on students as autonomous, independent, self-motivated managers of their own time and learning process
More emphasis on sensitivity to student learning styles	Discussion of students' own work in the classroom
Teacher–learner power structures erode observation of the teacher's expert performance or just learning to 'pass the test'	Emphasis on knowledge use rather than only Emphasis on acquiring learning strategies (both individually and collaboratively) Access to resources is significantly expanded

also point to the importance of established school subject subcultures and that there can be a juxtaposition of personal style and subject cultural factors (p. 105).

Whilst teachers remain crucial, the exploitation of the full potential of ICT fundamentally changes traditional assumptions:

> (In) some classrooms there is indeed a genuine shift taking place from seeing technology less as a patient tutor to more of a tool which can facilitate inquiry and critical thinking. However, in so doing teachers have to accept that learning in such an environment is often chaotic, messy, may have no tangible beginnings and ends and might breed more confusion before genuine understanding occurs.
> (John and Sutherland, 2004, pp. 106–7)

In view of the absence of widely shared criteria for evaluating ICT applications, familiarity with the findings from (educational) psychology is a useful starting point for gaining a better understanding of how ICT applications can contribute to the learning process as well as of the role of the teacher *vis-à-vis* the computer – subject domain – learner triangle.

THEORIES OF LEARNING AND THEIR IMPLICATIONS FOR ICT USE

In this section, I will discuss a number of theories of learning and examine their implications for ICT use.

Alex Moore (2000, p. 1) makes the pertinent point that every teacher operates according to a theory of learning and within a certain philosophical context be they explicit/conscious or implicit/unconscious. He goes on to note (p. 2) that the presence of explicit theory in educational policy has been conspicuous by its absence. This is also true for ICT policy where very often financial exigencies, in particular the hope for making savings on staffing, apply.

Barbara MacGilchrist, Kate Myers and Jane Reed, in their book *The Intelligent School*, distinguish a 'traditional' model of learning, which views learning as 'the reception of knowledge, the learner as passive and the appropriate learning style as formal' (the behaviourist tradition) and a 'progressive' model, which sees learning as 'discovery, the learner as active and the learning style as informal' (the cognitive, humanist and social interactionist traditions) (MacGilchrist *et al.*, 1997, p. 20). Learning is seen to occur by making sense of knowledge one is exposed to and with which one interacts by way of mental processes and/or interaction with other people. The role of new technologies in bringing about learning is increasingly coming into view.

Behaviourism

A central premise of **behaviourism** is the notion of learning as *conditioning*, the idea that it is possible to explain human behaviour in terms of responses to stimuli and that, dependent on the nature of the stimulus, varying kinds of human responses can be provoked. This principle was subsequently extended by the idea that human behaviour can be accounted for through what is observable, that environmental rather than genetic factors result in learning, that there exists a range of behaviours that are possible and that reinforcement is imperative:

> (behaviourist) theory thus came to explain learning in terms of *operant conditioning*: an individual responds to a stimulus by behaving in a particular way. Whatever happens subsequently will affect the likelihood of that behaviour recurring. If the behaviour is reinforced (i.e. rewarded or punished) then the likelihood of that behaviour occurring on a subsequent occasion will be increased or decreased.
>
> (Williams and Burden, 1997, p. 9)

Behaviourist ideas are prevalent in many spheres of education, notably teacher education in England, where what teachers need to know, do and understand is articulated by the government in a comprehensive list of competences to be demonstrated by student teachers. In ICT terms, applications in the behaviourist tradition tend to follow an instructional pattern. Learning is broken down into a sequential series of small steps each covering a piece of the subject domain or a particular skill. A computer program or application models the role of the tutor by offering some input or paradigm which the learner can 'drill and practise' followed by the provision of feedback. This is, for example, the case with so-called Integrated Learning Systems (ILS), designed to help children develop specific skills often in the areas of numeracy and literacy, which are widely used in schools. ILSs present questions, record responses, provide feedback and automatically select tasks based on user responses.

Mark Warschauer (1996) identifies the following rationale behind these programs which he considers to have value:

- Repeated exposure to the same material is beneficial or even essential to learning.
- A computer is ideal for carrying out repeated drills, since the machine does not get bored with presenting the same material and since it can provide non-judgemental feedback.
- A computer can present such material on an individualised basis, allowing students to proceed at their own pace and freeing up class time for other activities.

In this context Charles Crook notes that teachers might find this mode particularly appealing because they consider such experiences to be important and 'furnishing the necessary opportunities is not the easiest or most rewarding part of their responsibility' (Crook, 1994, p. 14).

One of the particular problems with 'drill and practice' software is that it can potentially create 'a passive mentality which seeks only the "right" answers, thus stifling children's motivation to seek out underlying reasons or to produce answers that are in any way divergent' (Bonnett, 1997, pp. 157–8).

More advanced hybrids of the computer-as-tutor software tradition, such as artificial intelligence, intelligent tutoring or integrated learning systems, preoccupied with '(1) individualisation (of) problems and questions tailored to the (changing) needs of particular learners, and (2) the delivery of constructive feedback' (Crook, 1994, p. 12), have proved very difficult to develop. One of the important arguments Crook (1994) advances in his critical evaluation of the tutor model of educational computing is that,

> 'tutoring' talk is something that is organised at levels superordinate to that of the current moment. In other words, effective tutoring dialogues are embedded in more extensive contexts of shared experience. Such dialogues are normally made possible by the history of this experience.
>
> (Crook, 1994, p. 15)

The value, therefore, of interactions with human tutors lies in the fact that, unlike computers, they are able to draw on their knowledge of the learner gained through previous interactions in similar and different contexts. Given the complexity of the processes involved, it is very difficult to program it through mathematical algorithms.

Task 13.1
Evaluating software packages I

Identify the most widely used software packages in your department. How far do they break down the subject (domain) into small parts and build on the behaviourist stimulus-response-feedback model? What particular aspects of the subject (domain) do they focus on and what specific contribution do they make to the learning process? In your opinion, what are the advantages/disadvantages of computer-mediated compared with teacher-mediated modes in relation to the aspect of the subject (domain) covered by the applications?

Cognitive theories

Cognitive theories of learning see the learner no longer as a passive recipient but as a mentally active participant in the learning process. Two main schools of thought can be distinguished, *information processing* and *constructivism*. The former tries to explain the workings of the brain in terms of rules and models of information intake, storage and processing and how this helps to explain human behaviour. Research on intelligence or intelligent behaviour,[4] which can be seen as 'the appropriate use of cognitive skills and strategies within specific contexts' (Williams and Burden, 1997, p. 20), has been significantly informed by the information processing model of cognitive psychology. According to Howard Gardner, who has been promoting a particular model of human intelligence, for instance, learners are potentially able to develop at least seven types of intelligence:

> 1. linguistic: the intelligence of words
> 2. logical-mathematical: the intelligence of numbers and reasoning
> 3. spatial: the intelligence of pictures and images
> 4. musical: the intelligence of tone, rhythm, and timbre
> 5. bodily-kinaesthetic: the intelligence of the whole body and the hands
> 6. interpersonal: the intelligence of social understanding
> 7. intrapersonal: the intelligence of self-knowledge.
>
> (MacGilchrist *et al.*, 1997, pp. 23–4)

From this it follows that, as teachers, we need to present the subject (domain) and requisite skills in ways that meet the varied learning needs and types of intelligences of our pupils; ICT can make a significant contribution to this process.

The work of constructivists such as Jean Piaget and his followers has been concerned with how human beings construct the world around them through personal meaning rather than simply through the accumulation of knowledge and facts or the development of skills.

> Constructivists postulate that there is no reality independent of the human being. Reality is always constructed by the human being and exists, therefore, only subjectively in his or her brain.
>
> (Wolff, 1997, p. 18)

Piaget advanced the notion that human beings pass through a number of stages from the use of basic senses to more sophisticated ones, in particular abstract reasoning.

> Piaget saw cognitive development as essentially a process of *maturation*, within which genetics and experience interact. The developing mind is viewed as constantly seeking *equilibration*, i.e. a balance between what is known and what is currently being experienced. This is accomplished by the complementary processes of *assimilation* and *accommodation*. Put simply, assimilation is the process by which incoming information is changed or modified in our minds so that we can fit it in with what we already know. Accommodation, on the other hand, is the process by which we modify what we already know to take into account new information. Working in conjunction, these two processes contribute to what Piaget terms the central process of cognitive *adaptation*.
>
> (Williams and Burden, 1997, p. 22)

In ICT terms the theories of cognitive psychologists can be seen to inform software following the 'revelatory' paradigm of discovery-based and problem-solving oriented learning and simulation (see Collins *et al.*, 1997, p. 16). The most notable proponent of using the potential of new technologies to help learners 'construct new understandings through their exploratory activity' (Crook, 1994, p. 16) is Seymour Papert with his notion of a 'microworld':

> Papert's proposal is driven by a compelling image. If you wish to learn to speak French, he argues, you go to France. This surely makes good sense to us. But if France is where you go to command French, where do you 'go' to command, say, mathematics? What must be discovered in that case is a sort of 'Mathsland'.
>
> (Crook, 1994, p. 16)

State-of-the-art multimedia and hypermedia simulation software, combining and integrating the written and the spoken word as well as various kinds of images, has a huge potential for presenting to learners near-to-life microworlds modelling and (re)creating diverse aspects of subjects. There remain, of course, problems which should guard us against over-reliance on ICT-based approaches. True representations of reality are often – if not always – impossible, there exists the danger of (over)simplification as well as of working in isolation and at one stage removed from reality itself. There is also the question whether ICT-based activities add or subtract authenticity to classroom-based learning activities.

Theories of cognitive psychology also allow us to understand the impact of applications and tools which help users process information, engage them in abstract thinking, allow them to make the knowledge-construction processes transparent and help them to build classificatory systems. Generic software, such as word processors, databases, spreadsheets etc. fall into this category. There is some consensus amongst commentators that these applications are liberating and empower the user to engage in cognitive and creative thinking.

Task 13.2
Evaluating software packages II

Following on from Task 13.1, analyse the most widely used software packages in your department with a view to answering the following questions: how far do they help pupils in processing information, in engaging in abstract thinking, in solving problems, in making sense of the world around them etc? What are the advantages/disadvantages of computer-mediated compared with teacher-mediated modes in relation to these applications?

Learning styles

Other important lessons to be learnt from (cognitive) psychologists relate to **learning styles**, the characteristic cognitive, affective and physiological behaviours that serve as relatively stable indicators of how learners perceive, interact with and respond to the learning environment ... Learning style is a consistent way of functioning, that reflects underlying causes of behaviour.

(J. Keefe, 1979 quoted in Ellis, 1994, p. 499)

It is a widely held view that it is beneficial for teachers to be aware of pupils' preferences *vis-à-vis* their learning environment and the nature of interactions in it. Furthermore, there has been considerable interest as of late, particularly in the field of foreign languages teaching, in making pupils aware of their preferences and dispositions in order to become more adaptable to the requirements of specific learning tasks and activities or the learning process more generally. Key terminology in this field are 'learner strategies' and 'learner training'. Rod Ellis notes a number of distinctions that have been made by various researchers over the years in relation to learning styles such as *focusers* (concentrate on one aspect of a problem at a time and proceed in a step-by-step manner) versus *scanners* (tackle several aspects of a problem at the same time and allow ideas to crystallise slowly), *serialists* (operate with single-proposition hypotheses) versus *holists* (operate with multiple-proposition hypotheses), *impulsive* versus *reflective* thinkers, *divergent* versus *convergent* thinkers and *field dependence* ('perception strongly dominated by the overall organisation of the surrounding field') versus *field independence* ('parts of the field are experienced as discrete from organised ground') (see Ellis, 1994, p. 500).

Other studies have identified differing perceptual learning modalities:

1   visual learning (for example, reading and studying charts)
2   auditory learning (for example, listening to lectures and audio tapes)
3   kinaesthetic learning (involving physical responses)
4   tactile learning (hands-on learning, as in building models).

(based on Reid, 1987 in Ellis, 1994, p. 506)

Yet another study identified the four general learning styles summarised in Table 13.2.

In his discussion of this and other studies, Ellis points out that our concept of learning styles is still ill-defined, that the strength and nature of motivation seems to impact on learning styles and that environmental factors appear to be at least as important as innate qualities (see Ellis, 1994, pp. 506–7).

Irrespective of these shortcomings as well as the fact that there is still uncertainty which learning style works best, this aspect of (cognitive) psychology is of relevance for teaching in general and the use of ICT in particular. There appears to be a tendency amongst beginning teachers to teach how they themselves would like to be taught. In order not to provide too narrow a range of teaching styles it is important for teachers to be aware not only of their own preferences but also of the diversity of preferences amongst pupils. Given the variety of preferences amongst pupils about the learning environment and their interactions with it, teaching approaches and methods need to be varied. New technologies offer one (of many) possibilities to provide varied learning opportunities.

Table 13.2 General learning styles according to Willing 1987 (in Ellis, 1994, p. 506)

General learning style	Main characteristics
1 Concrete learning style	Direct means of processing information; people-oriented; spontaneous; imaginative; emotional; dislikes routinised learning; prefers kinaesthetic modality.
2 Analytical learning style	Focuses on specific problems and proceeds by means of hypothetical-deductive reasoning; object-orientated; independent; dislikes failure; prefers logical, didactic presentation.
3 Communicative learning style	Fairly independent; highly adaptable and flexible, responsive to facts that do not fit; prefers social learning and a communicative approach; enjoys taking decisions.
4 Authority-oriented learning style	Reliant on other people; needs teacher's directions and explanations; likes a structured learning environment; intolerant of facts that do not fit; prefers a sequential progression; dislikes discovery learning.

**Task 13.3
Personal learning and teaching
styles and ICT use**

1. Consider what you believe to be your preferred learning style. What learning activities do you associate with this learning style?
2. Discuss with your pupils what their preferences are. How representative are your preferences in comparison with those of your pupils?
3. What activities, including those relating to ICT use, can you think of in the context of the topic you are currently teaching that would cater for the wide range of learning styles prevalent amongst your pupils?

Social interactionism

A further school of thought of (educational) psychology is **social interactionism** which adds the importance of the location of human learning within a socio-cultural environment to the idea of learners constructing their own knowledge and understanding.[5]

The best known proponent of social interactionism is the Russian, Lev Vygotsky, whose work, whilst conceived in the 1930s, did not become available in the West in translation until the 1960s and 1970s. Put simply, the premise of his work revolves around the importance of interaction with others as part of the learning process:

> Vygotsky took issue with the Piagetian view that from the time of their birth children learn independently by exploring their environment, and with the behaviourist view that adults are entirely responsible for shaping children's learning by the judicious use of rewards and punishment.
>
> (Williams and Burden, 1997, p. 39)

Vygotsky afforded great importance to the role of language in the interaction of learners with one another: '(it) is by means of language that culture is transmitted, thinking develops and learning occurs' (Williams and Burden, 1997, p. 40). According to social interactionism, learning takes place through engagement with contextualised and situationalised socio-cultural environments and through 'contact with a culture of material and social resources that everywhere supports cognitive activity' (Crook, 1994, p. 32). A crucial part is played by other significant people in learners' lives, be they parents, teachers or peers, who enhance the learning of others by 'selecting and shaping the learning experiences presented to them' and who help them 'to move into and through the next layer of knowledge or understanding' which Vygotsky called the *zone of proximal development* (Williams and Burden, 1997, p. 40).

ICT can also be seen to have mediatory potential in the Vygotskyan sense. This view is, however, not unproblematic. In light of the insights afforded to us by social interactionism I consider it to be vitally important for teachers to be aware how the use of ICT (in the classroom) impacts on teacher–pupil, pupil–teacher and pupil–pupil interactions as well as on (inter)personal relationships. Also, there are the issues of the impact of ICT on the status of the teacher and the role of new technologies as mediators of learning. Given the importance of interpersonal exchanges in such a view of learning, questions need to be asked as to whether ICT does, indeed, have this mediatory potential or whether use of ICT will undermine the social quality of education and deprive learners of vital 'scaffolded social encounters' (see Crook 1994, pp. 61, 80). Charles Crook, in his 1994 book *Computers and the collaborative experience of learning*, repeatedly points out the need to employ computer-mediation very carefully and deliberately and to ask searching questions as to its potential to provide interactions that are actually significant in bringing about learning. The communicative potential of computer-mediated communication via the internet, therefore, warrants more detailed investigation.

The discussion of theories of learning in this section, then, suggests that in view of the limited availability of intelligent software, learning is as – if not more – likely to take place via the interactions of pupils with peers and the teacher whilst using ICT applications as it is via the interactions with ICT itself.

Task 13.4
ICT use and social interactions

Observe a number of lessons in which ICT is being used.

1. Describe the nature of social interactions taking place: do pupils work individually, in pairs or in groups?
2. What interactions can you observe under the following headings:

    - teacher–pupil;
    - pupil–teacher;
    - pupil–pupil;
    - pupil–computer.

3. What types of questions do pupils and teachers ask, i.e. questions related to technical issues or questions about the subject domain?
4. What kind of 'scaffolding' of learning is evident, i.e. mediation from the teacher or peers?

What evidence is there of learning taking place?
    Overall, do you think the use of ICT was instrumental in bringing about learning?

MAKING USE OF FINDINGS FROM OTHER RELATED DISCIPLINES

Other useful starting points for gaining a better understanding of how ICT applications can contribute to the learning process can be found in research into other related disciplines such as the study of literature or film.

In an interesting article in the *British Journal of Educational Technology*, Lydia Plowman (1996, pp. 92–7) argues, for instance, that interactive multimedia challenge traditional definitions of narrative and that their relative lack, for instance, of redundancy and fixed sequences has serious implications *vis-à-vis* comprehension and cognition in educational contexts. She posits that the potentially beneficial attributes of interactive multimedia, such as their multimodality, the integral part of group discussions or periods of individual reflection as well as the control of the user in navigational terms, are double-edged in so far as interaction with the computer can potentially disrupt the narrative structure which, she claims, is central to our cognition (see also Laurillard, 1998 and Laurillard *et al.*, 2000).

EVALUATING ICT APPLICATIONS

As with any other teaching tools, ICT applications have to be judiciously vetted by teachers for their effectiveness in facilitating learning to take place. One particular challenge of ICT applications relates to the fact that they obey specific conventions and rules which differ significantly from those of more traditional tools. They make use of a wide range of semiotic systems in that they can, as in the case of hypermedia, combine the written word, the spoken word as well as images. Their user-interfaces predicate faculties which have been termed 'critical media literacy' (Collins *et al.*, 1997, p. 62) in order to facilitate success-ful intake, processing and storage of the information contained therein. There is insufficient space in the context of this chapter to analyse these characteristics in detail; teachers along with all other users will, nevertheless, need to pay great attention to developing (in their pupils) the requisite skills. As well as the hypermedia nature of new technologies, their move away from sequential to random modes of information presentation is a very important feature for teachers to be aware of. No longer is the recall of facts and figures central but, instead, the ability to locate, select and re-use appropriate material. An additional problem in this context is the comparative lack of skills in teachers to make judgements on the basis of 'professional' experience:

> (the) very nature of multimedia, vast, non-linear and readable only through the computer screen, means that it is difficult to assess the scope and quality of a title or source without spending considerable time on it. There is no equivalent to picking up and flicking through a book which will give an experienced teacher a clear view of its coverage and relevance.
>
> (McFarlane, 1996, p. 4)

It is important to bear in mind that software developers make a number of assumptions in the process of the conception, production and evaluation stages of a new application. These include assumptions about the process of learning, the teaching methodology and the knowledge/skills base of the intended users, including their cognitive abilities. To some extent their possibilities are constrained by the technical capabilities of their chosen delivery system. For the purposes of selecting appropriate and effective ICT applications, the checklist in Table 13.3 may prove helpful.

Task 13.5
Evaluating ICT applications

1. Put the criteria in Table 13.3 in order of your preference. What do you consider to be most important in ICT applications for your subject area?
2. Use this checklist for the evaluation of an ICT application. Also, ask your pupils what they think. Then compare your views with those of your pupils.

TEACHER LEARNING AND TECHNOLOGY

A discussion of learning theories and ICT should also give some consideration to the learning process teachers themselves engage in when learning to make effective use of ICT in their teaching.

A literature review of relevant research by Meskill *et al.* (2002) suggests that there are conceptual and practical differences between novice and expert teachers. They note (pp. 46–7) that teachers who use technologies effectively can be seen as conceiving of technology as a means to an end rather than an end in itself, of seeing themselves as being in an advisory role and of viewing newness and variety as being desirable. Another of their characteristics is an eagerness to expand their repertoire. Novice teachers, on the other hand, appear most concerned with mastering the routines and rituals associated with new technologies.

Meskill *et al.*'s own research (p. 49) identifies four novice–expert continua from which a number of practical training and development implications flow, see Figure 13.1.

Table 13.3 Checklist for the evaluation of ICT applications

Criterion	Comment
What assumptions are made about how pupils learn?	
What assumptions are made about pupils' cognitive abilities, i.e. what are the prerequisites for the use of this application?	
In what socio-cultural context is learning situated? What types of pupil–teacher, pupil–pupil, pupil–application and teacher–pupil interactions are facilitated?	
Are the conceptual and linguistic/semantic assumptions clear and appropriate? Is the wording effective and appropriate?	
Are the scope and the aims of the application explicit?	
Can links with existing learning objectives / schemes of work be easily established? Is there an appropriate indication as to the possible contexts of use?	
Is the application user-friendly and interactive? Does it have the potential for differentiated access?	
Has appropriate use been made of hypermedia – is the layout clear and consistent? Is the material well organised and attractively presented?	
Does the concept work and is functionality given?	
Is the user able to pursue her own path through the material? Are examples of possible navigational structures available?	
Are teacher's notes as well as a user guide available?	
Is the authorship transparent and subject expertise given?	
Is the content accurate, reliable and up to date?	
Is the application comparable with similar resources, e.g. what does it do that a book doesn't /can't do?	
Is on-line help available and are error messages clear?	
Are there technical/compatibility problems?	

	Novice teacher		Expert teacher
Locus:	Machine	↔	Learners
Focus:	Self	↔	Student learning
Practice:	Managing students	↔	Empowering students
Emphasis:	Product	↔	Process

Figure 13.1 Differences between novice and expert teachers using ICT

Their research suggests that ICT-related training may not be sufficient for the conceptual development needed to use technology expertly. They note (p. 54) that novice teachers who had received 'state of the art' technology training were far less comfortable in its implementation than more experienced teachers with no formal training with computers but a great deal of classroom experience. Effective ICT use, therefore, seems to be predicated, at least to some extent, on a sound pedagogical understanding and any technical training and professional development needs to build on and go hand in hand with pedagogical concerns.

Task 13.6
Expert and novice teachers

Where would you place yourself on the four continua identified by Meskill *et al.* (2002)?

SUMMARY

In this chapter I have tried to demonstrate the importance of theories of learning for effective ICT-related pedagogy. This includes an awareness on the part of the teacher of the assumptions made by ICT applications and their creators about how learning takes place. This is, of course, not to argue technological determinism, i.e. to suggest that technology determines human behaviour, social relations and organisation. Instead, it recognises that technologies do not operate in a contextual vacuum and that the effect of a particular medium is never intrinsic in a medium but instead mediated by type of use and contexts (see Luke, 2000, p. 74). Careful selection of applications and types of uses on the basis of knowledge about learning are key to effective ICT use.

NOTES

1   See e.g. <http://www.ictadvice.org.uk/index.php?section=te&catcode=as-pres_02>.
2   See also <http://www.becta.org.uk/leaders/leaders.cfm?section=5&id=3155>.
3   See <http://www.interactiveeducation.ac.uk>.
4   William and Burden note that intelligence is but a '*hypothetical construct*, a term of convenience to account for something that doesn't really exist' (Williams and Burden, 1997, p. 19) and that it is preferable to think about it as a term describing someone 'acting more or less intelligently or demonstrating intelligent behaviour in a particular circumstance' (Williams and Burden, 1997, p. 20).
5   Yet another school of thought of (educational) psychology is humanism, which affords us valuable insights in terms of whole-person development beyond the development and use of cognitive skills; unfortunately, there is insufficient room here to discuss these. For a brief overview see e.g. Williams and Burden (1997, pp. 30–8).

REFERENCES AND FURTHER READING

Becta (2003) *What Research Says about Interactive Whiteboards*. Coventry: Becta. Online. Available HTTP: <http://www.becta.org.uk/page_documents/research/wtrs_whiteboards.pdf>.

Bonnett, M. (1997) 'Computers in the classroom: some values issues', in A. McFarlane (ed.) *Information Technology and Authentic Learning: Realising the Potential of Computers in the Primary Classroom*, London: Routledge.

Collins, M. and Berge, Z. (1996) 'Facilitating interaction in computer mediated online courses'. Background information paper for a presentation at the FSU/AECT Distance Education Conference, Tallahassee, Florida. Online. Available HTTP: <http://www.emoderators.com/moderators/flcc.html>.

Collins, J., Hammond, M. and Wellington, J. (1997) *Teaching and Learning with Multimedia*, London: Routledge.

Crook, C. (1994) *Computers and the Collaborative Experience of Learning*, London: Routledge.

Cuban, L. (2001) *Oversold and Underused. Computers in the Classroom*. Cambridge, MA: Harvard University Press. Online. Available HTTP: <http://www.hup.harvard.edu/pdf/CUBOVE.pdf>.

Ellis, R. (1994) 'Individual learner differences', in R. Ellis (ed.) *The Study of Second Language Acquisition*, Oxford: Oxford University Press.

Glover, D., Miller, D. and Averis, D. (2004) 'Panacea or prop: the role of the interactive whiteboard in improving teaching effectiveness', paper presented at the Tenth International Congress of Mathematics Education, Copenhagen.

Haughton, E. (1999) 'Look what they've done to my brain, ma'. *The Independent Education*, 3 June, p. 2.

Higgins, J. (1988) *Language, Learners and Computers: Human Intelligence and Artificial Unintelligence*, London: Longman.

John, P. and Sutherland, R. (2004) 'Teaching and learning with ICT: new technology, new learning?' *Education, Communication & Information*, 4(1): 101–7.

Laurillard, D. (1998) 'Multimedia and the learner's experience of narrative', *Computers and Education*, 31: 229–42.

Laurillard, D., Stratford, M., Luckin, R., Plowman, L. and Taylor, J. (2000) 'Affordances for learning in a non-linear narrative medium', *Journal of Interactive Media in Education*, 2: 1–19. Online. Available HTTP: <http://www-jime.open.ac.uk/00/2>.

Luke, C. (2000) 'Cyber-schooling and technological change. Multiliteracies for new times', in B. Cope and M. Kalantzis (eds) *Multiliteracies*, London: Routledge.

MacGilchrist, B., Myers, K. and Reed, J. (1997) *The Intelligent School*, London: Paul Chapman.

McFarlane, A. (1996) 'Blessings in disguise', *TES Computers Update*, 28 June, p. 4.

McFarlane, A. (2001) 'Perspectives on the relationships between ICT and assessment', *Journal of Computer Assisted Learning*, 17(3): 227–34.

Meskill, C., Mossop, J., DiAngelo, S. and Pasquale, R. (2002) 'Expert and novice teachers talking technology: precepts, concepts, and misconcepts', *Language Learning & Technology*, 6(3): 46–57. Online. Available HTTP: <http://llt.msu.edu/vol6num3/meskill/>.

Moore, A. (2000) *Teaching and Learning: Pedagogy, Curriculum and Culture*, London: Routledge Falmer.

Noss, R. and Pachler, N. (1999) 'Building new pedagogies: the ICT challenge', in P. Mortimore (ed.) *Understanding Pedagogy and its Impact on Learning*, London: Paul Chapman.

Pittard, V., Bannister, P. and Dunn, J. (2003) *The Big pICTure: The Impact of ICT on Attainment, Motivation and Learning*, London: DfES. Online. Available HTTP: <http://www.dfes.gov.uk/research/data/uploadfiles/ThebigpICTure.pdf>.

Plowman, L. (1996) 'Narrative, linearity and interactivity: making sense of interactive multimedia', *British Journal of Educational Technology*, 27(2): 92–105.

Resnick, M. (2002) 'Rethinking learning in the digital age', in G. Kirkman (ed.) *The Global Information Technology Report 2001–02: Readiness for the Networked World*, Oxford: Oxford University Press. Online. Available HTTP: <http://www.cid.harvard.edu/cr/pdf/gitrr2002_ch03.pdf>.

Warschauer, M. (1996) 'Computer-assisted language learning: an introduction', in S. Fotos (ed.) *Multimedia Language Teaching*, Tokyo: Logos International.

Williams, M. and Burden, R. (1997) *Psychology for Language Teachers. A Social Constructivist Approach*, Cambridge: Cambridge University Press.

Wolff, D. (1997) 'Computers as cognitive tools in the language classroom', in A.-K. Korsvold and B. Rüschoff (eds) *New Technologies in Language Learning and Teaching*, Strasbourg: Council of Europe Publishing, Education Committee: Council for Cultural Co-operation.

14 The Evidence Base for Effective ICT Practice in Literacy Learning

What Systematic Reviews Reveal

Carole Torgerson and Allison Freeman

INTRODUCTION

In this chapter we present the results of an overview (a tertiary review) of all the identified systematic reviews in the area of information and communication technology (ICT) and literacy learning, which were written or published in English since 1990. Before we present the results, however, we first outline the significance of the research in ICT and literacy learning; and we clarify the role of systematic reviews in informing practice, policy and scholarship.

OBJECTIVES

- To provide an overview of the history and processes of systematic reviews;
- To provide an overview of the implications for practice of systematic reviews in ICT and literacy learning.

ICT AND LITERACY LEARNING

Information and communication technology (ICT) is widely used in education. Governments around the world have invested heavily in ICT provision for schools in the belief that this will improve ICT use per se and have a beneficial impact in the fields of literacy and numeracy learning. There is some evidence, however, that ICT may not always be beneficial to literacy outcomes and there is even a suggestion of negative effects in some numeracy learning (Angrist and Lavy, 2002). It is therefore important for the role of ICT practice in literacy learning to be clarified for practitioners, policy makers, pupils and parents.

SYSTEMATIC REVIEWS

Traditionally, reviews have taken the form of 'narrative' (or non-systematic) reviews, whereby a subject expert presents evidence within given areas and draws conclusions. The problem with this approach is that the reader is left uninformed about whether the evidence presented is a true representation of *all* the research within that field. The reviewers may have been selective in their choice of research studies to include in the review. Alternatively, the reviewers might simply have been misled about the strength of the evidence. Due to widespread publication bias in educational research, positive or exciting results are more likely to be published than less exciting or negative results (Torgerson, 2003). Consequently it is important to identify, if possible, all the relevant (published and unpublished) studies within any given field of endeavour. It is also important to make the processes of searching for, identifying and synthesising included studies transparent to the reader so that, if necessary, the review can be replicated by an independent expert if the findings are contrary to received opinion.

A key advantage of a systematic review is that it is less likely to be biased than a non-systematic review. Because great efforts are made to identify both published and unpublished literature within a topic area, those unexciting 'no result' studies are included within the overall evidence base. The process of systematic reviewing also places an emphasis on making explicit the methods for searching for, including, synthesising and quality appraising all the studies included in the review. It does this through the development of a protocol, or plan, of the review which is written before the process begins, and which explicitly states all the methods for the review and the criteria for including or excluding studies. All things being equal, the results from good-quality studies are more reliable than ones from poor-quality studies, whether they are published or not. Similarly, most systematic reviews are undertaken by a group of researchers who undertake a process of quality assuring the review to ensure that any mistakes are rectified during the review process.

Limitations of systematic reviews

Systematic reviews can themselves be susceptible to publication bias. If a negative study has not been published, or is not available as a thesis, then it simply cannot be identified and included in the review. Statistical techniques have been developed to assess the extent of publication bias but these can often only detect extreme forms of such bias and systematic reviews may contain misleading conclusions because of a failure to include all the evidence. Systematic reviews can also suffer from interpretation bias, in the sense that the conclusions may not always arise from the actual data identified in the review, or a positive gloss may be placed on positive, but relatively thin, evidence. These drawbacks also affect traditional non-systematic reviews but the point is that they do so in a more extreme fashion.

History of systematic reviews

Systematic reviews have a long history. In the James Lind Library, Chalmers argues that the first recognisable review was undertaken in the 18th century by James Lind, who examined the causes and treatments for scurvy. In the field of education, systematic reviews were undertaken in the 1970s and 1980s long before their current widespread use in health care. Indeed, many of the statistical techniques used in quantitative systematic reviews were originally developed by educational researchers (Glass, 1976). Although systematic reviews have been widely used in educational research they have often been given different names. For example, Slavin described systematic reviews as 'best evidence synthesis', whilst the term meta-analysis is often used as a synonym for the term systematic review (Slavin, 1986). More recently, however, meta-analysis as a term has been used to describe a particular method of synthesising quantitative data. In a meta-analysis, a reviewer will take some or all of the studies identified in a systematic review and combine them statistically in order to generate a more precise estimate of the effect size of a given intervention.

Recent systematic review initiatives

Policy makers are increasingly recognising the importance of systematic reviews to inform evidence-based decision-making and a number of initiatives to address this demand have been established. An example of an international initiative is the Campbell Collaboration (modelled on the very successful Cochrane Collaboration in health care), which aims to identify all the experimental research in the field of education and the social sciences. A series of review groups have been established to collate, synthesise and interpret this evidence. The Evidence for Policy and Practice Information and Co-ordinating Centre (EPPI-Centre) is an example of a UK based initiative which aims to identify and synthesise a range of evidence including non-experimental evidence. This 'explosion' in evidence synthesis should produce more robust decision-making in the future and help to identify gaps in the literature where further research would be the most fruitful.

TERTIARY REVIEWS

Whilst a systematic review searches for and includes primary research studies as its data, in a tertiary review systematic reviews *are* the primary data source. The advantage of a tertiary review is that it can give an overall broad picture of the evidence identified in several reviews in a given field and possibly draw policy conclusions that a single review may not be able to do. One limitation of a tertiary review is that the included systematic reviews may be so different in their conceptualisation of a field that it becomes problematic to synthesise them.

In this chapter we present a tertiary review undertaken in the area of ICT and literacy learning. The conceptualisation of 'literacy' is a complex issue, and many of the included reviews define it in specific and different ways. For our tertiary review we adopted a broad definition of literacy in order to be inclusive. However, because the definitions within the included reviews vary we have not attempted to synthesise the reviews, but rather to present the scope of the research in the field. It is worth emphasising that a tertiary review is only as good as the systematic reviews it includes. In this tertiary review we attempted to minimise this by adopting a rigorous definition of 'systematic review' in our inclusion criteria. However, we did not undertake a full quality appraisal of the included systematic reviews and acknowledge that they vary in quality.

IDENTIFICATION OF STUDIES

We included reviews if they had used systematic review methods throughout, including the use of systematic searching of electronic databases, pre-established inclusion/exclusion criteria and some quality appraisal of their included studies. We adopted broad definitions of 'literacy' (including psychological and social/cultural definitions) and 'ICT', and included reviews if they focused on any ages or characteristics of learners. We only included reviews reporting on studies in literacy learning in English.

Initially we identified potentially relevant reviews for the tertiary review through the work of the EPPI English Review Group. Between 2001 and 2004 researchers in the English Review Group (co-ordinated by Richard Andrews and Carole Torgerson in the Department of Educational Studies at the University of York and funded by the DfES, through the EPPI-Centre) undertook a series of five systematic reviews in the field of ICT and literacy. As part of the review process, all of the previous systematic reviews undertaken in the field of ICT and literacy between 1990 and 2004 were identified and located (five further reviews were thus identified).

In 2003, a research team in the Department of Educational Studies at the University of York (co-ordinated by Richard Andrews) was commissioned by the Teacher Training Agency (TTA), and also supported by the EPPI-Centre, to undertake a further systematic review in the field of ICT and literacy (see <http://eppi.ioe.ac.uk/reel/home.aspx?page=/reel/review_groups/TTA_ICT/home.htm>). Both this review and two further systematic reviews identified in the process of undertaking the TTA review are included in this tertiary review.

All of the systematic reviews retrieved in the way described above were screened according to our inclusion criteria and then included in this tertiary review.[1]

RESULTS: REVIEWS IDENTIFIED

A total of thirteen systematic reviews are included in this tertiary review of the evidence base for the effective use of ICT practice in literacy learning: six EPPI-Centre reviews (including the TTA review) and seven further reviews identified in the process of undertaking the EPPI-Centre reviews.

The EPPI-Centre reviews (Andrews *et al.*, 2002; Burn and Leach, 2004; Locke and Andrews, 2004; Low and Beverton, 2004; Torgerson and Zhu, 2003 and the unpublished TTA review) are the result of work undertaken by members of the English Review Group. Initially, a systematic mapping study was conducted of research from empirical studies from 1990 to 2002. This identified the range and type of research studies addressing the impact of ICT on literacy learning in English for pupils aged 5 to 16. The methodology was devised by the Evidence for Policy and Practice Information and Co-ordinating Centre at the Social Science Research Unit, Institute of Education, University of London. Subsequently five 'in-depth' reviews were undertaken in the areas of: networked ICT and literacy, moving image texts and literacy, literature-related literacies, ICT, literacy and English as a second or additional language, and effectiveness of ICT on literacy outcomes.

Five further systematic reviews undertaken in the field of ICT and literacy since 1990 were identified whilst drawing the overall systematic map to describe the research in the field (Andrews *et al.*, 2002). These reviews were: Bangert-Drowns, 1993; Blok *et al.*, 2001; Fulk and Stormont-Spurgin, 1995; MacArthur *et al.*, 2001; and Torgerson and Elbourne, 2002. These reviews synthesised research in various aspects of literacy: spelling (Fulk and Stormont-Spurgin, 1995; Torgerson and Elbourne, 2002); writing (Bangert-Drowns, 1993); verbal and vocabulary development (Blok *et al.*, 2001). In some of the reviews the included studies focused on participants with specific learner characteristics, for example pupils experiencing learning disabilities (MacArthur *et al.*, 2001; Fulk and Stormont-Spurgin, 1995). Most of the reviews included papers of all study types (MacArthur *et al.*, 2001; Fulk and Stormont-Spurgin, 1995), whilst others were restricted to experimental research: randomised controlled trials or controlled trials (Torgerson and Elbourne, 2002; Blok *et al.*, 2001; Bangert-Drowns, 1993).

The TTA review (also an EPPI-Centre review) sought to examine the evidence for effectiveness of different ICTs in the teaching and learning of English for students aged between 5 and 16 years. A systematic mapping study was carried out, which focused on research published between 1998 and 2003 and an in-depth review was then conducted to investigate the effectiveness of different ICTs within the area of written composition.

Two further reviews not previously identified were located through the process of undertaking the TTA review (Bryant *et al.*, 2003; Hall *et al.*, 2000).

Table 14.1 provides a summary of the included reviews.

THE REVIEWS IN DETAIL

Writing

Bangert-Drowns (1993) conducted a meta-analysis of 32 studies using an experimental method to evaluate the effectiveness of using the word-processor to write assignments and published between 1983 and 1990. Each included study compared two groups of students who received identical instruction in writing, apart from the medium used for the writing process (word-processor or by hand) and measured treatment outcomes quantitatively. The author mixed different study types in the review (all were trials but only some used random allocation to groups) and this might have led to a misleading conclusion, as non-randomised studies are more susceptible to bias. The author concluded that the word-processing groups (especially the weaker writers) improved the quality of their writing more than the control groups.

Table 14.1 Summary of details of reviews included

Author, date	Area of literacy	Area of ICT	Number and type of studies included in review; type of synthesis	Findings of review as presented by authors
Andrews, 2004	Writing	Word-processing, multimedia, software	9 experimental studies; narrative synthesis	Findings were inconclusive. The evidence suggested that CAI and word-processing might lead to improvements in written composition when combined with strategic instruction. However, there were insufficient trials of high quality to demonstrate this conclusively.
Andrews et al., 2002	Reading, writing	Networked ICT	16 (various study types); narrative synthesis	Findings were inconclusive. The high-quality studies suggested that ICT use with regard to literacy development increases motivation and/or confidence in pupils and that 'empowerment and ownership are important factors to bear in mind in an increasingly diverse digital world' (p. 6).
Bangert-Drowns, 1993	Writing	Word-processing	32 experimental studies (with random and non-random assignment to groups); meta-analysis and narrative synthesis	The author concluded that the word-processing groups (especially the weaker writers) improved the quality of their writing more than the control groups. 'Word processing in writing may provide lasting educational benefits to users because it encourages a fluid conceptualization of text and frees the writer from mechanical concerns' (p. 69).
Blok et al., 2001	Vocabulary learning (word meaning)	Computer-assisted instruction (CAI)	5 experimental studies (with random or non-random assignment to groups); qualitative research synthesis	Results were equivocal. 'Only one study produced unequivocal evidence for superior learning in a computer-assisted condition' (p. 99).
Bryant et al., 2003	Vocabulary learning	CAI	6 experimental studies; narrative synthesis	In all the studies, students demonstrated gains within a short duration of instruction and the majority of studies documented that instruction occurred several times weekly, thus showing that vocabulary instruction need not necessarily take up great amounts of class time to produce results. 'CAI is a promising tool' (p.119).
Burn and Leach, 2004	Literacies associated with the moving image	Moving image	9 studies, varying in type including qualitative and quantitative research; narrative synthesis	Some studies concluded that work in the moving image had observable benefits for children's writing; several studies concluded that moving image work needed to relate to children's cultural experience.
Fulk and Stormont-Spurgin, 1995	Spelling	CAI	9 studies; 2 experimental studies, 7 single-subject designs (case study)	Eight out of the nine studies in CAI reported positive effects for CAI.
Hall et al., 2000	Reading	CAI	17 experimental studies; narrative synthesis	13 out of 17 studies reported an increase in student performance.
Locke and Andrews, 2004	Literature-based literacies (7 were concerned with response to text, 1 with composing texts and 1 with researching around texts)	Various including word-processing (1 study), multimodal software (6 studies), on-line discussion (1 study), hypertext (1 study)	7 (various study types); narrative synthesis	Teacher discourses strongly mediate reading practices around ICTs. There is a mismatch between many multimedia literature software packages and theories of literary response. Electronic storybooks can motivate and enhance literary response but can de-motivate over time. Online discussion encourages student articulation and sharing of responses to texts.

Author, date	Area of literacy	Area of ICT	Number and type of studies included in review; type of synthesis	Findings of review as presented by authors
Low and Beverton, 2004	Reading, writing	CAI, CALL, word-processing, software	8 studies (1 RCT, 6 experiments, 1 unclear); narrative synthesis	'There is an insubstantial body of evidence pointing in any direction regarding the research question' (p.119).
MacArthur et al., 2001	Word identification skills, reading comprehension, writing	CAI, software, electronic texts, word-processing, tools to support transcription	Word identification skills (14 experiments), reading comprehension (14 studies – various types), writing (20 studies – various types)	All 14 studies supported efficacy of CAI and software, for reading comprehension results were equivocal, for writing research found 'qualified support for the beneficial effect of assistive technology' (p. 297).
Torgerson and Elbourne, 2002	Spelling	Computer-assisted instruction	7 randomised controlled trials; meta-analysis and narrative synthesis	There was a small (not statistically significant) effect in favour of computer interventions. 'This review suggests that the teaching of spelling by using computer software may be as effective as conventional teaching of spelling, although the possibility of computer-taught spelling being inferior or superior cannot be excluded due to the relatively small sample sizes of the identified studies' (p.129).
Torgerson and Zhu, 2003	Spelling, reading, writing	Computer-assisted instruction (CAI), networked computer system, word-processing software packages, computer-mediated texts, speech-synthesis systems	12 randomised controlled trials; narrative synthesis and meta-analysis	For 5 different ICT interventions, overall 20 comparisons were included from 12 RCTs: 13 were positive and 7 were negative. These data suggest that there is little evidence from effectiveness research to support the widespread use of ICT in literacy learning.

Spelling

A recent systematic review and meta-analysis of randomised controlled trials (published 1980–2002) evaluating the effectiveness of ICT interventions in the teaching of spelling (Torgerson and Elbourne, 2002) suggested at best only a modest (not statistically significant) effect in favour of computer interventions on spelling. The authors of the review concluded that the teaching of spelling using ICT software may be as effective as conventional spelling instruction, although the possibility of computer-taught spelling being inferior or superior could not be confidently excluded due to the small sample sizes and generally poor quality of the included studies. Furthermore, none of the studies were undertaken within a UK setting.

Vocabulary learning

Blok *et al.* (2001) investigated whether or not computers enabled young children to learn vocabulary more effectively than traditional teacher-led approaches. This 'effectiveness' review restricted inclusion by study type and therefore only studies with an experimental design were reviewed. Five studies were included, only one of which demonstrated a positive effect for the computer condition. The review included a discussion of the quality of the five studies and concluded that there was little difference in effectiveness in vocabulary acquisition for pupils using computers or for pupils not using computers.

Research in populations of students with specific learner characteristics

MacArthur *et al.* (2001) reviewed published research on the use of ICT to teach or support literacy in populations of students 'with mild disabilities'. They reviewed research in technology and three literacy areas: word identification, reading comprehension and writing. This review included only studies with either an experimental design or studies where quantified learning outcomes were reported. Fourteen studies were identified which focused on technology and word-identification skills and within this area two major approaches were detailed: computer-assisted instruction (CAI) in phonological awareness and decoding and computer software that delivered speech feedback to students as they read. 'All of the studies supported the efficacy of CAI in improving the phonological awareness and decoding skills taught by the programs' (p. 279). In the area of speech synthesis, research indicated that 'the provision of speech feedback in meaningful reading contexts may lead to improvements in word identification for students with reading disabilities' (p. 282). However, these results should be viewed with caution, as control groups involved in the studies received no literacy intervention. Fourteen studies investigating technology and reading comprehension focused on the use of electronic texts to improve students' comprehension. Results here were equivocal with some studies showing a positive effect and others demonstrating no beneficial effects. In the area of technology and writing, twenty studies were identified, the majority of which concentrated on word-processing and on tools that supported transcription. MacArthur *et al.* found that 'research in writing provides qualified support for the beneficial effects of assistive technology' (p. 297).

Bryant *et al.* (2003) undertook a systematic review of research on vocabulary interventions involving students with learning disabilities, published in special education journals between 1978 and 2003. Six studies were identified based on the following intervention research variables: word selection procedure, materials, instructional design and procedures, duration of the intervention, mastery criterion, measures of vocabulary learning including reading comprehension, maintenance and generalisation. The interventions outlined in the studies were categorised into four areas, including computer-assisted instruction. CAI was used to deliver vocabulary instruction to students as they worked independently without teacher intervention. Researchers examined the effects of practice routines and the amount of vocabulary taught. Positive findings led the authors to conclude that 'CAI is a promising tool' (p.119) to be used independently for additional vocabulary practice.

Hall *et al.* (2000) examined studies of computer-assisted instruction in reading for students with learning disabilities published in refereed journals with a publication date between January 1980 and November 1997. Studies had to be empirically based research in which an experimental or quasi-experimental design was used. Seventeen studies were identified which fulfilled the criteria. All participants in the reviewed research were aged between 5 and 16 and numbers in each study ranged from 2 to 93 subjects. In thirteen out of the seventeen studies students with learning disabilities receiving computer-assisted instruction in reading increased their performance in reading decoding or reading comprehension. The three main findings from this review are: having computer-assisted instruction technology available in the classroom may be able to help overcome the Matthew effect (that is the paradoxical situation in which although we are aware of the existence of reading problems and remediation practices, students with learning disabilities tend to receive less reading time than their more able peers); the effective systematic instructional procedures used in reading instruction appeared to be available with carefully designed CAI software; and applying systematic, elaborate corrections resulted in the most efficient and effective learning. Authors of this review commented that many of the studies had a very small sample size, implying that the results were not able to show a statistically significant effect and were, therefore, not generalisable.

Fulk and Stormont-Spurgin (1995) reviewed published research on the effectiveness of four techniques for improving spelling, one of which was computer-assisted instruction (nine studies) for pupils with learning difficulties. The authors of this review concluded that eight out of the nine studies in CAI reported positive effects for CAI. However, only two out of these nine included studies that used an experimental design with random or non-random allocation to intervention (CAI) or control (traditional paper-and-pencil methods). The positive effects reported in the seven one-group studies could have been explained in other ways than by a causal relationship with ICT. These other explanations include: the statistical phenomenon of regression to the mean, where 'extreme' values either improve or decline, depending on which extreme of a distribution they lie; the Hawthorne effect, where merely the act of observation provokes a beneficial response; or temporal effects, whereby children tend to improve their spelling abilities irrespective of any intervention over the course of time.

THE FIVE EPPI REVIEWS

These five reviews, undertaken by members of the English Review Group between 2001 and 2004, are published on REEL (the EPPI-Centre website) and in Andrews, 2004.

Networked ICT

Andrews *et al.* (2002) looked at the impact of networked ICT on literacy learning in English for pupils aged 5 to 16. Sixteen relevant studies were identified ranging across a variety of study types. The review concluded that ICT use with regard to literacy development increases motivation and/or confidence in pupils and that 'empowerment and ownership are important factors to bear in mind in an increasingly diverse digital world' (p. 6). The included studies began from the assumption that networked ICT makes a positive impact on literacy development and attempted to explore how this impact is made. Most of the studies revealed a narrow conception of literacy, based on pre-digital notions of reading and writing. The authors of the review recommended that future policy should focus research funding for large-scale studies and give consideration to the balance of study type expertise in research teams.

Moving image texts and literacy

Burn and Leach (2004) conducted a systematic review of the impact of ICT on the learning of literacies associated with moving image texts in English for 5 to 16-year-olds. Their main aims were to review and evaluate accounts of the relationship between ICTs related to the moving image and the impact of their use on literacies associated with the moving image. In this review 'literacy' was defined as meaning principally the ability to make ('write') moving image texts using digital editing software, though it also meant writing *about* the moving image; and writing which is improved as a consequence of working with the moving image. Nine studies were included, spanning the years between 1990 and 2002. Four main findings became apparent: firstly, many of the studies found a link between media literacy and the cultural experience and preoccupations of young people, 'suggesting that curriculum content which recognizes this factor is more likely to motivate high quality work'; secondly, gains in literacy could result from incorporating moving image media in curriculum programmes; thirdly, the collaborative nature of media production was highlighted; and finally, the majority of included studies claimed positive motivational aspects, although one exception documented a negative effect in the case of girls and computer games. However, as the majority of the research reported small qualitative case studies, Burn and Leach noted that these outlined benefits of ICTs for moving image literacy were only 'suggested by the evidence and not conclusively demonstrated' nor could the findings be regarded as generalisable.

Literature-related literacies

Locke and Andrews (2004) set out to determine the impact of ICT on literature-related literacies in English for 5 to 16-year-olds. Seven studies, appearing between 1990 and 2002 were identified. The research consisted of studies using a range of study types which were judged to be of high to medium quality overall. Findings were as follows. The input of the teacher (the ideology, values and practices of the teacher or teachers who set up the interaction) mattered more than the technology. There was often a mismatch between the commercially available multimedia literature software packages and response-based teaching. Although many studies suggested that there was a motivational impact when ICT was introduced into a literature programme, there were also signs that duration of exposure to a technology could affect motivation.

ICT, literacy learning and English as a second or additional language

Low and Beverton (2004) reviewed the impact of ICT on literacy learning in English of learners between 5 and 16 years old, for whom English was a second or additional language. Their review concentrated on written literacy-related ICT research studies for 1990–2002, examining their impact on English as a second language and English as an additional language students and their teaching and learning environments where possible. Eight studies were identified, four of which were carried out with primary school age pupils and four of which were carried out with secondary age pupils. All studies collected and analysed a defined body of empirical data. With respect to the review questions the quality of the studies was variable for a variety of reasons: uncertainty of classification, methodological and analysis problems. It was impossible for the authors to find a clear impact pattern. Word-processing, it seemed, could improve writing and editing quality under certain conditions. On the whole, students found computer-assisted sessions enjoyable and helpful. Teachers reported a change of their role within class towards that of facilitator. Evidence could suggest only tentatively that students' learning and motivation were increased by a high-support user-friendly environment, the use of collaborative work resulting in a concrete end product and the integration of computer-assisted language learning into regular class procedures and activities. The main finding of this systematic review was that there is not enough evidence to support policy decisions about increasing the role of computers in language learning education. The authors noted that the included studies lacked details about classroom practices and aspects of bilingualism and, as the included studies were carried out in the early 1990s, they did not focus on internet-based teaching and learning or use of modern hardware, therefore impact within this area of ICT was not considered.

ICT and literacy effectiveness review

Torgerson and Zhu (2003) investigated whether or not ICT is effective in improving young people's literacy learning in English. As the focus of the review was 'effectiveness', papers using rigorous methods to assess effectiveness were required. Studies were only included in the review if they had randomly allocated pupils to an ICT or no-ICT treatment for the teaching of literacy. Twelve randomised controlled trials (RCTs) were included in the review. In synthesis (1) for five different ICT interventions, overall 20 comparisons were included from the 12 RCTs: 13 were positive and 7 were negative. The authors concluded that these data suggested that there is little evidence to support the widespread use of ICT in literacy learning in English. In synthesis (2) the authors undertook three meta-analyses: one for each of the three literacy outcome measures. They concluded that in spelling and reading the small effect sizes were not statistically significant. In writing there was weak evidence for a positive effect, but only 42 children altogether were included in the meta-analysis. The authors highlighted some of the limitations of the review: all of the included studies were undertaken in the USA; all of the participants in the studies were either very young children in the beginning stages of literacy, or slightly older children who were experiencing difficulties or disabilities in learning in literacy.

THE TTA REVIEW

The TTA review sought to examine the evidence for the effectiveness of different ICTs in the teaching and learning of English for students aged between 5 and 16 years. A review of nine non-randomised controlled trials was conducted to investigate the effectiveness of different ICTs in the teaching and learning of English, 5–16, within the area of written composition. The ICTs most frequently used in trials to attempt to improve the quality and accuracy of pupils' written composition were computer-assisted instruction or learning, software, multimedia and word-processing. Whilst the evidence suggested that CAI and word-processing may bring about improvement in written composition when combined with strategic instruction, the results of this review are non-conclusive as there was insufficient high-quality research to answer the research question.

SUMMARY

We identified thirteen systematic reviews in the field of ICT in literacy learning in English. Our tertiary review has described the scope of this research but we have been unable to synthesise these reviews because of their disparate nature in terms of: the conceptualisation of literacy adopted in the individual reviews; the varying ways of measuring of literacy outcomes; the many different ICT interventions investigated; and the fact that all the reviews were heterogeneous in terms of their inclusion criterion for study types. The current fragmented nature of the evidence base for practice as touched on in this chapter provides a challenge for government agencies and researchers to develop approaches which support evidence informed practice for teachers. During your teaching career, you can expect to see the work described in the chapter develop to provide you with more reliable research to support your work in the classroom.

ACKNOWLEDGEMENTS

We thank Andrew Burn, Diana Elbourne, Terry Locke and Graham Low for their helpful comments on a previous version of this chapter. We thank Alison Robinson for compiling the references and for proofreading the document.

NOTE

1   We know of one further systematic review being undertaken by the EPPI-Centre Post-Compulsory Education Review Group. This systematic review examines the impact of ICT on progress in literacy and numeracy for young people and adults with basic skills needs. However, we have not included it here because it has not yet been published on REEL. The protocol can be accessed at <http:// eppi.ioe.ac.uk/reel/home.aspx?page=/reel/review_groups/post-16/post-16_home.htm> and the review will be published on REEL in the near future.

EDITORS' NOTE

You may have become aware that teachers are expected to base their work on research and evidence where possible. Ways of supporting teachers in accessing the evidence base for practice are being developed nationally and internationally. In this chapter, you are introduced to this work, specifically the idea of research synthesis – the systematic reviewing of the evidence base for practice. In the chapter, the outcomes of systematic reviews in the context of ICT and literacy learning are reported and discussed (see <http://eppi.ioe.ac.uk> for further details).

REFERENCES

Included reviews

Andrews, R. (2004) *The Impact of ICT on Literacy Education*, London: RoutledgeFalmer.

Andrews, R., Burn, A., Leach, J., Locke, T., Low, G. and Torgerson, C. (2002) A systematic review of the impact of networked ICT on 5–16 year olds' literacy in English' (EPPI-Centre Review), *Research Evidence in Education Library (REEL)*, London: EPPI-Centre, Social Science Research Unit, Institute of Education (<http://eppi.ioe.ac.uk/reel>).

Bangert-Drowns, R.L. (1993) 'The word processor as an instructional tool: a meta-analysis of word processing in writing instruction', *Review of Educational Research*, 63: 69–93.

Blok, H., Van Daalen-Kapteijns, M.M., Otter, M.E. and Overmaat, M. (2001) 'Using computers to learn words in the elementary grades: an evaluation framework and a review of effect studies', *Computer Assisted Language Learning*, 14(2): 99–128.

Bryant, D.P., Goodwin, M., Bryant, B.R. and Higgins, K. (2003) 'Vocabulary instruction for students with learning disabilities: a review of the research', *Learning Disability Quarterly*, 26(2): 117–28.

Burn, A. and Leach, J. (2004) 'A systematic review of the impact of ICT on the learning of literacies associated with moving image texts in English, 5–16', *REEL*, London: EPPI-Centre, Social Science Research Unit, Institute of Education (<http://eppi.ioe.ac.uk/reel>).

Fulk, B.M. and Stormont-Spurgin, M. (1995) 'Spelling interventions for students with disabilities: a review', *Journal of Special Education*, 28(4): 488–513.

Hall, T.E., Hughes, C.A. and Filbert, M. (2000) 'Computer assisted instruction in reading for students with learning disabilities: a research synthesis', *Education and Treatment of Children*, 23(2): 173–93.

Locke, T. and Andrews, R. (2004) 'A systematic review of the impact of ICT on literature-related literacies in English, 5–16', *REEL*, London: EPPI-Centre, Social Science Research Unit, Institute of Education (<http://eppi.ioe.ac.uk/reel>).

Low, G. and Beverton, S. (2004) 'A systematic review of the impact of ICT on literacy learning in English of learners between 5 and 16, for whom English is a second or additional language', *REEL*, London: EPPI-Centre, Social Science Research Unit, Institute of Education (<http://eppi.ioe.ac.uk/reel>).

MacArthur, C.A., Ferretti, R.P., Okolo, C.M. and Cavalier, A.R. (2001) 'Technology applications for students with literacy problems: a critical review', *Elementary School Journal*, 101(3): 273–301.

Torgerson, C. and Elbourne, D. (2002) 'A systematic review and meta-analysis of the effectiveness of information and communication technology (ICT) on the teaching of spelling', *Journal of Research in Reading*, 25(2): 129–43.

Torgerson, C. and Zhu, D. (2003) 'A systematic review and meta-analysis of the effectiveness of ICT on literacy learning in English, 5–16', *REEL*, London: EPPI-Centre, Social Science Research Unit, Institute of Education (<http://eppi.ioe.ac.uk/reel>).

Further references

Angrist, J. and Lavy, V. (2002) 'New evidence on classroom computers and pupil learning', *Economic Journal*, 12 (October): 735–65.

Glass, G.V. (1976) 'Primary, secondary and meta-analysis', *Educational Researcher*, 5: 3–8.

Slavin, R.E. (1986) 'Best evidence synthesis: an alternative to meta-analytic and traditional review', *Educational Research*, 16: 5–11.

Torgerson, C.J. (2003) *Systematic Reviews*, London: Continuum Books.

Torgerson, C. and Elbourne, D. (2002) 'A systematic review and meta-analysis of the effectiveness of information and communication technology (ICT) on the teaching of spelling', *Journal of Research in Reading*, 25(2): 129–43.

Summaries and full texts of all the EPPI-Centre reviews can be accessed at <http://eppi.ioe.ac.uk/reel>.

Index